This INCURABLE EVIL

Mapuche Resistance to Spanish Enslavement, 1598–1687

EUGENE C. BERGER

The University of Alabama Press
Tuscaloosa

The University of Alabama Press
Tuscaloosa, Alabama 35487-0380
uapress.ua.edu

Typeface: Arno Pro

Cover image: Mapuche scepter, Metropolitan Museum of Art, The Michael C. Rockefeller Memorial Collection (purchase, Mrs. Bliss Parkinson Gift, in honor of Rene d'Harnoncourt, 1965, CC0 1.0); *background*, map of Chile by Willem Jansz Blaeu, 1630
Cover design: Lori Lynch

Cataloging-in-Publication data is available from the Library of Congress.
ISBN: 978-0-8173-2158-1 (cloth)
ISBN: 978-0-8173-6110-5 (paper)
E-ISBN: 978-0-8173-9452-3

FOR CAROLL

Contents

Illustrations

Acknowledgments

This project could not have been undertaken without funds from the Program for Cultural Cooperation between Spain's Ministry of Education, Culture, and Sports and United States Universities, the Herbert and Blanche Henry Weaver Fellowship, the William Campbell Binkley Graduate Education Fund, a Vanderbilt University Travel Grant, a Vanderbilt University Graduate Fellowship and Teaching Assistantship, and the J. León Helguera Fellowship.

I would like to thank the very patient staff at the Archivo Nacional and Biblioteca Nacional in Chile and the Archivo de Indias in Sevilla. From the Jean and Alexander Heard Library at Vanderbilt University, I would like to thank Paula Covington, and the Interlibrary Loan Department. Wendi Schnaufer at the University of Alabama Press saw the potential in my research before I did. She not only reached out to me at a conference years ago but was incredibly helpful during the entire writing process: from prospectus to the final draft.

I am grateful for the support received from Missouri Southern State University (MSSU) and Georgia Gwinnett College (GGC). I am especially grateful to Pres. Jann Joseph and GGC's Office of the Provost for granting me professional leave in the fall of 2020. I received a number of GGC School of Liberal Arts travel grants to present my preliminary research at conferences. I would also like to thank my supportive colleagues at MSSU and GGC, especially Michael Gunther and Ryan Gaston, who helped me develop the final version of this book.

I am very grateful to my advisor, Prof. Jane Landers, for her patience and guidance over the course of my entire graduate career and my first years as an assistant professor. Her knowledge of the field guided my research and her generosity with Latin Americanist colleagues across the country opened many doors for me. I would also like to thank my late mentor, Prof. Simon Collier. An expert on nineteenth-century politics, Professor Collier of course taught me about Andres Bello, Diego Portales, *pelucones* (bigwigs), and *igualitarios* (liberals). But his expertise also extended into the colonial era, where he and Professor Landers helped me craft my own research agenda. In what seemed to me an offhand comment at the time, Professor Collier told me that Chile was lacking a study of the colonial hacienda elite. This statement confused me as I was becoming familiar with the work of historians he knew, such as Jorge Pinto, Mario Góngora, and Alvaro Jara, all of whom had written about seventeenth-century economy and society in Chile. But Professor Collier's comment stuck with me, and twenty years later, I think I finally know what he meant. The late Prof. J. León Helguera was also a great supporter of mine and constantly encouraged me to publish even as I took on a heavy teaching load. I would also like to thank my other mentors at Vanderbilt University, Profs. Marshall Eakin, Carlos Jáuregui, Daniel Usner, and Edward Wright-Ríos.

I would like to thank my parents, George and Virginia, for supporting me in so many ways but always giving me the freedom to find my professional path. I would like to thank my son who grew up alongside this project and who has always inspired me. I am so proud of you, Matthew.

I would especially like to thank my family in Chile and in particular *mi suegra*. My mother-in-law always made sure I felt at home in Talagante and helped get me out the door and on the way to the archive on cold winter mornings. Thank you to my wife, Caroll. She has always been the biggest fan of my work and always reminded me of José Martí's advice. Without her, there would be no tree, no child, and certainly no book. *Gracias, mi amor.*

THIS INCURABLE EVIL

MAPUCHE SCEPTER. Courtesy of Archivo Fotográfico Museo Chileno de Arte Precolombino.

Introduction

Indigenous Slavery and Slave Societies

> "Este mal es incurable. . . . Y hacen reventar trabajando y de una y otra suerte no ay yndio que descanse ni asista a sus pueblos" (This evil is incurable. . . . They make them burst from overwork and no Indian ever rests nor is able to return home).
>
> —Francisco González de Salcedo, Obispo de Santiago de Chile, January 20, 1630

"Incurable evil" is how Archbishop of Santiago Francisco González de Salcedo described the treatment of Mapuche servants (*encomendados*) and Mapuches who were enslaved by Spanish soldiers in Santiago and in Chile's colonial south. González de Salcedo wrote to the young Spanish king Philip IV multiple times in 1630, observing that captive Mapuches were branded on the face, had their hands bound, and were sold to merchants heading to Peru.[1] The actions described by González de Salcedo were part of a Spanish network of taking and exporting of the enslaved Mapuche that not only served landowners of Chile's expanding seventeenth-century *latifundia* (large estates) but also became an important source of enslaved laborers for mines, workshops, stables, and galleys in Peru.

This book describes not only how this export expanded over the seventeenth century but more importantly how the Mapuche transformed their society to resist it. The Mapuche would resist this truly incurable evil until a literal movement of heaven and earth in the form of an earthquake and epidemic of stem rust (a fungus particularly damaging to wheat) interrupted the trade and the sale of enslaved Mapuches to Peru.

For even the most casual of observers visiting Chile, the history of the Mapuche indigenous people is omnipresent. When bands like Green Day, Deep Purple, or Soda Stereo have concerts in Santiago, they perform at the Teatro Caupolicán, named for the Mapuche *toki* or war leader of the 1550s. If one is in the Cerrillos neighborhood and needs some work done on one's car's front axle, there is a shop on Paicaví street named for a 1612 Mapuche-Spanish peace parley. With apologies to fans of rival clubs like "La U" or "La Católica," Colo-Colo (named for a Mapuche contemporary of Caupolicán) is Chile's most popular professional soccer club (fig. I.1).

Despite these popular representations, we lack a deeper appreciation of Mapuche contributions to colonial history. This book's goal is to look at a

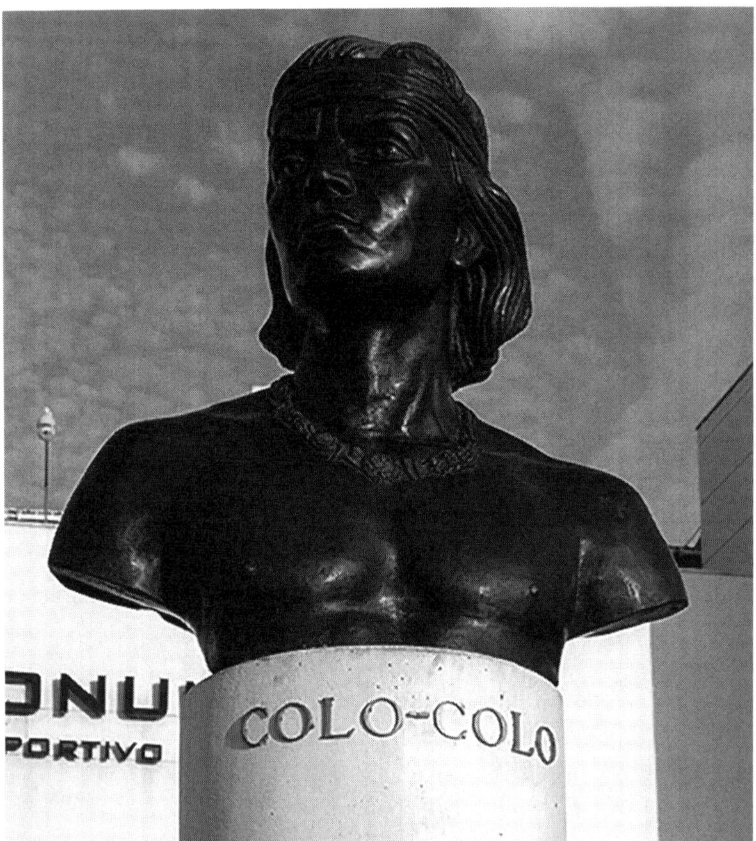

FIGURE I.1. Bust of Colo-Colo outside of Estadio Monumental, Santiago, Chile, 2020. Photograph by Carlos Figueroa, CC BY-SA 4.0.

lesser known and unappreciated part of the Spanish conquest: enslavement and export and how the Mapuche resisted the practice. Spanish colonists, soldiers, and their Native American allies enslaved thousands of Mapuches, many of them forced on ships heading toward Lima or across the Andes to Potosí. This demand for Mapuche labor both inside and outside of Chile created more than a century of immense pressure upon the indigenous people of Chile's south. This was a process obscured to both seventeenth-century writers and to modern historians alike by the larger "War of Arauco," a Spanish campaign that promised but failed to deliver the long-delayed conquest of South America. At first glance, the War of Arauco may seem like a series of attempts to win back lost territory south of the Bío-Bío River, thwarted by brilliant Mapuche tactics and military skill. Many of these Spanish offensives however, especially in the mid-seventeenth century, were in fact raids for enslaving disguised as "just war," repelled by generations of Mapuche tokis. The changing nature of these raids, the reasons for them, and the growing and successful Mapuche resistance to them are the subjects of this book.

The Mapuche and the Araucanía

Chile's marked geographical features produced a diverse population of roughly half a million pre-Columbian inhabitants. The ethnic and linguistic diversity would be a source of frustration for Spaniards who had just benefitted from the mitae (reciprocal) labor system of Peru, instituted and managed by a vast Inka Empire. There were no such labor expectations or tributary states south of Chile's Maule River.[2] South of the Maule were the coastal Mapuche,[3] mountain peoples such as the Pehuenche, Chiquillán, and Puelche, and farther south the Huilliche and Patagones. Although in frequent contact with one another, these groups were racially, culturally, and linguistically distinct.[4]

The pre-Columbian Mapuche lived in the region of Chile between the Choapa River and the island of Chiloé (fig. I.2). Archaeologists describe multiple phases of migration during the peopling of the Americas, where the Pacific Coast peoples were largely isolated by the Andes after their initial settlement.[5] While there was no empire in the south of Chile, the indigenous population did share a language and a rather homogeneous culture, which anthropologist Ricardo Latcham argues was only interrupted by a more recent migration. Latcham traces how the arrival of hunter-gatherer Moluches from Argentina "interrupted the [Mapuche] racial homogeneity." Only with

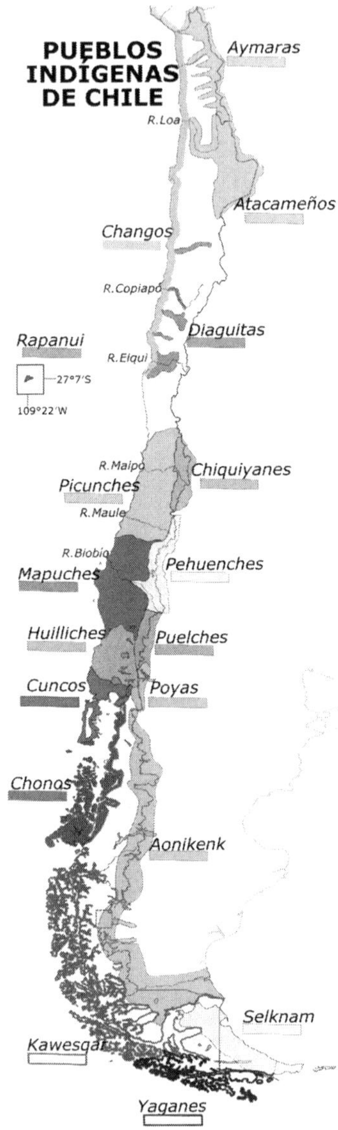

FIGURE I.2. Map of indigenous peoples of Chile.
Map by Createaccount, CC BY-SA 3.0.

this later Moluche migration did Mapuche-adjacent ethnic groups like the Puelches, Huilliches, Pehuenches, and Chiquillanes come to exist.[6]

The Moluche would find a region bordered by the Andes and the Pacific and one that sees heavy rainfall year-round. Much of the territory is beech and cedar forests, but the "historic core of Mapuche settlement" is nestled in a fertile valley with milder weather between the smaller Cordillera de la Costa and the dense forests of the piedmont.[7] The diet of Mapuches closer to the Andes had *piñones* (pine nuts) from the Araucaria tree as its base (fig. I.3), and meals of those living closer to the Pacific featured abundant sea life. We also know from ceramic traditions that closer to the arrival of Europeans, the Mapuche had developed a "fully agricultural and sedentary way of life."[8]

The abundance of food and relative lack of precious stones and metals meant little competition and led to the existence of a fairly egalitarian Mapuche society. Each Mapuche family generally maintained its own farmland, without a need for large group labor or town-like settlements. Each family's dwelling (*ruka*) might be within sight of their neighbor's but never adjacent.[9]

Archaeologist Tom Dillehay argues that Mapuche political organization and iconography show Andean and Amazonian influences with their "duel spatial and political organization" and in their "myths, tales and legends." Mapuche

FIGURE I.3. *Araucaria Araucana* tree, Conguillío National Park, Chile, 2019. Photograph by Delahimalaya-alosandes, CC BY-SA 3.0.

FIGURE I.4. Pitrén culture ceramic jars, Museo Andino de Santa Rita, Chile, 2018. Photograph by Velvet, CC BY-SA 4.0.

iconography shared images of "felines, snakes and raptorial birds" with other Pacific Coast cultures. Mapuche ceremonial fields were often aligned in the same "U" shape one might see at Chavín de Huantar in Peru, and Mapuche ceramics included double-spout jars (fig. I.4) similar to those from Peru's Moche civilization.[10] There is also ample evidence of Inka Empire influence on the Mapuche, including "symbols of authority which were embodied in *kero* [wide-mouthed stone or wooden decorative] drinking vessels [and] religious codes." More importantly for our purposes, however, is the fact that the Mapuche concept of "reciprocal labor arrangements between kin groups, or *mingaco*, is derived from the Quechua [language of the Inka Empire] term *minga*."[11] For the relatively egalitarian Mapuche, their encounter with the Inka was the first time outsiders had tried to "establish themselves, dominate the population and put it to work." From this experience, the Mapuche seem to have developed the word winka (outsider or foreigner) "derived from *pu Inka*, that is 'the Inkas' in *mapungú[n]*."[12]

This settlement pattern of small, kin-based settlements may have seemed haphazardly scattered across the central valley, but beneath it was a well-developed trade network and a great deal of mobility and intergroup contact. Intergroup alliances before and during the Spanish conquest were dynamic and complex. The Pehuenche, Chilquillán, and Puelche of the Andes were neighbors and culturally similar to the Mapuche but could at times be in conflict with them or with the Huilliche, another linguistically similar group inhabiting territory including Chiloé. The absence of a central village meant the absence of a central authority. A *lonko,* usually an elder or descendent of a previous leader, served as the head of a familial unit, but his power was limited.[13] A *machi* or shaman was important in Mapuche ceremonies but had little day-to-day influence. In times of war, a toki or warrior chieftain was named to make strategic decisions, but in times of peace he had little power.[14] Although war often brought a toki to power, it ultimately limited Mapuche hierarchy as conflicts over land made political organization more difficult.[15] There were some decisions made at bi- or triannual meetings called *reguas* or *cahuínes* where lineage-based clans came together. While some political discussion went on at these gatherings, their central feature was a reciprocity ceremony. More infrequent were larger gatherings of several cahuínes. In these *levos,* clans traded, contracted marriage, performed religious ceremonies, and made or organized wars.[16]

This decentralization limited larger conflicts and helped the Mapuche resist both the Inka and Spanish Empires. However, decentralization also makes other things more difficult when discussing the indigenous people in Chile and Argentina unified by the above traditions and the Mapuzugún language. For example, there is still much discussion about what to call speakers of Mapuzugún. While "Mapuche" is fairly universal in modern and colonial usage alike, a good number of scholars use the word Araucanían or *Araucano* to describe these same people. Arauco is also a Mapuzugún word derived from *ragco,* meaning "muddy water," and *Auca,* from the indigenous Quechua term *purum aukas,* meaning "enemy, rebel or wild."[17] Ragco became the region of Arauco where early Spanish explorer and founder of Santiago Pedro de Valdivia established a fort in 1553 near the Carampangue River. The Carampangue feeds into the Bahía de Arauco, and the Mapuche "heartland" is the Araucanía, extending from the Bío-Bío River to Chiloé.[18]

Mapuche Ethnography and Historiography

Finding sources to write an overview of Mapuche culture, much less a book on their resistance to enslavement, has only become possible in recent decades. As mentioned, the Mapuche are quite popular but equally misunderstood in Chile's national imagination. The earliest colonial literature was epic poetry, lauding the bravery and exploits of Mapuche warriors. Alonso de

Ercilla, a Spanish soldier and poet, penned the "first American epic," *La Araucana*, published in 1569. Ercilla was a page to the future King Philip II, and after rubbing elbows with several European monarchs, Ercilla knew the formula for writing a popular European epic: a bloody conflict in a faraway land between two very different but equally matched armies, with plenty of tales of chivalry and tragedy.[19] Mapuche leaders like Colocolo and Caupolicán were lauded for their bravery and the Mapuche in general were described as "unshackled" and with "necks unbending, traits that some scholars argue doubled as reflections Spanish authors had of themselves."[20] The Spanish hoped to be "gentlemanly, prideful and religious" like *La Araucana*'s Mapuche protagonists. For one scholar, Ercilla's celebration of the Mapuche even extended into the national period, with generations of Chileans "breathing Ercilla" without even knowing it.[21]

While Ercilla wanted to boost the fortunes of the monarchy by seeing Spanish values reflected in the Mapuche, independence era intellectuals used Mapuche history to reject Spain's legacy. Latching on to any heritage that was not European in origin, many Chilean independence leaders regarded themselves as "the true heirs of the [Mapuche]." One patriot intellectual "toast[ed] the Chileans as the 'sons of Caupolicán, Colocolo and Lautaro,'" while another proclaimed that the ancient Mapuche would look "with pleasure on the youthful and glorious exploits of Colombia, Peru and Buenos Aires."[22] The Liberator himself, Simón Bolívar, referred to the Mapuche as *fieros republicanos* (fervent republicans) in his famous Jamaica Letter, while Chilean statesman José Miguel Infante was more specific, referring to the Mapuche form of government as "Federalist."[23] Ultimately, patriots from both in and outside of Chile were impressed by Mapuche success, impressed perhaps by a lack of a Mapuche authoritarian or monarchist tradition. A patriot publication, the *Almanak Nacional*, in 1824 even published a chronology of "tokis araucanos" dating back to the "Spanish invasion." This list gave the reader the misleading yet amusing impression that the Mapuche had predicted an uprising of white and mestizo creoles. This creole uprising would be the culmination of Mapuche rebellions of the past, rescuing the Chilean "fatherland" from European invaders.[24] Finally, in 1829, exiled Chilean liberator Bernardo O'Higgins spoke nostalgically of his childhood experiences with the Mapuche and crafted a plan for an "Amerindian Empire" led by indigenous groups like the Mapuche who had successfully resisted generations of monarchs.[25]

Having such a flattering view of the "free" and "unbending" Mapuche in the Chilean national literature certainly serves the needs of nationalism and keeps the Mapuche in the historical memory. But when it comes to understanding attempts by the Spanish to capture and ultimately enslave thousands of Mapuches during the colonial period, viewing them as superhuman/federalist caricatures does not help create an accurate view of Chile's indigenous past. Fortunately, historians and anthropologists of the late nineteenth and into the twentieth centuries began to explain the larger history of Chile's south and humanized the aborigines, detailing both their pre-Columbian history and their relationships with the Spanish. Chile's most eminent historians like Diego Barros Arana and Benjamín Vicuña Mackenna began to include more detailed accounts of Chile's indigenous people in their general histories, and in 1900, Tomás Guevara published the first volume of *Historia de la civilización de Araucanía*. This landmark work was the first general tome to detail how the culture and politics of the Mapuche affected their relationship with the Spanish.

With the growing influence of anthropology and archeology, twentieth-century historians like Nathan Wachtel, Alfred J. Tapson, and Alvaro Jara were able to explain the strategic and societal changes in indigenous society that kept the Spanish at bay while also shedding more light on Spanish mistakes and abuses.[26] Jesuit historians like Ralph Foerster and Eugene Korth have also made important contributions to our understanding of how a Spanish "spiritual conquest" generated several meetings between Mapuches and ecclesiastics, and produced ethnographic sources.[27]

Today, the history of Chile's aborigines continues to gain popularity. The fieldwork of the prominent American archaeologist Tom Dillehay and archival research from historians like Jaime Valenzuela Márquez have bolstered our understanding of the region.[28] Even veteran historians like former director of the Biblioteca Nacional Sergio Villalobos have written about Mapuche-Spanish interaction.[29]

Indigenous Slavery and the Colonial Americas

The history of Native American resistance to enslavement is one that can be linked to the larger field of slavery and abolition in the Americas as a whole. Although our sources and training do not always overlap, the work of Middle Passage scholars significantly helps historians of indigenous slavery. In 1975, Edmund S. Morgan asked, "How heavily did American economic opportunity and political freedom rest on Virginia's slaves?"[30] Morgan suggests that the Virginia aristocracy of the early republic was just as moved to action by their common ownership of enslaved people as they were by ideas from John Locke or Jean Jacques Rousseau. After all, he argues, "aristocrats could more safely preach equality in a slave society than in a free one."[31] In referring to the national period, Morgan asked, "Is America still colonial Virginia writ large?,"[32] a query we could certainly make of former Ibero-American colonies like Cuba, Brazil, or Chile. Ira Berlin has provided thousands of history undergraduates and professional scholars alike with an extremely elegant way of understanding slavery in England's North American colonies as either "slave societies" or "societies with slaves." Berlin helps us understand that the colonial worlds that owners of enslaved people created were directly connected to the "long and notorious history" of planters.[33]

In the twelfth-century Levant, the commodity was sugar, and sugar planters expanded across the Mediterranean world, eventually making their way to the Atlantic coast of Africa, a society largely mimicked in colonial Brazil. Berlin wrote that in these American slave societies "the masters' authority radiated from the great estates to the statehouses, courtrooms, countinghouses, churches, colleges, taverns, racetracks, private clubs and the like."[34] Again, Berlin and Morgan describe owners of enslaved Africans, but can this "radiation of authority" exist where indigenous slavery is predominant? In other words, were there "indigenous slave societies" in Chile or elsewhere?

Finding indigenous slave societies in the colonial record requires us to examine regions where scholarship has often subsumed indigenous slavery into the narrative of the transatlantic trade. One of these areas is the neighboring English colonies of South Carolina and Georgia. Peter Wood's *Black Majority* sets a foundation for much of our work, as he explores the earliest and indigenous origins of plantation society in South Carolina. Allan Gallay expands on Wood's research, discovering that indigenous slavery was not transitory but in fact essential to understanding slave society in Georgia and the Carolinas. Gallay adds that the persistence of indigenous slavery in South Carolina sent this colony on a trajectory different from that of its neighbors in the Chesapeake: "South Carolina, by contrast [to the Chesapeake], became thoroughly enmeshed in imperial competition with Spanish Florida and French Louisiana, while its powerful Indian neighbors played an even larger role in influencing the colony's economic and political development."[35]

For Gallay, indigenous slavery was central to "how the South [became] the South." Gallay writes that "the plantation culture we associate with the antebellum South did not magically appear fully developed in 1820" but was instead created by frontiersmen like Jonathan Bryan.[36] Bryan's father, Joseph, had been an ally of one of South Carolina's "largest slave traders," and Jonathan inherited his father's knowledge of alliances and enmities with groups like the Yamasee and the Apalachee.[37] For Gallay, successful frontiersmen like Bryan were all prospective planters in that they had to "amass capital, make decisions about which lands to accumulate and develop, purchase appropriate laborers and effectively manage them, market crops, and usually develop alternative money-making enterprises in case of crop failure."[38] For Bryan, his brothers, and their neighbors, this capital amassed on the frontier went directly to the purchase of enslaved people and converted frontiersmen to planters in their lifetime.[39]

Gallay explains that, while "Native American societies are traditionally viewed as external to the plantation system," the fact is that "the drive to control Indian labor . . . was inextricably connected to the growth of the plantations and that the trade in Indian slaves was at the center of the English empire's development in the American South."[40] Gallay adds that Indian slavery gave owners of enslaved people in South Carolina something of a "head start" on the cruelty and exploitation that would persist into the nineteenth century: "From first settlement, South Carolina elites ruthlessly pursued the exploitation of fellow humans in ways that differed from other mainland colonies, and they created a narcissistic culture that reacted passionately and violently to attempts to limit their individual sovereignty over their perceived social inferiors."[41]

Another scholar of the British Americas, Matthew Mulcahy, includes further detail on this connection between indigenous slavery and cruelty in *Hubs of Empire*. He reminds us that indigenous slavery and African slavery were part of the same circum-Caribbean networks, where indigenous slavery was a primer to the cruelty displayed against enslaved Africans.[42] Christina Snyder also describes the overlap with indigenous and African slavery. She details how settlement patterns and intertribal and interimperial rivalries helped determine the unpredictable nature of slavery in the North American Southeast.[43]

While these scholars help us better understand the development of slavery in the US South, regionalism in historiography often prompts us to ignore the universal role of indigenous slavery in this country. Of course, four different European powers colonized the future United States, a fact that permits us to select or reject certain legacies when actions (like taking of enslaved individuals) taken by one of these kingdoms are too uncomfortable to discuss. Daniel Usner elucidates this problem well in a 2014 article, where he points out that Francophobia from scholars like Ruben Thwaites hinders our understanding of plantation slavery's antecedents in Louisiana. Thwaites wrote that French colonists were "'paternally nurtured by their king'" and as such "'lacked initiative.'" This presumed lack of initiative gave generations of scholars license to ignore early Americans like Jonathan Bryan or Etienne Véniard de Bourgmont. Bourgmont was expelled from France in 1698, married the daughter of a Missouri Native American chief, and wrote an opera called *Les Indes Galantes*. But as Thwaites praised English settlers who he felt "abounded with individual enterprise," we similarly overlook French contributions to frontier exchange and any possible indigenous antecedents of an antebellum slave economy.[44] The same is true of the whitewashing of Spanish colonial legacies in US history and architecture.[45] Fortunately, the work of Bernard Bailyn, David Weber, and many others helps us see North America as part of the larger Atlantic world and its forced-labor dependent economy.[46] In Brett Rushforth's *Bonds of Alliance*, we even see the juxtaposition of forced-labor economies within France's North American and Caribbean colonial possessions.[47]

Historian Andrés Reséndez also reminds us to consider the role of Native American slave takers in multiple regions in the Americas. Reséndez starts with the Comanche in northern New Spain who enslaved neighboring groups. While the Comanchería, much like the Araucanía, never came close to reaching Caribbean, Brazilian, or even North American percentages of enslaved peoples in their society, Reséndez argues that percentages alone do not reflect how the Comanche used the sale of enslaved individuals to expand their influence across their region. Much like with allied Mapuches (*indios amigos*) in Chile, "slavery gave the Comanches the means to acquire horses and weapons and to use these as powerful levers to forge alliances, seek compliance, punish enemies and secure their borders."[48] Reséndez adds that focusing too much on numbers has limited our search for slave societies in another way: time. The international trade in enslaved Africans was banned in 1808, and, as a result, scholarly interest in slave societies in subsequent years often faded. However, captive taking by Native Americans and Europeans from within the Americas continued well into the nineteenth century, where Spanish colonists in particular "pioneered new practices of enslavement."[49] Reséndez's *The Other Slavery* helps us examine areas like the Araucanía or the Comanchería where for far too long indigenous slavery was deemed to have been fleeting or even nonexistent, somehow assumed to have evaporated because of demographic collapse or the acceleration of the transatlantic slave trade.

Indigenous Slavery and Latin America

In Latin America, by contrast, there is no dismissing indigenous slavery as part of a regional aberration, where free colonies like Pennsylvania or New York take on more weight when constructing national narratives. Latin American nations with slaveholding pasts must acknowledge and reckon with their colonial sins or try to abridge the entire colonial past. Most of us are incapable of imagining a Latin American colonial past without slavery. Brazilian historian John Monteiro, for example, notes that even though the 1690's Brazilian gold rush turned raiders into entrepreneurial placer miners almost overnight, the "master-Indian" patterns persisted into a new era of African slavery. Decades of *paulista* (from São Paulo) raids on indigenous groups like the Tupinikin, Tupinambá, and Tamoios had established this "master-Indian relationship [and] defined the framework of a larger structure of domination, thus laying the bases of a distinct slave society." This unequal distribution of resources began during the paulista era, and continued into the eighteenth century, when the introduction of enslaved Africans further exacerbated the "stark distinctions between a small minority of wealthy colonists and the vast majority."[50]

A Slave Society in Chile?

While nineteenth-century historians like Vicuña Mackenna acknowledge that indigenous slavery did exist in Chile, they often explain it away as the anomalous actions of a handful of backward colonists, who lacked the benefit of nineteenth-century modernist thought. For Vicuña Mackenna and his nineteenth-century colleagues, the transgressions associated with slavery were limited to the colonial period and unimportant to any national character. The most obvious example of this sealing off of the colonial past is the historiographic and popular treatment of La Quintrala. Catalina de los Ríos y Lisperguer or "La Quintrala" was a member of colonial Chile's prominent Lisperguer-Flores family and the subject of Vicuña Mackenna's 1877 biography, *Los Lisperguer y la Quintrala*. In the years before her 1662 death, de los Ríos was investigated by the bishop of Santiago for accusations that she tortured her servants. In a 2001 article, Ronda Ward explores both the origins of the fascination with de los Ríos and, perhaps more importantly, how this fascination has led us to a misguided sense of the colonial period as a whole. Ward traces much of the interest back to Vicuña Mackenna's work, arguing that the historian of the new republic sharply exaggerated the actions of a colonial woman to cover the sins of her male counterparts. By covering the actions of male landowners, Vicuña Mackenna helped to construct an apocryphal colonial heritage, one that ignores how holders of enslaved indigenous persons practiced Ira Berlin's "art of domination."[51]

In Vicuña Mackenna's stilted version of Chile's colonial elite, few owned enslaved individuals, and those who dared to be cruel risked infamy. Even some twentieth-century historians, while acknowledging the existence of slavery in Chile, called it "necessary" for the health of the colonial economy.[52] It would take Chile many generations to "blot out forever the foul and haggard crime; . . . the blight and mildew" of slavery,[53] and fortunately, more recent historiography has not found it necessary to excuse the conduct of colonial slaveowners. A closer look at colonial sources by historians like Mario Góngora reveals that ownership of enslaved people among Chile's elite was actually on the rise as the colonial period progressed, further blurring the "undulating lines" of aristocracy and producing more rivalries.[54] Góngora in fact details how colonial owners of enslaved people were ubiquitous, protecting their privileged status through the creation of a rural tenant farming peasantry. Hacendados (owners of haciendas) who owned enslaved people were able to both exploit and maintain the loyalty of these tenant farmers or *inquilinos*[55] by renting them land and extending them credit. This clientelism created a loyal inquilino peasant class and insulated owners of enslaved people from potential rebellion by them or servants. Alvaro Jara's invaluable archival research provides us new sources on the history of forced labor in Chile, and Rolando Mellafe's study on the routes of the African diaspora into Chile is an unparalleled resource.[56] More recently, Sonia Macarena Sánchez Pérez has given us a roadmap for future study of Mapuche enslavement, and Jimena Obregón Iturra looks at the Mapuche diaspora in Lima through archives in Peru.[57] Finally, Jaime Valenzuela Márquez has edited a comprehensive set of articles on forced migration in the Americas.

This goal of this book is to contribute an understanding of how the "art of domination" caused demand for Mapuche enslavement despite successful Mapuche resistance. This interplay between resistance and demand for forced labor dominated the cultural, economic, and political lives of Chile's residents for most of the seventeenth century. Chapter 1 explores the origins of Mapuche resistance to all forms of forced labor, beginning with the Inka mitae system. The sixteenth-century Mapuche continued to balk at Spain's demands that they mine gold and build cities for the empire, their resistance even culminating in general rebellions in 1554 and 1598. Chapter 2 explains what exactly the Mapuche were resisting. A trade in enslaved Mapuches and Mapuche servants extended from the Araucanía all the way to Lima, where hundreds of enslaved Mapuches and their descendants were scattered across several neighborhoods within the capital. Chapter 3 details how Mapuche society transformed its leadership and politics in the seventeenth century to combat a new and more virulent cycle of raids to enslave by the Spanish. By the 1650s, Mapuche resistance had succeeded to the point that "great tokis" called meetings with and made demands of Spanish officials. Chapter 4 explains how the resistance of rebel Mapuche communities had become so successful that the Spanish had to capture and export their Mapuche allies or "amigos" if they were to meet demand for indigenous laborers. This shift to allies caused another Mapuche uprising in 1655 and prompted discussions by Spanish colonists about abolishing Mapuche forced labor altogether. Chapter 5 details how Spanish governors in the 1660s and 1670s abandoned any hope of taking land in Mapuche-controlled territory, instead focusing their energy on raids to enslave designed only to profit them personally, unconnected to any strategic or political aims. This boldfaced corruption became endemic for Spanish governors, who, despite promises to the Crown to finish the conquest of Chile, were now realizing that this was impossible in the face of Mapuche resistance. This cycle of raids to enslave and corruption would only come to an end with a massive Lima earthquake in 1687. This earthquake changed the economic relationship between Chile and Peru, making the export of captive Mapuches out of the Araucanía much less profitable for Spanish soldiers and landowners.

1

Winka

The Sixteenth Century and Origins of Mapuche Resistance

Resistance to the Inka

In modern Chile, we hear hundreds of Mapuzugún words like *cahuín* (gossip), *laucha* (mouse), and *pololo(a)* (girlfriend/boyfriend) in daily Spanish-language conversations.[1] *Winka* is another commonly used Mapuzugún term, but with centuries-old relevance. This phrase dates back to before Spanish arrival in the 1530s all the way to failed attempts by Inka armies to conquer the Mapuche (fig. 1.1). Historian José Bengoa traces the term to the Mapuzugún *pu Inka* (the Inkas), the first of several groups of outsiders to see an attempted conquest stall in Mapuche territory.[2]

The Inka of course influenced dozens of indigenous groups throughout the continent, permanently transforming many of them through forced migration. The Inka presence in Chile was not a minor one. Much of the southern Inka province of Collasuyu was located within Chile, with Inka rule extending into what is now Santiago.[3] The Inka conquered the Pikunche of central Chile, panned for gold in the Marga-Marga River estuary near modern Viña del Mar, and attempted to extend their conquest further south.[4] According to Peruvian chronicler Inka Garcilaso de la Vega, the Mapuche dramatically turned back the Inka at the Battle of Maule during the 1470s or 1480s.[5] More recently, historians like Osvaldo Silva and Leonardo León Solís argue that the importance of this battle has been overstated and that the empire's slow expansion was just as important to the lack of Inka influence among the Mapuche.[6] Chile's northern region by contrast was fully incorporated in the empire. The central region and Aconcagua valley were in a period of "transition," and the area between the Maipo and Maule Rivers was one of "frontier and confrontation" (fig. 1.2).[7]

This Mapuche resistance to the Inka was surely in part due to Inka forced labor demands. We cannnot argue that the Mapuche resistance completely isolated them from the Inka, but none of the aforementioned Inka influences could be labeled as full-scale adoptions and did not extend to acceptance of Inka communal labor requirements. Tom Dillehay argues that in fact the

FIGURE 1.1. Battle of Maule. Illustration of the confrontation between the Mapuches (*left*) and the Incas (*right*), in Felipe Huamán Pomo de Ayala, *Nueva Crónica y Buen Gobierno*, c. 1615.

FIGURE 1.2. Inka road system. Map by Koen Adams, CC BY-SA 4.0.

Mapuche may even have co-opted the *minga* system for their own purposes, instead of being absorbed into Inka labor obligations. "The Araucanian concept of . . . *mingaco* ('reciprocal labor arrangements') is derived from the Quechua term *minga*," and we know that for hundreds of years, Andean *ayllus* (communities) used cooperative labor to great success. The Inka, however, adjusted this concept to imperial construction projects, building roads and palaces through the mitae or corvée system. The Mapuche rejected this state building obligation, instead seeing the Inka as a "group of organized foreigners whose objective was to . . . dominate the population." The Mapuche viewed these labor obligations as damaging enough that they would necessitate a "widespread resistance network," one that would be again deployed against the next winka no more than a generation later.[8]

Beginnings of Resistance to the "Incurable Evil"

After successfully resisting the Inka Empire, the Mapuche would be given little respite before confronting labor demands from the Spanish. Initially, the Spanish and several Inka nobles worked together as one "group of organized foreigners" in their colonization of Chile, but Spanish troops' lack of discipline would make it difficult to maintain any alliance. With the help of Paullo Topa, a son of Huayna Capac, Diego de Almagro led the first Spanish exploration of Chile from Peru in 1535 and conquered several Andean provinces on his way southward.[9] As they approached central Chile, three of Almagro's men deserted or simply wandered off into the Huasco valley (near modern Vallenar) to *ranchear* (pillage/raid). Two of Almagro's soldiers were killed by district residents angered by the "bad deeds and poor treatment."[10] Enraged, Almagro responded by "order[ing] the *Ülmen* [elder] of the district, called Marcando, his brother, and twenty of the principal inhabitants to be brought thither, all of whom . . . he delivered to the flames."[11]

It is unclear whether the Mapuche had advanced notice of this *almagrista* (Almagro's group) violence (from Spanish soldiers loyal to Diego de Almagro) as it made its way south, but they certainly recognized Almagro's lieutenants as a threat. The Mapuche met Almagro's lieutenant Gómez de Alvarado at the Itata River in 1536. Gómez de Alvarado's advance column battled there with a "great number of natives," a clash that would become known at the Battle of Reinohuelén (Reynogüelén). Nineteenth-century historian Vicente Carvallo Goyenche put the number of Mapuche attackers at more than twenty-four thousand,[12] but sixteenth-century chronicler Alonso de Góngora Marmolejo referred to them as "disorganized and untrained."[13] Whatever the balance of forces, both sides suffered casualties, and Almagro and his men soon left Chile, worried that they were losing their share of Inka Empire spoils while meeting significant resistance in Chile.

Michimalonco: The Pikunche Roundly Reject More Mine Work

After the almagristas were driven back at Reynogüelén, future Spanish columns would initially avoid the Mapuche, settling instead among the Pikunche, a group previously conquered by the Inka in the fifteenth century. A handful of Pikunche chiefs had become Inka regional governors, some like Michimalonco were even received as diplomats in the Inka capital of Cuzco.[14]

The Spanish would abandon Chile from 1537 to 1540 while Almagro and the Pizarro brothers fought for control of Peru. Pedro de Valdivia, a new arrival to South America and veteran of European wars, allied with the victorious Pizarro camp and was tasked with organizing another expedition from Peru to Chile in 1540. Eager to exploit the *oro* (gold) *de Chile* that was well-known in Peru,[15] Valdivia immediately sought indigenous laborers to mine it. However, Almagro's violence from four years before was fresh in the minds of the residents of the Huasco valley, and upon his arrival there, Valdivia found it mostly deserted as the Diaguita residents were *alzados* (in rebellion) and had taken up strategic positions out of sight of the Spanish. With the Diaguita people out of sight, Valdivia could not force them to provide food. Before pushing south, the Europeans resorted to surviving on the small dogs that they found near abandoned villages.[16]

Unable to gain a foothold in the Huasco and Choapa valleys, Valdivia found allies in Atepudo and Quilicanta, as he moved farther south. Atepudo and Quilicanta both begrudged Michimalonco for his cooperation with the Inka. Valdivia settled in the fertile Mapocho valley, where he could cement his alliance with Atepudo and Quilicanta by waging war against Michimalonco. After three months of construction on the new Spanish capital of Santiago, Valdivia organized an attack on Michimalonco's fort defended by four thousand Pikunche troops. After ninety minutes of attacks, Michimalonco surrendered the fort, emerging dramatically at the wall with bow and arrow in hand and proclaiming "Inchi/e Michimalonco" (I am Michimalonco). After his spirited surrender, Michimalonco was released quite anticlimactically after the Pikunche leader promised to show Valdivia where to find more gold.[17]

FIGURE 1.3. Four scenes from Michimalonco's 1541 attack against Concón (near Marga-Marga) and Santiago. Commemorated four hundred years after the attack in the weekly children's magazine, *El Colegial* 1, no. 2 (1941). From Memoria Chilena, Biblioteca Nacional de Chile.

Michimalonco did eventually guide Valdivia's troops to the Marga-Marga estuary, but balked when Valdivia demanded 1,200 Pikunche laborers to pan for gold there.[18] Instead, Michimalonco told Pikunche farmers around Santiago to hide their food from the Spanish and began to prepare an army to move against both the Spanish at Marga-Marga (where he set fire to a Spanish ship) and the city of Santiago itself. Michilalonco's army eventually grew to sixteen thousand Pikunche and Mapuche troops, with even his former rival Quilicanta feeding him information about Spanish troop movements. On September 11, 1541, Michimalonco's army fell on Santiago, destroying much of it in a day-long assault (fig. 1.3).[19] Valdivia had already set out toward Rancagua to try to avoid a Mapuche-Pikunche alliance, but the famous Spanish colonist Inés de Suárez helped avoid the city's total destruction by executing two captive chiefs, an act that disoriented their advancing comrades.[20]

Lautaro: Assassination as Resistance

Michimalonco had left most of Santiago in ruins and escaped to the south. Valdivia would spend much of the next two years attempting to reedify the capital and secure food. He also obviously had to adjust expectations. The conquest of Chile (if even possible at that point) would be difficult. Valdivia's letters to the Crown reflected not necessarily his triumphs but rather his struggles in bringing Chile under Spanish control. He began to hope that his "labors of hunger" (*trabajos del hambre*) and his sacrifices, rather than the usual "labors of war" (*trabajos de la guerra*), would please the Spanish monarch.[21] Valdivia had already weathered one attempted mutiny in 1540 even before the attack on Santiago. He knew that he would somehow have to handsomely reward his followers if these "labors of hunger" were to succeed.

The most important of these rewards would ultimately come in the form of *encomiendas* for almost all of the members of his 150-man expedition.[22] Once the groups of indigenous workers were distributed to his allies, Valdivia asked few questions of how the encomienda workers were treated. Valdivia even freed all the members of his expedition of their debts and of their obligations to him, dramatically tearing up their IOUs.[23] While Michimalonco's successful resistance did certainly stall European advance into Chile, some things did not change: the Spanish thirst for gold and their distaste for manual labor. These two factors proved strong enough to require a renewal of Mapuche resistance to forced labor a half a century after the Battle of Maule.

After his difficulties at Santiago and Marga-Marga, Valdivia sought a new

Pacific port and new sources of gold. In 1550, Valdivia and his lieutenants arrived at the mouth of the Bío-Bío River, where they erected the town of Concepción. Valdivia also sent Gerónimo de Alderete and Francisco de Villagra on separate expeditions to find the "Lost City of Caesars" and the "North Sea" (the Atlantic Ocean).[24] The Spanish had long heard of and imagined a large and rich empire in the Andes (Cuzco), but it took them over thirty years of a presence in the Caribbean and Mexico to reach the Inka capital. Perhaps there would be a similar lost kingdom in the Chilean Andes.

Valdivia might have done better, however, to worry about real indigenous warriors than mythical ones. These multiple myth-chasing expeditions left the Spanish at a disadvantage, no more evident than in 1553 when Mapuche troops, commanded by the toki Lautaro, killed Valdivia. Lautaro was the son of a principal cacique (chieftain), which afforded him the "privilege" of working closely with Valdivia as a hostler. Like Michimalonco, however, Lautaro saw little hope for advancement as a Spanish ally. Lautaro left Valdivia's service around 1550 and soon became a toki near Tucapél, and his knowledge of the Spanish and their horses made him an indispensable military leader. In the weeks before Valdivia's assassination, there had been skirmishes in the area surrounding Fort Arauco, but Valdivia seems to have been a target of opportunity. Upon spotting him, however, the Mapuche clearly knew who he was and turned his killing into a ceremony filled with symbolic rejection of growing Spanish incursions.

Diego de Rosales, a seventeenth-century Jesuit missionary and historian, collected accounts of the killing from Mapuche and Spanish oral histories and wrote the most extensive and most accepted account of the killing: "An infinite multitude had congregated . . . women, children and elders along with the troops of soldiers, that there were, they made a ring, and planted in the middle of the *tokis*, the lances, and arrows, making a great circle, the chiefs and ancients from all around, they called to bring out Valdivia, and in the middle of the wheel, they would take his life." Valdivia was felled by a blow to the head with a club. With that, his captors

> raised their voices, and their lances over the dead body, stomping the earth with their feet, and making it shake, to make it understood that the earth trembled with their bravery. Upon this one arrived, and ripping him open from the throat to the chest with a knife, he reached his hand into him, and removed the heart by ripping it out, and while beating, and squirting blood, he showed it to everyone, and smearing the tokis

> and the arrows with blood, he cut it into small pieces, that all the chiefs ate, and the rest licked up the blood, and all of those in the group that touch a part of the body, are sworn to unite their arms, and to have their hearts against the Spanish. They cut off his head soon after and made flutes from his thighbones and (his head) put on a stake, they sang a victory song around it, and had a long celebration with toasts and acts of joy, at seeing their nation liberated.

Later, "they took the head and nailed it to the door of the house of the great Caupolicán, principal author of this trophy, and around it put the heads of some Spaniards, distributing others among different provinces, to bring devotion to them. Finally, they cooked the head of Valdivia, and while all were intoxicated yet solemn, Caupolicán took out the head, and drank *chicha* from the skull, offering a toast to all of the chiefs greater than him. This head kept watch outside of his house, as if it were a link to an ancestor, and they pass it down to his descendants."[25]

This exocannibalistic ritual was not just a "sensory experience" for the Mapuche, but eating the heart was a spiritual one as well.[26] For the Mapuche, the heart or *piuke* "was considered the place of decision, will . . . and feelings." This means that the best way for the Mapuches to "assimilate the qualities of the enemy" was to literally "digest" him. The victor achieved a "symbolic gaining of the life substance of the captive's body."[27] The making of flutes out of Valdivia's leg bones also begins to make sense in the context of this incorporation of qualities. The verb *zugún* means to both talk and to play music. By playing the bone flutes, the soul of Valdivia would "sing or speak," providing the Mapuches with more Spanish knowledge and power. Contacting their dead through music was an important Mapuche practice. Perhaps the contacting of the Spanish dead would also prove useful.

Decapitation also was also an act of assimilation. The head was a "symbol of the enemy's bravery . . . and the source of his prestige."[28] The person in possession of a severed head absorbed some of its qualities, as thought and perception were believed to reside there. The skull was incorporated into traditional Mapuche rites as a drinking vessel, and a hat could be fashioned from a jawbone. This process came from a tradition where the victorious hunter would wear the jaw of his ferocious prey, just as the victorious warrior's cap could display their bravery and ferocity.[29] There is also the possibility that this decapitation was a response to Suárez's assassination of captive caciques during the siege of Santiago in 1541.

How Mapuche society maintained and expanded resistance in future decades is discussed subsequently, but already in the 1550s, Lautaro knew that resistance was the only path forward. As a bilingual war commander, Lautaro's experience told him that it would take more than the assassination of Chile's governor to deter the Spanish, and he began to plan a major assault that could drive Europeans out of Chile entirely. Lautaro's offensive began in 1557, destroying several Spanish towns and threatening to once again level Santiago. As Lautaro neared the capital, a Spanish column led by interim governor Villagra intercepted and killed him.[30] While Lautaro's general uprising had failed, resistance to the Spanish and the *mal mayor* (worst evil) of forced labor had already become an integral part of a changing Mapuche culture.

Tokis, Machis, and Cahuínes: Societal Transformation as Resistance

As mentioned, Mapuche and Spanish generals of the past are well known to everyday Chileans. But the story of seventeenth-century Mapuche resistance is not one that can be boiled down to an image of brave commanders leading their troops from a parapet. Instead, Mapuche leadership took multiple paths and reorganized multiple times in the face of increasingly unrestrained Spanish enslavers. Recently, scholars like Tom Dillehay, Guillame Boccara, Horacio Zapater, and José Bengoa have looked beyond Tucapél or the multiple attacks on Santiago to help us understand the complexities and adaptability of Mapuche leadership.[31]

As mentioned, meetings of multiple Mapuche clans before the seventeenth century were infrequent and usually did not involve future planning. In the seventeenth century, however, levos or cahuínes transformed from infrequent gatherings to the centers of a "widespread resistance movement against the Spanish invaders."[32] As Spanish pressure on Mapuche territory increased, multiple (up to nine) levos could be combined to create "tierras grandes" or *ayllarehue*.[33] By the 1600s, multiple ayllarehue were organized into *butunmapu*, a confederation that posed a significant challenge to the Spanish, so much so that the Europeans began to refer to the butunmapu as "estados" (states).[34] Dillehay argues that Mapuche understandings of said territory made confederation building even more important and that political organization was not a function of "strict geographical boundar[ies]" but rather a "networking arrangement."[35] For the Mapuche, sovereignty was community; it was the Andean ayllu or the Athenian *ecclesia*. Without calling the Mapuche protofederalist, we can still acknowledge that their concept of constantly negotiated sovereignty was important to their resistance. As one historian puts it, "myth and rites are the central axes of Mapuche cohesion and identity."[36]

Part of negotiated sovereignty was of course establishing a leadership process. Bringing together multiple lineages with thousands of members to face a winka threat required new leadership roles and the adjustment of old ones. Tokis or *gentokis* became exclusively military commanders, while an *ülmen* would lead a levo. The seventeenth-century Mapuche also had multiple spiritual leaders like the "machi, hechicero, reñi, boquivoye (huecubuye, boquibuye) and nguillatufe."[37] There is quite a bit of overlap involving their roles, but for the purposes of resistance, these leaders would oversee rituals, help determine when it was time to go to war, and also consult with Pillán.[38]

Not only did Mapuche leadership positions change during the seventeenth century but so too did the process of promotion to positions of power, especially when it came to status earned through resistance. In the 1560s and 1570s for example, we see the appearance of a type of "Indian mercenary" who worked for a prearranged payment.[39] Warriors also began to ascend through the ranks of Mapuche society, something unseen in peacetime when social status was largely hereditary. An ülmen could become a toki through his war deeds. A toki could become a gentoki, or "possessor of the stone hatchet, a symbol of his function."[40] Toki referred to both the leader and the leader's staff or hatchet, the object that symbolized their power. Thus, through the ritual murder of a Spaniard with toki, a gentoki retained a constant reminder of the source of his power and his title. The hatchet could be "considered as an ancestor or as a part of a petrified mythical ancestor."[41] The Mapuche revered their ancestors, and the fact that the ancestors were present in ritual assassination integrated violent resistance even more into Mapuche society. The hatchet was a tremendously powerful symbol of leadership that helped reorganize Mapuche society around these new war chiefs.

Resistance itself was not enough to transform Mapuche society; it had to be successful. The seventeenth century saw a myriad of successful tactical changes from Mapuche soldiers, detailed by historians like Louis de Armond and Nathan Wachtel. For one, the Mapuche quickly incorporated Spanish horses into both their daily life and their combat, so much so that they would earn a religious significance. The Mapuche became superb riders and developed saddles, which were made of small pieces of wood and wool cushions and were lighter than those imported by the Spanish. This meant that

Mapuche horses did not tire as fast and that the Mapuche cavalry was faster and more mobile. The Mapuche horse's burden was also lighter because the riders used little metal in their weapons or riding implements.[42]

Mapuche tactical advantages went beyond their use of horses. In the desert north, the Spanish did encounter resistance, but there were no dense forests to disorient them nor was there rain to spoil their gunpowder. Southern Chile by contrast was full of rivers and forests where Mapuche combatants could hide, and the rainy climate would often dampen Spanish fuses and gunpowder.[43] Pre-Columbian Mapuche were already excellent swimmers and frequently used canoes in the south's many navigable rivers. As seen in chapter 4, there were multiple cases of Spanish soldiers drowning in their attempts to capture Mapuches. Some of these rivers were wide enough to contain lagoons and small islands. Small islands in the Purén River, in particular, were important natural forts and contributed to the Purén valley's development as a center of Mapuche resistance.[44]

Rivers and Resistance

Chile's rivers were also important to the question of political decentralization and resistance. The Spanish decision to found Concepción at the mouth of the Bío-Bío River meant that Mapuches in coastal provinces like Arauco were susceptible to Spanish raids, while the province of Purén was tucked into inland wetlands and not easily accessible to Spanish arms.[45] As we disaggregate terms like *Indian* or *Araucanian*, we start to understand (quite logically) that differing proximities to Spanish settlements meant there could not be a universal Mapuche resistance strategy, and as such, it is difficult to say that "the Mapuche thought this" or "the Mapuche did that."

The Mapuche of Arauco and Tucapél and the Huilliche near the Spanish port town of Valdivia often became indios de paz or indios amigos. Making peace with the Spanish and participating in the conquest of Chile (as indios amigos did) can certainly be viewed as an act of capitulation. But indios amigos also could be freer in their movements, were subject to less forced labor, and, since their communities were larger, could still resist as the center of general uprisings. For these Spanish "auxiliaries" who grew up in the shadow of a Spanish town or Spanish fort, becoming a Spanish ally was often the only path to some autonomy. Some observers even claimed that some auxiliaries or *indios de servicio* were interested in prolonging and expanding the war to keep the relative freedom that working with the Spanish army offered.[46] Ironically perhaps, many unconquered communities of Mapuches also tried to prolong the war "and preferred death in battle to becoming subjects of a people who had committed so many wrongs against them without justice or reason."[47]

While there were sporadic attempts by the Spanish to retake territory lost to Lautaro's rebellion, most of the military activity around the Bío-Bío in the 1560s and 1570s could be classified as "frontier violence." As seen in later chapters, the Spanish would conduct raids on Mapuche frontier levos just to please the viceroy of Peru, while the Mapuche would benefit from these raids for their commercial potential. As historian of North American frontiers James F. Brooks points out, only focusing on the "corrosive" effects of frontier violence "diffuses its major contributions to intercultural trade, alliances, and communities among groups often antagonistic to Spanish modernizing strategies."[48] Historian Richard White adds that within a "war" the periods of actual armed conflict are very brief and can blur our attempts to understand frontier exchange. Violence was often "inextricably bound up with commerce" in that it was an "option both for acquiring goods and for protecting them."[49] We cannot argue that the Mapuche asked the Spanish to raid them, but they certainly knew when to expect Spanish infantry and used them to resupply, seizing or trading for swords, armor, and gunpowder.[50]

Intergroup relationships through frontier violence were also very important to "ethnogenesis."[51] The sons of Mapuche men and Spanish women made up much of the Mapuche hierarchy and were afforded a unique status by the Spanish. Mapuches and Spaniards were duty bound to rescue captives, but those who went unredeemed contributed to increasing *mestizaje* on both sides of the frontier. Mapuche women also maintained relationships with Spanish soldiers from nearby forts or encampments.[52] Even frontier Mapuches who had resisted for years could *dar la paz* (make peace) with the Spanish, allowing them to return to or normalize contact with colonists.

These low-stakes Spanish raids not only netted credibility for Mapuche war leaders who resisted but also helped cement inter-levo alliances with items bought or plundered during these raids like beads or dogs.[53] It was in fact so common for the Mapuche to have Spanish goods that the Jesuit Diego de Rosales described how a Spanish cavalry patrol stumbled upon a group of Mapuche soldiers. The Spanish cavalry actually hailed the mounted Mapuches, believing them to be another Spanish patrol, but when they approached were shocked to discover that these were in fact Mapuches donning almost exclusively Spanish equipment and clothing.[54]

Purén Indómito: The Core of Resistance Takes Shape

Much further from permanent Spanish settlements was the Purén/Lumaco region, the center of Mapuche resistance and an area with a very different reality than that of the Mapuches already described. Already by the 1560s, the Spanish had begun to identify the four nearest Mapuche provinces of Arauco, Mareguano (modern Marihueñe), Tucapél, and Purén. Arauco and Tucapél were the provinces of the northwest and southwest and were relatively accessible from Concepción. Mareguano in the northeast was farther inland but near the navigable Bío-Bío.[55] But we have long understood through seventeenth-century sources that the southeastern province of Purén was autonomous for much of the colonial period. One of Chile's best-known colonial works of literature is the seventeenth-century epic poem, *Purén Indómito* (Purén unconquered) by Diego Arias de Saavedra. Purén and Lumaco had an "outsized" role in Mapuche resistance first because of "highly productive and geographically formidable wetlands, or *ciénagas,* that protected it from Spanish armies."[56] The Spanish were further hampered by the lack of a Pacific port nearby, and even today, there is very little ocean access along the 150 kilometers between Lebu and Saavedra. The Purén and Lumaco valleys were also the site of one of the largest mound groups in the region.[57] These mounds (*kuel*) are "socially built mound(s) where ancestral spirits reside, important people are occasionally buried, and public rituals are performed" (fig. 1.4).[58] In the sixteenth and early seventeenth centuries, these kuel were the sites of multiple reguas, important gatherings for recruitment and strategizing. Relatively safe from Spanish raids, the kuel of Purén also served as landmarks where other displaced Mapuches or even Spanish deserters could regroup and develop new "social spaces" around "the multimound *rehuekuel* of multiple lineages."[59]

In the same way that the *vida fronteriza* (frontier life) provided opportunities for sporadic Mapuche resistance, areas like Purén and Tucapél saw Mapuche armies preparing for larger and successful attacks on Spanish cities and forts. One such attack was led by Lautaro, who not only killed Valdivia but also twice expelled Spanish colonists from Concepción. After his victory over Valdivia at Tucapél, Lautaro led the 1554 sacking and destruction of Concepción. Spanish colonists fled to Santiago and tried to return and rebuild Concepción two years later. They managed to last a month in Concepción before Lautaro's army appeared and, after a brief battle, forced the

FIGURE 1.4. *Kuel* in the Purén Valley, 2008.
Photograph by Len60, CC BY-SA 4.0.

Spanish out of the city again.[60] After Lautaro's death, the toki general Caupolicán led the third attack on Concepción in four years. In 1557, the Spanish had arrived by ship, setting up a temporary fort in Talcahuano Bay. This time the Spanish managed to disembark but faced off against Caupolicán's army outside of Concepción in the battles of Lagunillas and Millarapue.[61]

Caupolicán's death in 1558 would lead to three years of calm that ended with the killing of Spanish captain Pedro de Avendaño in Purén. In 1561, a measles outbreak occurred among the Mapuche when the Spanish attempted to repopulate the Araucanía, but the epidemic did not prevent the Mapuche from destroying new Spanish settlements at Cañete and Tucumán. In 1563, the Spanish abandoned Fort Arauco, and Concepción was again under siege. This year represented perhaps the strongest Mapuche position since Valdivia's death. The Maule River, not the Bío-Bío, had become the frontier, with the Spanish "ashamed [that] they found themselves in larger numbers since the beginning of the conquest, yet [militarily] weakened."[62]

Chile was becoming, then, not the capstone of Spain's South American conquest but rather a center of indigenous resistance to forced labor. The success of resistance from Purén in particular made this part of the Araucanía attractive to any number of refugees fleeing Spanish forced labor. As noted, Spanish operations were seasonal, meaning that hundreds of Spanish soldiers brought servants with them to frontier campaigns and left them there when they returned to Santiago every winter.[63] In their arrogance, the Spanish expected the same servants to aid them again when they returned months later, and some did. Many, however, simply returned to their *reducciones* or levos. The seasonal migration of Spanish soldiers contributed to a larger trend of "vagabondism" in the Chilean countryside that would continue into the national period. Historian Mario Góngora describes not only seasonal migrations from Santiago to the Araucanía but also constant movement between Santiago and La Serena, Santiago, and Mendoza and in and out of Andean valleys led by the Pehuenche and Puelche.[64]

This wandering existence was largely prompted by the demands of Spanish employers and soldiers, but it could also be beneficial to individuals who sought to escape poor conditions or simply believed that conditions would improve elsewhere in the colony. The same Andean passes used by the Pehuenche, Puelche, and Huarpe also proved a common escape route for enslaved Africans, with many colonial authors describing daring Andean escapes. Rosales, for example, provides details on how three groups of enslaved Africans made their way out of Santiago and across the Andes in 1633, 1644, and 1649.[65] Twentieth-century historian Góngora details how "mestizos, mulattos and zambos" in colonial Chile (and other frontier areas in the Americas) would often be free to wander as local hierarchies did not tie them to any particular place within the colony. In fact, itinerant people of all ethnicities across the colonial Americas could often find agency or community among autonomous indigenous groups like the Mapuche. For example, Jane Landers describes how Seminoles in Spanish Florida captured enslaved Africans from Francisco Phelipe Fatio's Saint John's River plantation. While on the surface, these enslaved Africans traded one type of bondage for another, dozens of them never returned to plantation life, eventually gaining "the freedom that Seminoles typically granted their black vassals in the nation."[66] Indigenous communities also welcomed Spanish deserters, who, far from Lima or Madrid, may have tired of the discipline of army life.[67]

Wanderers escaping to the margins of Spanish society would of course reject any attempts to force them back, and as such, we have dozens of accounts of former "vagabonds" joining or even leading resistance from several Mapuche levos.[68] These Mapuche-mestizo alliances first appeared only two decades after Lautaro's victories and continued well into the seventeenth century. In 1577, a mestizo named Alonso Díaz and a cacique from Lebu named Juan led an attack on Angól. Juan took a Spanish first name after having been enslaved by the first Spanish conquerors in Chile, sent to Peru, and brought back to Chile as a servant to Governor Melchór Bravo de Saravia in 1568. Juan soon escaped to Lebu and began to organize *malocas* against the Spanish with Díaz.[69] Díaz seems to have reappeared in 1584, this time leading an ambush near Angól against the new governor Alonso de Sotomayor. The Spanish learned that Díaz had since abandoned his Spanish name, now calling himself Paineñameu. Spanish arquebusiers eventually repelled the ambush, finding Paineñameu hiding in a marsh. Several Spanish officers argued for Paineñameu's immediate execution, but his life was spared after he agreed to cooperate and lead the Spanish to the positions of other rebels. Paineñameu eventually led the Spanish to the hiding place of an unnamed rebel of African descent, who despite being discovered was able make a narrow escape by swimming across a river.[70] With developments like these, the Spanish had to be asking themselves whether they were generating more resistance fighters than they had apprehended.

The Road to Curalaba: More Forts and More Cahuínes

Evidently frustrated by his first foray into the Araucanía region, Sotomayor later returned to Marihueñe, and began to methodically burn Mapuche crops.[71] Despite clear setbacks, both Sotomayor and his successor Martín García Óñez de Loyola were determined to take territory unoccupied by the Spanish since Lautaro's time. But the Mapuche resistance was now even more organized than it had been under Lautaro. Something would have to give, and it would in the form of the Curalaba Uprising.

Recognizing that Sotomayor was interested in more than summer raids, the Mapuche organized a more robust response. Chief (probably toki) Cayencura of Marihueñe , in defense of his smoldering fields, prepared a general uprising to drive out the Spanish who had set up camp near Angól.[72] Cayencura sent messengers bearing a bloody arrow (*flecha ensangrentada*) to more than 150 levos, eventually raising a force of thousands of warriors ready to attack the Spanish arsonists.[73] The toki Lonconabal brought two thousand soldiers, among them the famous captains Liencura, Aramoco, and Quelicante. Anteleubu from Purén brought one thousand pike men, among them Catuguanquen, Talcamavida, and Millapoa. Three thousand Puelches left the mountains to join the attack, under the command of Milladoto. Once all had arrived, the Mapuche conducted a parley where they settled on a three-pronged attack with one of the columns led by the same outlaw who had swum out of reach of the Spanish only weeks before. The plan was also aided by a double agent named Andrés, a teenager and former servant to Captain Fernando Albarez de Toledo in Chillán. As a Spanish officer, Albarez de Toledo likely lost track of Andrés while wintering away from the front, and Andrés was able to provide valuable intelligence to the Mapuche about Spanish positions.[74]

Cayencura's army did surprise the Spanish with a nighttime attack on their position near Angól in January 1585. Spanish arquebusiers were able to fend off the invaders, but Sotomayor was left shaken. Rather than waiting for reinforcements, the governor immediately began construction on two forts: one on the Bío-Bío called Santísima Trinidad and another in Purén called Espiritu Santo.[75] Sotomayor would order these forts dismantled not three years later as Mapuche resistance proved too dynamic for him to make any real progress on resupply.

The same Puelches who had joined the attack on Angól quickly regrouped under the command of a new toki, a Puelche woman named Anuqueupu or Yanequo (Janequeo). Anuqueupu's brother Quechuntureo and husband, Guepotaén, were both rebel leaders, and multiple chroniclers cite the death of Guepotaén as motivation for Anuquepu's attacks. It was clear, however, that Anuqueupu was not simply a grieving widow, as she seamlessly put together a force of four thousand troops through a cahuín and through the ritual murder of two Spanish officers captured between Osorno and Villarrica.[76] While it is unusual to see a female toki, Mapuche women held multiple leadership positions in the early colonial period. Anuquepu's ascension was representative of an increased call to resistance and more frequent meetings to organize among the Mapuche, Puelche, Pehuenche, and Huilliche in response to Sotomayor's insistence on taking back territory lost to Lautaro's uprising.

In October 1590, Sotomayor would lead his last summer campaign into Mapuche territory. This campaign would not have been particularly noteworthy but for the fact that it would be Sotomayor's last and more importantly prompted a measles outbreak. This pestilence took the lives of a handful of Spanish soldiers but decimated the *yanaconas* (indigenous servants) who accompanied the Spanish; one chronicler estimated that 1,300 lost their lives.[77] Despite the loss of his yanacona servants to the outbreak, Sotomayor remained confident in his progress and traveled to Lima to ask for reinforcements.[78] Instead of rewarding Sotomayor, however, the viceroy removed him as governor and replaced him with Óñez de Loyola.

While the Spanish were changing governors in Lima, a number of caciques met near Arauco to discuss how to keep the virulent Europeans at bay. Curaquilla, Pengueregua, Millarapue, Chibilongo, and Curilemo met in a cahuín, sacrificed a sheep, and tried to inspire other tokis to join them in an attack on the Spanish.[79] Spanish troops were informed of the meeting, however, and scattered the participants. In the late sixteenth century the Spanish became particularly insistent that the Mapuche not meet in great numbers, as they assumed that such a meeting of several levos was a plot against them. Sometimes this assumption was correct, but the Spanish presence also created peacetime problems like infectious disease, which would require a meeting of multiple levos to organize a response. Spanish officials, however, cared little about this nuance and would break up these *borracheras* (drunken parties), as they called them, if they had an opportunity to do so. This pattern of creating the need for a cahuín, then violently breaking up the cahuín, contributed to an even larger Mapuche response in the form of the Curalaba Rebellion of 1598.

The Resistance Triumphs at Curalaba: The End of *La Conquista*?

Increasing Spanish attempts to take territory provoked more energetic Mapuche campaigns to drive them out, especially when the Spanish dared challenge the core of Mapuche resistance. As new governors were inclined to do, Óñez de Loyola created quite a scene upon his 1593 arrival in Chile. There were parades in his honor in Santiago and Concepción, soon followed by processions for his wife, Beatríz Clara Coya, the niece of the "Last Inka," Túpac Amaru (fig. 1.5).[80]

Óñez de Loyola made peace with several groups of Mapuches fronterizos near Concepción, a typical hollow gesture of goodwill with little strategic value. Next, however, Óñez de Loyola did something not seen by Spanish commanders in decades. He foolhardily (or bravely according to some chroniclers) established a fort in an empty marsh at Lumaco, the core of Mapuche resistance. The Mapuche tokis would react swiftly to this new tactic, with results that still reverberate today.

After much ceremony with Mapuches fronterizos and "founding" forts that were already there, Óñez de Loyola made a significant push toward Arauco with 200 Spanish infantry and more than 650 indios amigos. After scorching Mapuche fields, the Spanish were turned back from Tucapél, the resistance

FIGURE 1.5. Marriage of Captain Martin Óñez de Loyola to Beatriz Ñusta. Cuzco School, oil on canvas, 1718. Collection of Museo Pedro de Osma. This painting is more family tree than wedding portrait. Óñez de Loyola and Beatríz Clara Coya appear on the left; the couple on the right is Lorenza de Loyola, their daughter, and Juan de Borja, their son-in-law, who were present only in spirit at the wedding. (*Ñusta* means "princess.")

inspired from toki Paillamacho of Purén. In August 1593, spring was near and it was time for the Spanish to set out toward Purén once again. This time, the Spanish sent a capitán de amigos (leader of indios amigos) to the wetlands to try to convince Paillamacho to make peace. Instead, the Purén Mapuches attacked the captain and returned to the wetlands with his severed head. The Spanish stayed nearby, burning fields for two weeks and searching for Mapuche instigators. Eventually, two of the governor's most trusted soldiers and a group of indios amigos entered deep into the thickets and surprised a group of bathing *purenes* (residents of Purén), executing as many as they could catch.[81]

The Spanish insisted that the indios amigos make overtures of peace to the purenes but did little to protect them when the purenes reacted angrily. For example, when the amigos living in Fort Rangalí (near La Imperial) warned the local *corregidor* (mayor) in 1595 of an impending attack, the corregidor insisted that the amigos were crying wolf. Instead of protecting Rangalí, the corregidor sent one hundred amigos out of the fort to *dar la mita* (fulfill their labor quota) at nearby gold mines. While the fort's best defenders met their forced labor obligations (never mind that soldiering is also labor), the purenes attacked Rangalí, killing the hundreds of women, children, and elderly who remained. Predictably, Óñez de Loyola responded with a punitive campaign after those he had left unprotected were victimized in such a fashion. Soon, 1,000 amigos and yanaconas along with 135 Spaniards found themselves wading in chest-deep water toward an island in the wetlands of Purén. This island was a well-known and isolated *rebelde* (rebel) hiding place where the Spanish again set fires, stole Mapuche cattle, and took prisoners.[82]

In 1597, Óñez de Loyola himself led almost 200 Spanish troops and 1,500 indios amigos into Purén. The goal of this expedition was not to take captives but rather territory, as the Spanish broke ground on a new fort in Lumaco, initially supplied by one thousand bushels of stolen Mapuche wheat. The Mapuche simply could not have a Spanish fort neighboring their kuel, and called at least two major cahuínes. Spanish troops broke up the first, but after Óñez de Loyola (and all but 140 soldiers) had retired to Concepción, the Mapuche met again and planned a successful assault. Anganamón from Purén was elected toki general and set upon the Lumaco fort with seven thousand troops. The siege lasted two days and finally ended through negotiated surrender after the Mapuche destroyed a Spanish resupply caravan.[83]

Óñez de Loyola had found, yet failed to topple, the core area of Mapuche resistance. His plan was to keep raiding and pillaging neighboring areas like Tucapél and Arauco until they were no longer vulnerable to instigation from the purenes. Spanish occupation and a scorched-earth strategy were never going to succeed at winning the hearts of Mapuches in those interstitial communities, but Anganamón and Pelantaro were unwilling to wait for these strategies to fail on their own. The toki general and his lieutenant Pelantaro knew that Óñez de Loyola planned to winter, not in Concepción or Santiago, but instead in Osorno or La Imperial so that he could be closer to Purén and resume his campaign earlier in the spring.[84] Anganamón, Pelantaro, Guaquimilla, and as many as three hundred Mapuche troops followed

Óñez de Loyola into a mountainous area south of Angól, between the rivers Purén, Rehue, and Picoiquen.[85] As the Spanish slept near a creek named Curalaba, the Mapuche attacked and killed the governor of Chile.

For the second time in fifty years, the Mapuche resistance had assassinated Chile's top official. As was the case with Valdivia's killing, several chroniclers detailed the demise of the famous nephew of Saint Ignatius, some even getting first-hand accounts from Anganamón and Pelantaro years later. Many chroniclers focus on the days and hours before Óñez de Loyola's death, trying to excuse away the fact that the Spanish were underprepared. Some described that at some point during his retreat, Óñez de Loyola's saddle broke, sending him tumbling off his horse. For the superstitious soldiers escorting him, this was a bad omen and left the governor with only a company of seventy, a far insufficient number. Other authors argue that the group exercised a lack of caution as they set up camp at Curalaba without putting soldiers on watch for the night. Still others write that the Spanish were not careless but ambushed and outnumbered. Most concur, however, that Óñez de Loyola was decapitated, his head becoming the inspiration for the subsequent Mapuche assault.[86]

Pelantaro would later boast that he would not stop until he had "driven all Spaniards out of Chile" or had Spanish women "making chicha and dressing in blankets."[87] Less than two days later, the Mapuche had thirty thousand troops attacking different Spanish towns simultaneously. As the governor's executioner, Pelantaro became the recognized leader of the assault and a gentoki.[88] Soon, this small assault turned hundreds of small levos into an army, one that between 1598 and 1602 forced the Spanish to abandon Chillán, Osorno, Valdivia, Villarrica, La Imperial, Santa Cruz, and Arauco (fig. 1.6).[89] In the resulting "Disaster (or Victory) of Curalaba,"[90] more than three thousand Spaniards were killed and hundreds more taken captive.[91]

Curalaba was the end of the Spanish conquest of Chile. The Mapuche would maintain some level of sovereignty in the Araucanía well into the nineteenth century and even after Chile became an independent nation. Unfortunately, this did not mean that Mapuche communities would now be left alone. Not only Potosí but other urban areas throughout the viceroyalty would still demand gold, wheat, beef, leather, tallow, mules, and, most importantly, laborers from Chile. The Mapuche victory at Curalaba meant that their sixteenth-century resistance had worked. But they would need to remain vigilant and find new ways to combat the persistence of Spanish forced-labor demands, the mal incurable, for almost the entire next century.

Establishing the nature of this Mapuche resistance is important not just for the sake of the ethnohistorical record but also because the Spanish would test that resistance for more than a century with ever-expanding attempts to capture and enslave Mapuches. It is a testament to the complexity and malleability of this resistance that it continued well into Chile's national period.

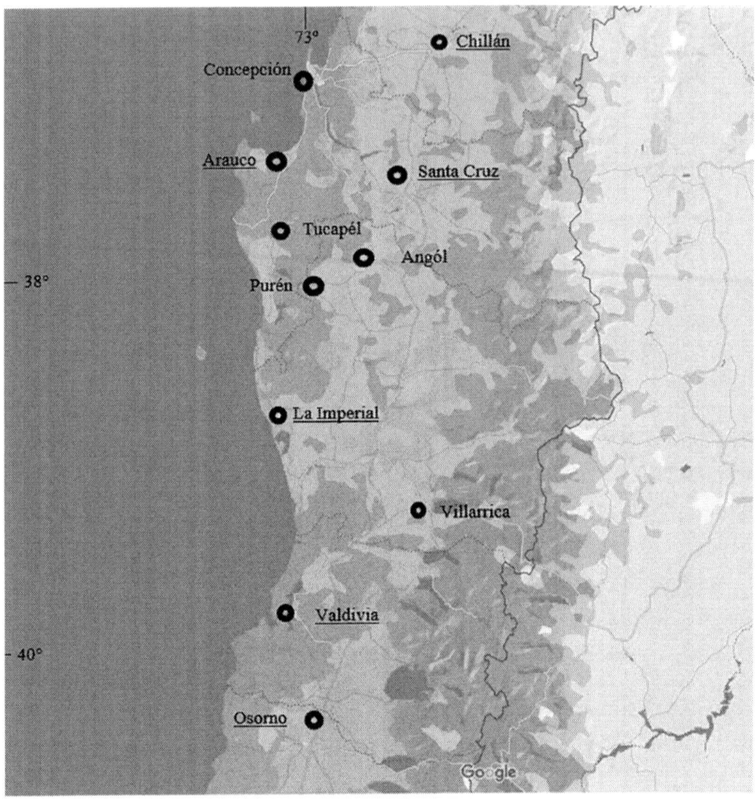

FIGURE 1.6. Spanish cities abandoned after the Curalaba Uprising are underlined. Concepción was not abandoned. Tucapél, Angól, and Purén were forts. Villarrica was abandoned in the 1550s. Map data 2021 © Google. Map by Eugene C. Berger.

2

A Pacific Coast Diaspora

The Incurable Evil and an Evolving Need for Resistance

The Curalaba uprising began in 1598, but the Spanish would not completely abandon Valdivia and Osorno until 1604. The only thing resembling a counterattack by the Spanish was a march of about five hundred soldiers from Fort Nacimiento toward Purén and Lumaco. There the Spanish directed *indios auxiliaries* (indigenous servants) to scatter cordwood (*fajina*) in an attempt to break up Mapuche resistance and interrupt crop production. But while the bulk of Spanish forces were in Purén, the Mapuche had snuck by them and begun to attack towns neighboring Concepción like Talcahuano and Hualqui.[1] When we read about the success of Michimalonco, Lautaro, and Pelantaro, it may strike us as odd that the Spanish did not abandon Chile entirely, but money and pride were at stake, which gave Spain tremendous staying power and a tremendous thirst for forced labor. This chapter looks at what the Mapuche resistance was really up against. I discuss attempts by the Spanish to curb indigenous abuse in the sixteenth century and how they were limited by powerful *encomenderos*. I examine the relationship between the transatlantic slave trade and raids to enslave into Mapuche territory. I also detail an expanding export of enslaved Mapuches out of the Araucanía and to Santiago, La Serena, and Lima.

Spellbound by Gold and Silver

Not settled by Europeans until fifty years after Hispaniola, Chile was to be the culmination of Spain's conquest of the Americas. Pride was at stake for the viceroy of Peru, but, more importantly, so was money. By 1545, the Spanish had begun to extract silver from Potosí in Upper Peru (now Bolivia), an undertaking that would require vast resources from throughout the viceroyalty of Peru. Potosí's "mountain of silver" consumed "mules from Córdoba, coca from Cuzco" and would soon attract "Indian slaves from Southern Chile."[2] The "gargantuan system of draft labor" providing many of Potosí's workers was based on the Inka mitae, and eventually, more than "two hundred Indian communities spanning a large area in modern-day Peru and Bolivia sen[t] one-seventh of their adult population to work in the mines of Potosí, Huancavelica and Cailloma."[3] But as we have seen, the Mapuche rejected incorporation into the Inka labor pool, and therefore, the Spanish would eventually turn to "just war" and the encomienda system to force Mapuches to Potosí and Lima.

Before Curalaba: Forced Labor and Moral Failure

The extraction of enormous wealth on the backs of the indigenous was of course not unique to Peru and continued unabated in the face of any official attempts to protect aborigines. All European nations with American colonies used some form of forced labor, with the Spanish in particular having developed guidelines for the categorization and treatment of "others" or "outsiders" long before setting foot in the Americas. Many of these guidelines dated back to the cross-cultural encounter of the Crusades. To the Spanish, Muslims captured in the Crusades or in the *Reconquista* of the Iberian Peninsula had attacked Christendom and ipso facto Christianity itself and were to be treated as slaves in the context of this "just war." Thirteenth-century cardinal Henry de Susa (Hostiensis) postulated, "When Christ came into the world, temporal as well as spiritual lordship over all its peoples passed immediately to Him." According to his argument, those who did not accept Christianity were "recalcitrant" persons against whom a just war could be waged.[4] Queen Isabella herself chose a more forgiving tone when it came to the inhabitants of the Americas. She argued that Native Americas had "become vassals of the Crown and as such were free" and even instructed Columbus to free the Tainos he brought back to Spain with him. However, there were two important exceptions to this freedom: Native Americans could be legally enslaved in a "just war" where they had attacked or rejected Spanish authority and could remain enslaved if they were already in the service of other natives.[5]

These exceptions meant that Hostiensis's ideas of "recalcitrant" persons were applied quite extensively in the Americas and affected how the Spanish used "The Requirement of 1514." The *requerimiento* declared that "only warring Indians could be enslaved" and required the reading of a proclamation in Latin informing the Indians that the resistance of "peaceful intercourse" would give the Spanish "just cause for war."[6] Rather than a means to separate warring from peaceful natives as it was intended, however, the requerimiento was used as a means to justify the enslavement of newly discovered indigenous groups. The requerimiento's proclamation rarely was translated into an indigenous language, and it was often read to those who were already imprisoned and destined for enslavement.

The indigenous people who were not immediately enslaved did not fare much better. These "pagans" were forced into the *repartimiento* system, where they were distributed to Spanish conquerors to be cared for, put to work, and instructed in the Christian faith.[7] In many areas, the repartimiento (system of forced labor similar to encomienda) and encomienda coexisted, and in others, the latter replaced the former. What links them in all areas, however, is the fact that neither actually became a means of protecting indigenous residents. Pope Paul III issued the bull *Sublimis Deus* in 1537 as a response to reports of Spanish cruelty in the Americas, but it had little immediate effect in Chile or anywhere else in the Indies. The bull however would influence future debate, by declaring that the indigenous were "true men" who were not to be enslaved.[8]

The real-world consequences of these debates of course played out first in the Spanish Caribbean, including Mexico, where coastal natives were sent from Tampico to Cuba and Hispaniola and bartered for cattle. This practice was so extensive that it would pave "the way for the ranching empire that would flourish in Texas in later centuries." In the 1560s, however, the "export" would shift back inland and was designed to provide laborers for the silver mines of Zacatecas region.[9] In Peru, the Spanish would employ some of the remaining Inka administrative techniques to find laborers for their own silver mine at Potosí. In Peru in fact, the Spanish pattern of employing conquered Indians in manual labor projects worked relatively seamlessly, as encomenderos became the new beneficiaries of the Inka mitae system of labor obligations, organized into local *ayllus* (family groups).[10]

The Crown had anticipated that encomenderos in Peru would relish their newfound authority and try to "transform themselves into a European-style hereditary nobility."[11] In an attempt to avoid class divisions among the conquistadors, the Crown made nobles out of very few of them and took steps to keep encomiendas nonhereditary, reinforcing the idea of service and reward.[12]

Competition for encomiendas curbed feudalism but still hurt Crown authority in that it led to political infighting and in some cases civil war.

King Charles V took a further step in 1542 when he issued the "New Laws." The New Laws reinforced the royal ban on indigenous slavery and dictated that encomiendas would revert to the Crown upon the death of their holder.[13] While the New Laws did slow enslavement of Indians to some degree, the latter provision infuriated encomenderos.[14] In New Spain, the viceroy got around the New Laws by allowing frontier Spaniards to label the indigenous Chichimec as "convicts" who could be held as enslaved people and almost in perpetuity.[15] In Peru, however, the viceroy was not even given the chance to manipulate the royal order as encomenderos openly defied the Crown. In 1546, the Pizarro brothers and their contemporaries rebelled against and decapitated Peru's first viceroy, Blasco Núñez Vela, whose unenviable mission had been to curb the siblings' power.[16]

It would come as no surprise then that encomenderos in Peru did a miserable job fulfilling their obligation to protect and instruct the natives entrusted to their care. As thousands of indigenous people in Peru begun to succumb to overwork and disease, the encomiendas could no longer be evenly distributed along ayllu lines. Indigenous laborers were moved from place to place in an attempt to create larger concentrations of mineworkers.[17] This trend worried the Crown and prompted additional yet equally unsuccessful attempts to control the encomienda institution. While there may not have been violent defiance from encomenderos in Chile, colonists there were no more willing to submit to royal restrictions of forced labor.

Encomiendas and Indigenous Slavery in Chile

Spain's addiction to forced labor in Chile began in the first days of their presence there and would not be remedied even with the dramatic defeat in 1598. As seen, in the leadup to Curalaba the Spanish were still willing to risk alienating their indigenous allies a half-century after Valdivia lost his life in pursuit of gold. Valdivia in fact had been willing to incur tremendous personal debt in search of Chile's precious metals, his second foray into Chile costing him 783,000 *pesos de oro* in loans, commodities, weapons, and ships.[18] Not content with returns from Marga-Marga, Valdivia founded Concepción near tributaries of the Bío-Bío for placer mining, near the coast to export the gold, and near relatively dense indigenous populations that could mine it (fig. 2.1).[19] Farther south, the Spanish would build Osorno, La Imperial, and

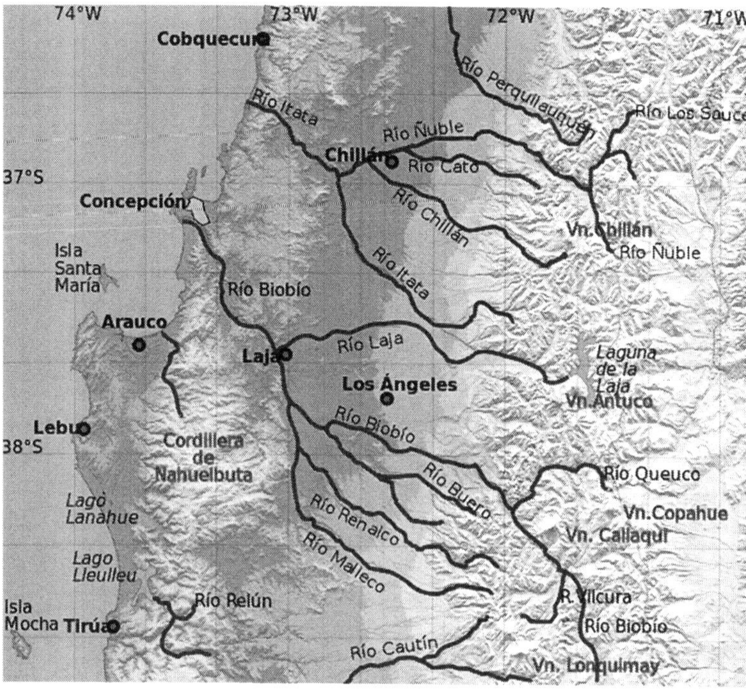

FIGURE 2.1. Watershed map of the Bío-Bío region.
Map by Createaccount, CC BY-SA 3.0.

Villarrica (rich town), the latter named as such for its promise of future gold strikes. Even after Valdivia's death in 1553, placer mining returned and extraction expanded to new levels.

While distinctions between types of labor (debt peonage, encomienda labor, personal service, slavery, etc.) did eventually emerge in Chile, the first major Spanish project there, placer mining, looked very much like the slavery seen in other parts of the Americas.[20] Since this type of mining involved partial immersion in water most of the day, it was not long before local workers began succumbing to these terrible conditions.[21] A seventeenth-century Augustinian and indigenous advocate claimed there had been as many as three hundred thousand indigenous workers between La Imperial and Valdivia providing gold to the Crown, most of whom disappeared due to "plague, continued wars and calamities."[22] To replace these people, encomenderos repeated the actions of their contemporaries in Peru and began to openly violate prohibitions against moving encomienda Indians, forcing them hundreds of miles from their homes to work on their estancias and in their mines.[23] In one case, encomienda workers from the trans-Andean province of Cuyo would make a seasonal trek over the hundreds of kilometers between Santiago and La Serena.[24] The Crown eventually acknowledged that mine work was dreadful and agreed that indigenous volunteers would be paid a percentage of the gold they extracted. However, little was or could be done from Spain to see that this royal order was enforced. In fact, the same order began with a statement on how important gold mining was to the royal treasury and a promise of royal help in aiding the extraction of the metal.[25]

Placer mining was never a year-round activity in Chile. Miners needed to stand in a river for hours every day, so Chile's "mining season" would start at the beginning of spring in October and last throughout the summer. This of course was also the time the Spanish army could lead campaigns; in the winter and fall, horse carts would become stuck in the mud, and rivers would be too swollen and too swift to ford. During the springs and summers then, one sector of Spaniards managed operations while at the same time another sought labor and territory. Predictably, Mapuche mineworkers could often join forces with the *indios rebeldes* who were trying to fend off Spanish incursions. Therefore, the value and status of encomiendas in cities like Concepción could vary greatly from year to year and create desperation for encomenderos trying to anticipate conditions.[26]

This all meant that Chile's sixteenth-century frontier economy was unique in that it was "an economy of conquest" or "transitory." Yes, there were mines and haciendas near Santiago and Concepción, but because of the unpredictability of supply and production, these mines and haciendas were not the apex of an emerging colonial elite (at least not in the sixteenth century). Instead, mines and haciendas, as well as Spanish forts, were at the center of a subsistence economy with a floating labor population, where products (including the enslaved individuals) could change hands multiple times.[27] In the earliest years of Spanish presence in the Araucanía, economic activity centered on forts. Food was stored in forts during the winter, and if that supply ran out, colonists would eat *fascicularia* roots or wade into the ocean to find mussels. It took at least a decade if not more for Concepción and the forts of Cañete and Angól to be self-sufficient. The Araucanía needed constant resupply with ships from Valparaíso, ships whose cargo on return voyages increasingly included enslaved "rebel" Mapuches taken in "just war."[28] With that instability in mind, Philip II established the Real Audiencia (superior court) in

Concepción in 1565. The Audiencia was designed to "guarantee stability for encomenderos in the possession of or right to indigenous labor."[29]

The arrival of more soldiers in the 1570s marked the transition from a gold extraction economy to a farming economy, largely to feed said soldiers who would be staying in and around Concepción.[30] More reinforcements did not mean an end to shortages, and these soldiers would find themselves obligated to conduct raids for their own subsistence. As more soldiers arrived, more agricultural workers were needed to feed them, more raids occurred, and warfare became more frequent and more intense. That last piece of information was usually the most important for the viceroy, who would send more soldiers. This cycle would continue for at least a century.

There was a bit more stability in Concepción from 1575 to 1598, demonstrated by the founding of Fort San Fabián de Conuco and the town of Chillán, which both sought to protect estancias (cattle ranches) and the indios de paz from *correrías de los araucanos y pehuenches* (raids from the Mapuche and Pehuenche). Even with increased stability, however, the economy of the Concepción region was "speculative," meaning high prices because of the high risk combined with the potential for great reward in placer mines.[31] Concepción's sixteenth-century economy had a tenuous señorial character at best, based on gold extraction, but one weakened by the need to use the limited resources for raids. Concepción's landowner class did not start to develop until the last decade of the sixteenth century, when petitions for *mercedes de tierra* (land grants) picked up.[32]

Landowners in Santiago during this time fared slightly better than their contemporaries in Concepción. They were spared the need to scour the Pacific for shellfish, and they were able to make capital improvements in the manner of other Spanish colonial capitals. These improvements had limitations, however. For example, in most parts of the Spanish Americas, the *adelantados* (military governors) would give way to more permanent *señores* (feudal lords), but in Chile, the encomenderos and their allies in government tried to be both. The land that these original hacendados owned was not nearly productive enough for Chilean elites to ascend to the seigniorial ranks they desired and in some cases not even enough to break even. Before the 1560s, encomenderos in Chile perhaps believed that gold mining would sustain them and ensure their legacy. However, despite attempts by Hernando de Santillán to organize the settlement and treatment of encomienda Indians in Santiago, there was a major demographic decline in indigenous population, especially around 1590. This meant a "radical transformation" of what we understand to be the encomienda in Chile. Especially in the last two decades of the sixteenth-century, gold mining declined and the "ruralization of personal service" began. In the seventeenth century, ranchers, not mine owners, would come to dominate politics and the economy. However, an ounce of beef fat will never be more valuable than an ounce of gold, and the ranchers needed a way to make up the difference while still maintaining their aristocratic pretentions. This would require the help of merchants to boost their market potential but also would involve buying on credit, selling titles, marrying into wealth, and the enslavement and sale of Mapuches.[33]

Resistance and a Slave Society

By the seventeenth century then, a seigniorial society in Chile was emerging thanks to an uptick in the capture, employment, and export of enslaved Mapuches. Della Flusche and Mario Góngora argue that increased slaving raids made rural labor more universally available and not limited to encomiendas as they had been in the sixteenth century. Many of the sixteenth century colonists who had their encomiendas subdivided pivoted to slavery as a source of their seventeenth-century labor. For example, Flusche traces how the Toro Mazote family became part of a new Santiago elite by making slavery their family business. Ginés Toro Mazote arrived from Spain in the 1560s as an infantryman, bearing no title, reputation, or connections. His service in the army and his time as a tallow merchant apparently connected him to both a source of enslaved people and the export business that they supported. Ginés's son Andrés parlayed his father's social climbing into a Lima law degree and an advantageous marriage upon his return to Chile. His wife, Luisa de Celada, listed in her 1656 will "a mill and a tannery," wine, real estate, and "thirty Black slaves and thirteen Indian slaves."[34] Andrés's brother Manuel was an active merchant like their father, with contacts in Buenos Aires and Lima. One of Manuel's transactions involved the import of twenty-five enslaved Africans from Buenos Aires to Santiago in the 1620s. Thanks to the business of slavery, in one generation the Toro Mazotes had joined the ranks of colonial "patricians."[35]

The importance of labor to upward mobility meant that encomenderos in Chile were often more insistent on their right to indigenous labor and less willing to curb the increase in the indigenous slave trade. They argued that since the Mapuche had never submitted to Spanish authority, their continued rebellion was deserving of punishment in the form of forced labor. As

Chilean historian Rolando Mellafe puts it, "the non-submission . . . meant a constant transgression on the part of the rebellious Indians, against judicial and spiritual order . . . [this was] the basis and justification of [indigenous] slavery. The real and concrete motivation, however, was the need for manual labor."[36]

By the late sixteenth century, regulations of forced labor meant that the enslaved individuals could be moved from place to place by a colonist but not transferred from one colonist/encomendero to another. Encomienda Indians, by contrast, could be transferred to a different colonist but had to stay near their communities of origin. Colonists could physically punish and brand the enslaved Indians, a practice not allowed with encomienda Indians. A sixteenth-century landowner allied with the governor might prefer to be granted a redistributed encomienda that he could supplement with *indios de guerra* (captured Mapuche warriors), while a soldier or merchant who needed a limited number of more mobile laborers might prefer a captured indio de guerra.

The first groups in Chile forced into encomiendas were not Mapuches but groups like the Diaguitas and Pikunches in north-central Chile who had been vassals of the Inka. The original encomenderos commonly moved the Pikunches in particular to *lavaderos* (placer mines), but as new *tasas* (taxes/duties) and other restrictions appeared, encomenderos found new loopholes. One particularly disturbing practice involved the removal of Huarpes across the Andes from Mendoza to Santiago. As Santiago grew, and La Serena still needed miners, more and more Huarpe encomienda Indians were "borrowed" by colonists in those two cities. If the Spanish intended to allow the Huarpes to return to their homes as was required under encomienda restrictions, they would have had to stop mining or building in the fall, allowing the Huarpes to return to Mendoza, and then wait until spring for their return. The Spanish of course were not likely to stop mining gold or building houses for six months. This meant that the Huarpe encomendados either became de facto enslaved for years at a time in La Serena or Santiago, or they would be "absent" from their encomiendas when snow blocked their paths out of Mendoza. These snowbound and "absent" Huarpes would often hide in caves or on islands in Andean lakes to avoid capture, as those who were caught were placed in collars and irons and forcibly taken across the mountains. The bishop of Santiago Francisco González de Salcedo denounced this practice, adding that in some cases Huarpes were even forced to continue their trek even after the person they were chained to had succumbed. According to

González de Salcedo, rather than remove the chains from the deceased, the Spanish would often sever a limb from the corpse. To end this practice, he ordered that encomenderos removing Huarpes from Cuyo (Mendoza's province) would be excommunicated and fined 100 pesos. He also offered a reward of 50 pesos per Huarpe to any potential whistleblowers.[37]

Not all examples of encomienda manipulation involved a tragic trek across the Andes. Colonists were also perfectly capable of bending rules to find laborers from within Chile. For example, an enslaved individual whose provenance was in doubt could be transferred temporarily to an encomienda, or to a specific project, long enough for the original provenance of the enslaved individual to become lost in the record. Once enough time had passed, that person could be sold as an indio de guerra or absorbed into an encomienda.

Encomienda laborers could also be removed from their homes through a "rental" arrangement. After enough time had passed, a native would often stay with the borrower through a prearranged agreement that was essentially a sale. This process also provided a way to evade restrictions on encomienda inheritance. An encomienda laborer could be listed as a slave then eventually reabsorbed into the encomienda, *por dos vidas* (for two lives). Usually encomiendas could be inherited only once, then there would have to be a transfer or a reorganization. Once that took place, the period of dos vidas would start again. So, in practice, as long as encomenderos were friendly with governors and willing to do some odious paperwork every two generations, they could have their encomiendas in perpetuity. The goal was always to erase the provenance of the servant or enslaved person through multiple transfers, thus removing any legal restrictions based on provenance or precedent.[38]

Encomenderos Take Advantage of the Expanding Trade

One example of this maneuvering is the case of Andrés Balón. In 1604, Balón worked for Lorenzo Núñez de Silva in Concón (near Valparaíso). However, Balón belonged to an encomienda recently granted to Andrés Enríquez, apparently as part of influence trafficking by Governor García de Ramón. García de Ramón had transferred an "abandoned" encomienda to Enríquez that had once belonged to Osorno refugee Joaquín de Rueda. To resolve any dispute over rights to Balón's labor, Enríquez and Núñez de Silva appeared before a notary and agreed that Balón would stay in Concón and in exchange, Núñez de Silva would send Enríquez an "Indian slave captured in war."[39]

This example adds yet another layer to the role of enslaved Mapuches in the economic and political life of the seventeenth century. These enslaved Mapuches had cash value, political value, value in resolving disputes, and value in frauds committed by encomenderos. Again, we turn to examples from the Middle Passage to understand how pervasive the slave trade could become within a given society. While we tend to focus on the torture and tragedy of the transatlantic journey, millions of African laborers, enslaved and free, never left Africa yet were involved in the trade. William St. Clair's study of Ghana's Cape Coast Castle describes "Castle slaves" who "came in through the land gate every morning to report for work and left before it closed in the afternoon." These "Castle slaves" were bricklayers, carpenters, blacksmiths, gunners, and cooks, and most never left Ghana.[40] In other words, while it is important that we try to reveal the previously "invisible" export of Mapuches, export is only a percentage of the trade itself, especially when we see enslavement being ubiquitous enough that public notaries recorded these kinds of transactions.

The more that encomienda Mapuches and war captives were treated interchangeably, the more frustrated officials became about regulating their treatment. This frustration would become an important part of the decision to legalize indigenous slavery in 1608. The belief was that with indigenous slavery legalized, the clandestine transfer to encomiendas would decline. However, by the seventeenth century, it was too late to change patterns. The War of Arauco had become a slave market, and encomiendas were now part of de facto slave plantations. Some of these patterns even emerged organically, without black market sales or illegal raids. For example, specie was exceedingly rare in Chile's mostly rural ranching economy. Encomienda workers did not demand payment in specie, nor did royal officials expect tribute in any form other than personal service. However, this established a troubling trend whereby laborers were less and less likely to receive a salary at all. Essentially then, an assumed lack of specie was making free and encomienda natives de facto slaves.[41]

Seventeenth-century demographic decline accelerated the trend of enslaved people replacing encomienda laborers. First, under the 1542 New Laws, encomienda Indians were not to be taken from their *pueblos reducidos*, their homes. Even had encomenderos wanted to strictly follow this restriction, it was difficult after the refugee crises in 1553 and 1598. As Chile moved into the seventeenth century, fewer original pueblos reducidos remained. As a practical matter therefore, most estancias and haciendas began to rely more and more on the enslaved workers who were forced to stay on the property, rather than encomienda laborers who maintained connections to their far-flung communities.[42] This fact also made it easier for landowners to manipulate the provenance of their workers in official records; both enslaved and encomienda natives were from far away. Rarely would a *protector de indios* have the resources to check whether a Mapuche was from where they said they were.

As encomienda numbers declined, encomendero landowners contracted Spanish soldiers to find and sell them enslaved Mapuches. Constant demand created price increases, and soldiers began to capture Mapuches without a clear buyer in mind. This of course led to more raids, more Mapuche resistance to them, and more Mapuches being categorized as indios rebeldes who could be legally enslaved.[43] From 1608 forward, then, it was Mapuches born in the Araucanía who were the majority of encomienda laborers, and all attempts to curb the mal incurable had failed or actually made raids to enslave worse. Toward the middle of the seventeenth century, Valdivia's original encomiendas had become more and more subdivided and their communities of laborers were in decline. This meant that enslaved labor was more and more in demand in Chile.

West Africa as an Alternative Labor Source?

Elsewhere in the Americas, colonists began to turn to enslaved Africans to supplant declining indigenous populations. Decades before the Middle Passage began in earnest, both free and enslaved Africans had a major presence in the Spanish Americas. They were instrumental in the armies of conquest in Peru with two hundred accompanying Pedro de Alvarado upon his arrival in 1534. One of the two hundred, Juan Valiente, eventually participated in Almagro's expedition to Chile, joined Valdivia's troops, became an encomendero, got married, and lived out the rest of his life in Chile.[44]

Toward the end of the sixteenth century, the "Atlantic" slave trade in fact extended well into the Pacific, meaning that after the trauma of the Middle Passage, enslaved Africans would have to continue their arduous journey on foot across Panama.[45] By 1640, there were some twenty thousand enslaved Africans in Lima. Eventually, not only Lima but "all the northern and central Andean coastal and interior cities had Black populations that by 1600 accounted for half of their total populations." Lima would stay "half black . . . for most of the 17th century."[46] At least one viceroy of Peru believed that exporting enslaved Africans to Chile could reduce the personal service burden on Mapuches.[47] Colonists in Chile were behind this idea as well. As early as the 1570s, colonial officials began to ask royal authorities to send larger and larger numbers of enslaved Africans to work in the mines and haciendas around Santiago. By 1613, for example, Juan Fernández de Castillo and other residents of La Serena petitioned for the import of one thousand enslaved Africans, claiming that the town's population had been decimated by war and disease.[48]

Throughout the colonial period, many colonists in Chile argued that the solution to Mapuche rebellion and to urban labor shortages was exile for the leaders of any uprisings. The petitioners in La Serena for example argued the entire colony would benefit by removing these captives 150 leagues away from the Araucanía.[49] Expanding this (obviously flawed) logic to enslaved Africans, some colonists believed that the vast distance from Chile to West Africa would make revolts by enslaved Africans unlikely as well. All of these factors meant that import of enslaved Africans increased gradually, with a total of 183 sold in Santiago in the year 1615.[50] This slow but steady growth meant that by 1620 the Black and "mestizo de color" population of Chile had reached twenty-two thousand.[51]

Throughout Chile's central valley, enslaved Africans were employed by hacendados in a number of tasks from rock breaking to cattle herding. Some supervised haciendas or public works projects.[52] Enslaved Africans on the Jesuit hacienda La Ollería made pots, tended cattle, and did laundry.[53] Other skilled tasks performed by Santiago's enslaved Africans included clock making, carpentry, tailoring, and metalworking.[54] These skilled Africans were quite visible and a very important part of public life in the capital. In fact, visibility was an essential part of their value for many owners. Enslaved Africans were often *negritos* or *negritas de alfombra*, a door person and status symbol for prominent *santiaguinos*.[55] Others worked in similarly prominent domestic service occupations like coachman, house servant, food carrier, and messenger.[56] Historian Benjamín Vicuña Mackenna claimed that in Chile, at least, working as an enslaved domestic ipso facto improved treatment. A negrito de alfombra showing obvious signs of malnourishment or mistreatment would cause embarrassment to the owner's family. Senior coachmen and messengers could become well-known representatives of prominent families, with messengers in particular often loaned by their owners to families announcing marriages or "grave matters."[57]

Not only were enslaved Africans status symbols for their owners, but the colonial aristocracy hoped that ownership of enslaved people could help forge a path to elite status for years to come. When we examine the guidelines of late seventeenth- and early eighteenth-century *mayorazgos* (entailed estates), there is discussion of the importance of enslaved Africans to the "work, conservation and growth of the haciendas." These prominent families considered how important a potential influx of enslaved Africans would be in increasing the value of the estate. These entailed families also made sure that miscegenation was to be avoided within their ranks, detailing that the inheritors of these mayorazgos could not "marry with one who has the bad race of moor, Jew, nor church penitent, nor *negro* or mulatto nor any other bad quality race that could cause dishonor."[58]

As was usually the case in colonial Latin American cities, there was the relative freedom of physical movement for Santiago's Black population. This allowed for some building of a diasporic community through periodic gatherings, despite the scorn expressed by White inhabitants who saw assemblies of Santiago's Black community as no more than exhibitions of "idleness and licentiousness."[59] Already in the early seventeenth century, Santiago's Black residents had annual processions on Three Kings' Day, and they had some opportunity for collective identity through militia units and in their own confraternities founded and supervised by Jesuits.[60] The Cuerpo de Pardos of Santiago eventually produced the Infantes de la Patria, which fought bravely on the side of Chilean Patriots during the Independence Wars.[61] Military service was an important and, perhaps the most direct, path to manumission for enslaved Africans.

If enslaved Africans were present in all parts of Chile's economic and cultural life by the early seventeenth century, why then was forced labor still expected of Mapuche war captives? As seen in subsequent chapters, there is more to the persistence of the mal incurable than weak supply of African forced labor, but this was a factor. Chile was only the "southern terminal of the *Pacific Circuit*" at the edge of a much larger commercial region, which meant that there were all kinds of reasons that an expected shipment of enslaved Africans might not reach Chile.[62] For example, fluctuating demand in Chile often brought enslaved persons who were not sold in Santiago or Valparaíso back to Lima.[63] Part of the status assigned to enslaving Santiago families was precisely attributable to how difficult it was to purchase and maintain enslaved Africans in Chile's capital. Owners of enslaved people were subject to heavy tax burdens,[64] following the trend of enormous expense and value attached to enslaved Africans. Enslaved Africans already living in Chile could also be sold to Lima to pay off debts, sometimes sold away from their families. This was especially troubling to many enslaved ladinos and creoles (people of African descent born in Chile), who saw a sale to Lima as a "permanent exile" from not only their families but their home colony as well.[65] The practice had become so common that in 1646 Governor Martín de Mujíca declared that enslavers and ships' captains taking the enslaved individuals from Chile to Peru would be fined 500 pesos for each exported person.[66] Despite the fines, however, this practice continued and by the mid-eighteenth century the bishop of Santiago, Manuel de Alday, sent a letter to the Royal Audiencia denouncing the practice and threatening not just fines but excommunication for captains who took enslaved Africans to Lima without a church license.[67] This example comes after a period when prices for enslaved people had actually begun to drop after the English were granted the *asiento* (license) in 1713. After 1713, the British were permitted to import double the number of enslaved Africans that had been coming into Buenos Aires in previous years, with four hundred per year destined for Chile and the "upper provinces" of Córdova, Tucumán, and others.[68]

While four hundred enslaved persons per year may seem like many for a smaller colony like Chile, residents there knew from past patterns that only a handful of them would stay. Most of the enslaved people arriving in Lima through Cartagena would stay there. The enslaved population available to Chile had often been labeled as "troublemakers" by their limeño owners who were anxious to sell them off.

Contraband and the Inshore Trade

These limitations on enslaved Africans imported from Lima might drive an owner of enslaved people in Chile to consider an overland purchase from Buenos Aires. But this trans-Andean trek had its own complications. Córdoba was becoming an important colonial city as a midpoint for the flow of goods out of Europe, Africa, Brazil, and across the Andes to Potosí, Lima, and Santiago. But this overland route was subject to frequent and often arbitrary restrictions as the Crown preferred that all trade be conducted along the Pacific route where they could tax it and escort it (it was mostly Potosí silver that they were worried about), leaving Peru to Panamá and across to Spain via the Caribbean. Already in 1594, a royal *cédula* (order) prohibited commerce between Buenos Aires and Angola (via Brazil), expressly mentioning human cargo. There were occasional exceptions to this prohibition, but on average, smugglers charged four times less for enslaved Africans than licensed shippers, making it no surprise then that for most of the colonial period it was contraband that led imports of enslaved Africans to Buenos Aires.[69]

There were colonists in Chile who did manage the obstinacy of colonial bureaucracy well enough to receive special permission to send a group of enslaved Africans through Buenos Aires, but the subsequent challenges were great as well. Lima may have been the vice regal capital, but Buenos Aires was still a major seventeenth-century city and would pull enslaved Africans out of caravans destined for Chile. Enslaved Africans worked in Buenos Aires as cooks, construction workers, artisans, musicians, bakers, hairdressers, and even exterminators. The open frontier outside of the city also permitted some *creoles* to move up in the social ranks as gauchos, leaving their urban jobs open to *bozales* (enslaved people who had been born in Africa).[70]

Those enslaved Africans who did leave Buenos Aires toward Chile then faced an incredibly daunting trek over the Andes.[71] The enslaved people had to be dressed for the cold of the Andes, and the traders had to take food, arms, soldiers, medicine, and usually a surgeon along with them. Such obstacles were "so prominent, that they almost completely paralyzed the legal slave trade." Thus, as in the Peruvian trade, with the costs incurred in the trek across Panama, the real profits were in the sale of contraband, under the auspices of the slave trade.[72]

The difficulties of such a trek over the Andes have been described by the surgeon Patricio Gedd, who accompanied a 1731 expedition conducted by the trader Joseph Norberto de Vicuña. Vicuña set off on March 1 from Buenos Aires with 285 enslaved Africans, 85 of whom belonged to Vicuña and the rest to the British South Sea Company. They made the journey in carts to the town of Mendoza. There the expedition sold a number of slaves, took stock of those who were in ill health (some had already died along the way), and traded the carts for mules. From there, they continued toward the "giant overhanging precipices and signs of violent earthquakes, landslides and avalanches" (fig. 2.2.) After days of walking, the "Africans forced along this road suffered horribly from the penetrating cold. The sweat they build up . . . on their daylong marches froze on their skin and made the night that much more horrible."[73]

On April 20, the journey on to Santiago continued on the backs of 184 mules, arriving in Santiago via the Aconcagua valley in early May.[74] Two hundred and forty-four slaves made it all the way to Santiago after the relatively "quick" trip of two months and eight days from Buenos Aires. One hundred

FIGURE 2.2. Nineteenth-century group near Portillo. This is the treacherous Mendoza to Santiago route that enslaved Africans travelled. ETH-Bibliothek Zürich, Bildarchiv/ Fotograf: Wehrlie, Leo/Dia_247-01271/CC by-SA 4.0.

and eleven were adult men, sixty-three were young men and boys, fifty were adult women, and twenty were young women and girls.[75]

Importing enslaved Africans into Chile meant a tremendous human and monetary cost, a cost that peaked (not coincidentally) at the same time enslaving malocas by the Spanish were picking up in the Araucanía. A 1626 declaration by the cabildo of Santiago stated that Chile needed four thousand enslaved Africans to "compensate for the diminished number of Indian workers,"[76] but as noted, no more than four hundred would ever arrive in Chile in a "good" year. The cabildo of Santiago was surely further dismayed after the Portuguese revolution of 1640 interrupted the activities of Portuguese traders and raised prices. In Chile, costs shot up from 250 pesos per enslaved person to 600 and 700 pesos during the initial years of the decade. This overnight increase forced Chilean governor Martín de Mujíca to prohibit the export of enslaved Africans from Chile to Peru in 1646. With the temporary interruption of imports from Cartagena and Buenos Aires, Mujíca knew that desperate Lima plantation owners and merchants would look to move enslaved Africans from within the viceroyalty. Mujíca soon removed the ban, but a list of sales from 1664 of enslaved people shows no drop in prices to pre-1640 levels. As late as 1686, there was no appreciable decrease, making enslaved Africans a "luxury" available to few Chileans in the late seventeenth century.[77]

Encomenderos as Feudal Lords

As it became more apparent that enslaved Africans would not satisfy demand in Chile, the encomendero class developed Mapuche-specific justifications for forcing them into service and permanent enslavement. With the background of the Crusades and the *Reconquista* always at the front of their minds, early Spanish chroniclers in Chile looked for idol worship or houses of worship they could extirpate in the name of Saint James the Great (Santiago). The Spanish did not find idols among the Mapuche but did mention that the Mapuche worshiped the sun and moon. The chroniclers also spoke of a "cult of the devil" (Pillán) who they believed the Mapuche worshiped through feasts and funerals. In breaking up cahuínes, therefore, the Spanish saw themselves preventing potential attacks and potential idolatry. Spanish priests in Chile had their own version of the Valladolid Debates, believing they had a duty to help organize indios de paz into reducciones, keeping them near the Spanish so they could learn how to "live as men." Without this, the Mapuche could not live according to "natural order."[78] Conveniently for landowners and Spanish officers, having Mapuches in reducciones also meant that they were available for personal service. This added another layer of urgency to Spanish attempts to keep indios de paz away from the influence of indios de guerra or indios rebeldes.

Ecclesiastics were especially helpful in justifying not only personal service but also just war and permanent enslavement for the Mapuche. By the late sixteenth century, a great number of Mapuches had been baptized (often in mass rites that they did not consent to), and, therefore, any who rebelled were considered apostates. Apostates were subject to "war of blood and fire," and their enslavement would serve a spiritual good. Juan de Vascones, an Augustinian vicar in Chile, added that after Curalaba, the Mapuche would have to be controlled with "firm bit and reins." The famous Spanish officer and writer Francisco Núñez de Pineda y Bascuñán sagaciously noted that indios de guerra could not be apostates as they had never lived with the Spanish and did not "know God." Núñez de Pineda added that the real barriers to evangelization were enslavement as well as the rape of Mapuche women by Spanish missionaries.[79] Ultimately, however, Curalaba meant that the proponents of "just war" as both a strategic and spiritual urgency would win out in Chile.

This export of the enslaved individuals, particularly to Coquimbo and neighboring La Serena, was becoming so frequent by the 1570s that a corregidor (judge) from Santiago was appointed as a *visitador y numerador de indios*. In other words, the town council of Santiago appointed a special investigator to visit La Serena and report on the conditions of the enslaved.[80] (La Serena did not have a town council of their own yet.) The visitador would have predictably little effect, and export of Mapuche captives would continue.

Genocide as Punishment and Policy

After the Mapuche attack on Angól in 1577, Governor Rodrigo de Quiroga was so incensed that he declared all indios de guerra as guilty of rebellion and sentenced them to death. Such a declaration was not only outside of his powers but also held no weight when none of these "rebels" were in Spanish custody. Nonetheless, the declaration did motivate the Spanish infantry, whose actions were now legally justified. Quiroga subsequently ordered a rare winter campaign where he ordered two hundred soldiers to raid the Pacific Coast south of Fort Arauco, taking 350 Mapuche prisoners and 6 "principal *caciques*" of Arauco and expelling them to La Serena.[81]

By 1590, those with the most experience in or near the Araucanía understood violence like that which so angered Quiroga was a direct result of Spanish labor demands. Bishop Augustín de Cisneros stated very clearly in that same year that "the principal occupation of the soldiers when they are not engaged in military campaigns is . . . hunting down Indians, both male and female for their personal service."[82] One author describes the 1590s as a decade of "enormous violence" in the south of Chile.[83] Rather than attempting to restrict slave raids, however, Spanish governors continued to blame the Mapuche for frontier violence and converted the export of Mapuche captives as punishment and policy. Sotomayor, for example, believed that constant punishment would lead to a Spanish triumph and the eventual extermination of the Mapuche. Sotomayor had little concern with territorial gains, concentrating his efforts along the southern shore of the Bío-Bío, near Concepción. In one case, the community of Catiray (modern Santa Juana) entered into eight different peace agreements during Sotomayor's administration, with every one of them eventually broken.[84] This pattern of course did little to advance Chile's development but did produce a steady source of Mapuche captives.

By the 1590s, captive Mapuches were being "crowded into hulls in a fashion that resembled Negro slavers" in Valdivia and sent to Valparaíso and points north.[85] Chroniclers describing Spanish malocas during this period noted that every Spanish soldier and indio amigo left the raid with at least one captive. Governor Óñez de Loyola brought 180 Spanish soldiers and 1,200 indio amigo infantry in one 1594 foray south of the Bío-Bío.[86] This meant that if it held to the pattern, the raid would have returned with more than 1,000 Mapuche captives. Spanish malocas in the 1590s were now almost always accompanied by the destruction of Mapuche crops and the theft of Mapuche cattle. The Spanish strategy was now to remove people from Mapuche lands, not to take the land itself.[87] Having more Mapuches severed from their lands of course worked out for slave traders as well, as this way they would have much less support from or communication with their communities of origin. As reducidos (subject) communities weakened, the Mapuche would instead turn to ayllarehues, which more and more organized around resistance.

Both an Opponent and a Protagonist: The Case of Óñez de Loyola

While officials in Chile had clearly decided that punishing Mapuches for their resistance was the only path forward, they were certainly not helped by any clear strategy from Peru on how to interrupt the mal incurable. Lima would promise then never send reinforcements and supplies, would become distracted by pirate threats (both real and imagined), and generally followed the Hapsburg lack of imagination for its American frontiers. It would be up to residents of far-flung outposts like Chile to construct their own political and cultural systems.[88] Officials in Peru were getting what they needed from Chile, at least for the time being, through support for the *carrera* (silver fleet) via the Pacific "inshore" trade, where Chile provided tallow, jerky, timber, mules, and enslaved Mapuches.[89]

Viceroys of Peru in fact had come to expect a modest inflow of Mapuche captives, so they were unlikely to try to interrupt the trade and, in some cases, participated in it directly. One colonial author wrote in 1607 that he had observed the public sale of Mapuche prisoners of war in Lima and that the practice seemed to have been well established.[90] In a 1630 letter, the bishop of Santiago González de Salcedo added that Mapuches were sent to the very daughters of Viceroy Diego Fernández de Córdoba.[91]

This demand from Lima also meant that the policy of punitive raids needed to continue, even if it made the Araucanía more volatile. Óñez de Loyola knew the punitive policy was not working. He denounced growing slave export, arguing that the shipment of enslaved Mapuches from Valdivia was becoming quite regular.[92] Many of these Mapuche captives had even come to the Spanish as allies and instead were placed in irons.[93] Óñez de Loyola also criticized his eventual successor for branding indios de guerra on the face and sending some of them to Arica where his brother had a vineyard.[94] Beyond Arica, Óñez de Loyola also recognized that Mapuches were still regularly sent to Peru, even catching his own lieutenant governor in the act.[95] Óñez de Loyola tried to close loopholes, issuing a prohibition against "bartering" for the enslaved people since barter had been used to get around the existing prohibition on sales. Even if no cash changed hands in an initial trade, this trade would assign a value to a laborer, a value that could become a cash price later.[96]

Óñez de Loyola also helped reveal that while raids in the Araucanía were supposed to secure southern cities against attack by indios rebeldes, they were instead making cities more vulnerable. As Santiago and other cities in the north demanded more labor, southern interests began to ship out the same Mapuches who had fed and supported the army on their campaigns. While their food and supplies diminished, the Spanish army was called upon to conduct additional raids, leaving them ill-prepared to deal with any attacks.

Óñez de Loyola also tried to address some of the more inhumane practices within this inhumane trade, principal among them punishment of escape attempts by mutilation.[97] *Desgobernar* (to dislocate) involved either cutting a nerve in one foot or cutting off toes with a machete and then putting the foot in boiling lard to stop the bleeding.[98] The colonial official Gregorio Sánchez had already denounced this practice to the viceroy in 1578, not because it was immoral and inhumane but arguing that maiming the enslaved individuals made them less valuable as mineworkers. The hobbled enslaved laborers could only work in the fields, added Sánchez.[99] Óñez de Loyola also recorded accusations of sexual exploitation as part of this trade. Many denouncing sexual exploitation were merely concerned with the products of nonconsensual Spanish-Mapuche relationships, lamenting increasing *mestizaje*. Others, however, did mention the "immoral purposes" at the root of the capture of so many Mapuche women and girls.[100]

While his public statements may have reflected concern about instability in the south, Óñez de Loyola still believed that Chile's economic fortunes would be boosted by a renewal of lagging gold mining around La Serena. Unfortunately, the miners were to come from the Araucanía, with Óñez de Loyola himself arranging transport.[101] He led campaigns into the Araucanía, even founding the new Spanish fort of Santa Cruz (near modern Santa Juana along the Bío-Bío River) (see fig. 1.6).

He also believed that order along the frontier was essential, but having entered into a strategic marriage himself, it would have been hard for him to pursue extermination over alliances. Instead of adopting Sotomayor's genocidal plans then, Óñez de Loyola opted for a more mixed approach toward Mapuches when he arrived in Concepción. He convoked a group of indios amigos and indios de guerra in the center of Concepción and promised better treatment. In response, the cacique Antipillán agreed that in exchange for better treatment, his community would help expand the Millapoa (Lumaco) fort mentioned in chapter 1.[102]

Quite ironically, however, Óñez de Loyola's assassination meant that future governors would pursue a war of revenge against the Mapuche in his name. Alonso García de Ramón (1600–1601, 1605–10), and Alonso de Ribera (1601–5) continued to conduct raids during their administrations. García de Ramón boasted that when thirty caciques reneged on a peace settlement, he had twenty of them killed and sent the remaining ten to "clean the viceroy's stables."[103] In 1608, García de Ramón led an army advance into the mountains southeast of Concepción (an area not usually subject to Spanish raids) and captured more than two thousand indigenous residents.[104]

Padrón de Indios de Lima: Mapuches "Reappear" in the Peruvian Diaspora

In 1631, Governor Francisco Laso de la Vega personally delivered Mapuche captives in Lima, using their capture as evidence that the War of Arauco was now over and organizing a parade to celebrate. Santiago de Tesillo, who served as a field marshal under Laso de la Vega, often traveled with the governor and detailed the parade's development. Tesillo wrote,

> As the news spread throughout that city general joy grew in it, the Royal Audiencia gathered in the palace [fig. 2.3] to congratulate the *virei* [viceroy], and he with holy and religious zeal went with the same

> audiencia to the cathedral to give thanks, to who so piously disposed of it and ordered letters to be written to all the cities of the kingdom so that the same yields of grace might be given in them, and it seemed convenient that those captives whom the governor had sent to the galleys of Callao [Lima's port district] should see the scope of the city of Lima; they were brought into the main square, where the number of people who came to the event was remarkable, and there was also a squad of soldiers who received them with salvoes of harquebuses and muskets, . . . this was a great day for the two heads of Peru and Chile, seeing the fruits of the expense and effort that had been made, and the other the work of achieving victory.[105]

The exuberance displayed by ordinary limeños reflected their belief that the War of Arauco had gone on far too long. In one case a group of prominent limeños collected alms to clothe any of the "forgotten and helpless captives" of the Curalaba uprising, who they hoped would be freed.[106]

What happened to the captive Mapuches Laso de la Vega used as props for his parade? Despite ending up more than three thousand kilometers from their homes, Lima's relatively robust record keeping meant that we do have at least one valuable source providing a glimpse of the Mapuche diaspora in Lima. More infrequently than historians would like, Peruvian viceroys would

FIGURE 2.3. Palacio Arzobispal, Lima, Peru, 2015.
Photograph by Diego Delso, CC-BY-SA.

order a census. Thanks to the particularly diligent scribe Miguel de Contreras in the employ of Viceoroy Juan de Mendoza, we have the so-called Padrón (census) de los Índios de Lima en 1613. The *padrón* is an excellent snapshot of the residents of more than 3,500 homes within the borders of Lima's Santa Ana parish in the year 1613. Among those residents were at least 82 "indios de Chile."[107]

Most of the native Chilean residents who appeared in the census remembered how long they had been in Peru, their age, their town of origin, and their cacique in Chile. Contreras also listed occupations when applicable. Many of those from Chile were young women or girls, following the preference for the enslaved indigenous female in the Americas.[108] Many of the enslaved males worked as tailors or butchers. If they were old enough to remember, the enslaved people listed their hometowns or ports of embarkation in Chile like Valdivia or Concepción, or smaller towns in the interior like Osorno, Chillán, or Angól. The "hometowns" listed seem to alternate between the areas where they actually grew up and the towns where their sellers had encomiendas.

Outside of family and occupational information, Contreras included details about the sale and travels of the enslaved Mapuches he interviewed in Lima. For example, Pedro de Raya told the scribe that the bishop of Panama had brought him to Lima seven years before. Raya had been gifted to the bishop by Governor Alonso de Ribera, after capturing him in "the war."[109] Another Lima resident was Francisca Carrillo. Francisca was from Santiago and brought to Lima with the permission (license) of Governor García de Ramón. So at least three governors (so far), García de Ramón, Laso de la Vega, and Ribera openly took and traded enslaved Mapuches and in fact used their involvement in the trade to grow their popularity and create a gifting cycle with influential figures in Chile. In the padrón, we also see a very liberal definition of "just war." Spanish officers were taken at their word as they brazenly lied and "certified" that indio amigo and indio de paz captives they sold or transferred were actually taken in war. In the padrón, we see dozens of Mapuche children under ten, in some cases toddlers, taken from Chile as "combatants." Other enslaved individuals like Barbara had arrived in Lima recently and remembered that it was Luis Gonzalez (the name of a ship's captain apparently) who had brought her from Chile.[110]

It was common to see enslaved Mapuches branded to distinguish them from encomendero or free Indians. As seen in the case of Melchora, an enslaved woman from Chile in the service of a silversmith named Diego de Requena, the brand was often on the face.[111] Some owners of enslaved people also remembered the details involving purchases and volunteered the information to the scribe Contreras. The Lima painter Augustín de Soxo (Sojo) had purchased the enslaved Chilean María from Domingo Sánchez de Solís for two hundred patacones.[112] In another case, Lima resident Geronima Vargas gave silver to Juan Amadóz so that he could travel to Chile and purchase an enslaved person. Once in Santiago, Amadóz bought *una muchacha india* (an indigenous girl) who now served Vargas's two daughters in Lima's Encarnación Convent.[113] Other indigenous immigrants from Chile lived in the Colegio Real in Lima, working for the adolescent sons of Lima encomenderos who aspired to be priests or lawyers.[114] As mentioned, censuses were infrequent, and only a handful of scribes shared Contreras's attention to detail. We do see Mapuches appearing in Lima documents, however infrequently, well into the 1670s.[115] It is also important to mention that because Indian slavery was "largely illegal, [its] victims toiled, quite literally in dark corners and behind locked doors, giving us the impression that they were fewer than they actually were."[116] This is certainly the case with enslaved Mapuches working in galleys in Lima, hidden below deck in the port of Callao.

Many historians of slavery are accustomed to often quite detailed descriptions of the Middle Passage. When we attempt to trace the export of enslaved indigenous people, we look for the same tragedy and trauma aboard slave ships that we saw in the Atlantic. While it is true that there were diasporic ocean voyages for the Mapuche aboard ships leaving Valparaíso or Concepción toward Callao, descriptions of those voyages are lacking in detail. Perhaps a cargo of mostly tallow with a dozen or so enslaved Mapuches in irons seemed unremarkable to sailors and merchants. If the details of the voyages were discussed, it was usually because something went wrong or because the chronicler was trying to prove a point. This was the case in 1633, when Governor Laso de la Vega (the same man who held the parade) wrote to Viceroy Luis Fernández de Cabrera to express how brave he had been in transporting Mapuches, considering the evidence he had of how dangerous such a voyage could be.

Laso de la Vega pointed to recent shipboard revolts as evidence, one in particular in Coquimbo where four enslaved indigenous men took over the ship that was to transport them to Callao. The conspirators stole a boat from a neighboring ship, and Spanish sailors pursued them through the harbor. The Spanish caught up to the escapees, and in the ensuing skirmish, all four captives and two Spanish sailors were killed. Laso de la Vega mentioned that there had been similar revolts in Concepción, and that Philip IV's plan to move all of Mocha Island's inhabitants to Coquimbo would also ultimately end in violence.

To bolster his case, Laso de la Vega detailed a 1631 revolt, this time in Valparaíso, where a number of Mapuche prisoners of war on their way to Callao forced their way off the ship transporting them. After killing at least two Spaniards and three enslaved Africans who were aboard, they made their way to shore and eventually back to the Araucanía. Laso de la Vega added that it was only through "God's mercy" that the escapees did not burn the ship, which had already taken on its principal cargo of wheat. According to Laso de la Vega, this saga only came to an end when the Spanish recaptured and executed the escapees in Purén, more than seven hundred kilometers away from Valparaíso.[117] More than two decades later, we have details about twelve captive Mapuches in collars waiting to be exported to Callao because the captain of *Las Ánimas del Purgatorio* was too afraid to set sail from Valparaíso with such dangerous passengers.[118] Aside from details from these "logistical failures," we have few descriptions of shipboard treatment or difficulties incurred in transit. Most enslaved Mapuches heading northward seem to have arrived without further incident.

Compounding the lack of detail about this human trafficking is the fact that much of it was lost in the volume of nonhuman trade between Chile and Peru during the seventeenth century. In the seventeenth century, the power of Lima merchants rivaled even that of mine owners, the former even lending money for new excavations. Lima merchants also had the ear of the viceroy, in one case forcing him to maintain restrictions on trade between Buenos Aires and Santiago.[119] Alonso de Ovalle wrote in 1646 that profits for Peru were so great that some "with forty thousand pesos or less of capital invested in lands, cattle and slaves. . . . They would [take out] every year between ten to twelve thousand, a profit of 25%, very considerable . . . taking into account the dangers and contingencies of the sea." Ovalle added that this did not necessarily require trips every few months since there are some goods that in a fifteen- to twenty-day Chile to Lima journey fetch a 200 to 300 percent profit.[120]

Chile was not a direct participant in the Spanish Flota de Indias (treasure fleet) that left Callao with silver every year in May or June. Goods brought on the return journey would make their way across Panama on mules, be loaded on ships again, and arrive in Callao in November or December. If there were remaining European goods after limeños had made their purchases, and if they were not on their way to Acapulco, goods would be loaded on ships for Valparaíso, where they would fetch prices that were double or triple those in

Lima.[121] Clearly, Chile could not live on scraps from the flota. Instead, the inshore trade between Chile and Peru, which often included nothing from Europe but included many enslaved Mapuches, grew more and more vibrant in the seventeenth century.

As the inshore trade was not a priority for royal officials, records of these voyages are thin. With the records that we do have, we see trade picking up between Chile and Peru in the latter half of the century. In an attempt to collect evidence about a smuggling case involving Governor Juan Henríquez, a court representative provided copious detail about exports leaving from Peru after 1665. The Royal Treasury records for the year 1665 for example show that *Nuestra Señora de los Angeles* left Valparaíso on January 12 carrying "tallow, jerky, cordovan, and other goods." *Nuestra Señora de los Reces [Reyes], Nuestra Señora de Buen Viaje,* and *San Francisco de Asis* also left that year, all with some form of tallow or leather destined for Callao. The tempo of this inshore trade stayed consistent for the next several years, with seven ships leaving Valparaíso in 1667, five in 1670, and nine in 1672.[122]

While an average of one ship every two months seems easy to trace, the manner in which these ships took on cargo in Valparaíso further conceals the process of Mapuche export. Valparaíso was a ghost town for much of the year, but between December and April, merchants from all over the Santiago region and as far away as Mendoza flooded the port.[123] Aside from the tons of tallow and leather that appeared during these summer months, one of the "specialties" of Valparaíso "consisted in the transport and sale of enslaved individuals." Wealthy Santiago families frequently found *piezas* (enslaved Africans in this case) in Valparaíso to work as domestic servants, often buying directly from the captains of these ships from Callao. The same captains would also buy enslaved Mapuches as they prepared for the return trip to Callao. For example, in 1663, Captain Pedro de Torres Figueroa sold a Mapuche named Gapolén for 300 pesos to the captain of *Nuestra Señora de Atocha.*[124] Another captain, Melchior de Los Reyes, had a fourteen-year-old enslaved Chilean boy named Juan in his home in Lima.[125]

The Internal Mapuche Diaspora

While we have sporadic shipping and census records to trace the export of enslaved Mapuches to Lima, we know the least about the enslaved Mapuches who stayed in Chile. While the six or seven Pacific voyages per year to La Serena and Callao represented much of Chile's trade activity toward Peru, most trade and communication actually took place over the remnants of the Inka Road. This overland trade is much more gradual, can take place in stages, and is harder to trace. Migrations to isolated regions produced no parish records that might trace marriages, baptisms, or deaths.[126]

In fact, in the mid-seventeenth century the inshore trade's point of origin even extended into Argentina and included the "pampa circuit." The pampa circuit began in the Argentine pampa and took cattle and salt across the cordillera at passes in the Neuquén region. Once in Chile, the cargo was delivered in Concepción and shipped north. Some of the cattle were fattened on estancias in the central valley, slaughtered, and cured with the Argentina salt, then sent on to Potosí.[127]

The cases of Juan and Gapolén are of course clear examples of how slave export in Chile often worked, but most records do not give us the name of the enslaved individual, the purchaser, the seller, and the destination all together. For example, debts could be settled informally through the transfer of an enslaved individual with no record of the transaction. Enslaved Mapuches were often exchanged for enslaved Africans with no name given for either, and sales of enslaved people could take place in a hurry where scribes did not bother to record the sale. Enslaved Mapuches were listed in wills simply as "grabbed in the southern war" or were referred to as *una niña/un niño auca* (a Mapuche girl/a Mapuche boy).[128] Chile infrequently sent ships to Lima between May and December, when winds began to blow southward and when Lima soap makers slowed production (affecting tallow imports) to stabilize prices.[129] Therefore, any remaining cargo in Valparaíso in May had to be sold quickly and often off book. Other transactions were made in the Araucanía and the enslaved individuals may have been exported from Chiloé, Valdivia, or Concepción without stopping in Valparaíso to converse with the scribes from the Santiago cabildo.

While most of these ships leaving Valparaíso were destined for Callao, some disembarked in La Serena. La Serena's gold deposits remained active well into the seventeenth century and is mined in the region even today. This meant that a trickle of laborers was not enough to meet demand for larger mining operations, as the encomenderos there had already made significant investments in mining infrastructure, including their own export fleet with their own records.[130]

Colonial officials had not stopped trying to find large pools of laborers for La Serena's mines since the 1570s. In 1576, former *oidor* (judge) Juan Torres de Vera wrote to the king from Potosí (the continent's largest mining town) that La Serena needed a thousand laborers. His suggestion was that the king take laborers from the Araucanía and resettle them in the same way that he had done with the *moriscos de Granada* (Moors of Granada). He added that a just punishment for "warlike and delinquent" Indians would be a death sentence; therefore, it was only fair that they receive the lesser sentence of forced labor.[131]

The Curalaba Uprising

Pelantaro and other *lonkos* (community leaders) witnessed all of this and understood that colonists had already discussed the immorality and illegality of indigenous slavery and not moved an inch to curb the practice. The public focus for most governors was on the difficulty of getting soldiers to the front, but privately, many believed that the only financial incentive to get them there was the black market in enslaved people and war materials. Over and over, incoming Spanish governors had a seemingly unique solution to the colony's instability, but no solution ever remedied the fact that indigenous forced labor continued to be Chile's most valuable commodity.

Coincidentally, two years before the Curalaba uprising, the Council of the Indies demonstrated their own concern with the relationship between Spanish creoles and the Mapuche. The council argued that the continued practice of "personal service" was an existential threat to Spain's American colonies. On the same page, quite literally, the council's scribe added that the body was concerned with how war in Chile was preventing the extraction of gold. While the council did not recognize how the two above developments were linked, the Mapuche certainly did. The extraction of gold caused the war, and as long as the Spanish wanted gold, the Mapuche resistance to forced labor would continue.

The Mapuche also observed how, over the decades, the Spanish continued to expand their definition of a "rebel" or a "slave." Recall the case of Andrés Balón in terms of how readily war captives were moved in and out of encomiendas to solve disputes between colonists. In the seventeenth century, the trade in enslaved Mapuches could even be counted upon to resolve future disputes. In 1605 for example, Diego de Cartagena gave Blas Pereira a four-year-old *India Auca, cogida en guerra* (Mapuche girl, captured in war) and a horse, in exchange for an indigenous servant named Blasillo who had been temporarily working for Pereira. This exchange included a clause stating that if the servant Blasillo were to run away or die or be claimed by his original owner, then Cartagena would be compensated with another enslaved individual. If the Mapuche girl died or her original owner appeared (probably her family) then Cartagena would pay Pereira thirty pesos. Finally, a third case demonstrates how colonists could use the mere idea or perception that an enslaved person had been captured in war to end a dispute. From 1607, we have the prohibited sale of *una india auca cogida en la guerra* for eighty patacones of silver, a sale prohibited because she had not actually been taken in war. This Mapuche woman was from a repartimiento near Osorno belonging to Mariana de Pliego, and, as seen, indigenous people from repartimientos and encomiendas could not be sold or moved.[132] It appears that Mariana de Pliego was not involved in the sale or available to resolve the dispute, so the rest of the document was a discussion of to whom the money would be refunded and what to do with the extralegally enslaved person who was not actually enslaved. This development helps explain the aforementioned clause explaining what to do if the encomendero or owner were to "appear." The ubiquity of actual prisoners of war provided by the Spanish army meant that there were hundreds of encomienda Mapuches who all parties simply assumed to be war captives. Rather than prevent illegal sales by confirming possession of enslaved people, colonists put these clauses in sales that could dissolve sales made illegally or in error. The Spanish had normalized the sale of Mapuche captives to such an extent that the forced movement of wage-earning Indians and the temporary transfer of encomienda Indians was now often problematic and, according to Bishop González de Salcedo, even "incurable."

While the Curalaba uprising was an important victory for the Mapuche, in future discussions they did not take the decision to attack lightly and would usually tie it to the increase in Spanish captive taking of the 1580s and 1590s. The avarice of colonists through the trade in enslaved people was such that it left an impression for decades. The toki Maulicán, in conversations with Spanish captives thirty years after Curalaba, still remembered the frequent export of Mapuche captives from Valdivia.[133] In 1643, a Spanish woman named Louysa Pizara was interviewed about the 1599 siege that drove her out of her native Osorno. More than four decades later, Pizara remembered that "the Spanish in Osorno were very well positioned and had been greatly esteemed; yes in such manner that an individual Castilian made use of 300 Indians as his subjects, who had to deliver to him a certain weight of gold as tribute weekly. Because of these and other unbearable burdens, cruelties, and tyranny, the Indians joined together in the year 1599."[134] The Mapuche would continue to join together to resist forced labor in the seventeenth century but in ways that went much beyond the violent uprising of 1599.

3

The Era of "Great Tokis"

In 1598, the Mapuche stopped the Spanish conquest of Chile. In response to their defeat, the Spanish legalized the enslavement of Mapuche captives, conducted multiple raids, canceled those raids, asked for more funds from the viceroy, and even established a permanent army along the Bío-Bío. None of those experiments put the Spanish back in a pre-1598 position. The story of the first half of the seventeenth century is not one of the Spanish finally figuring out the Araucanía but instead one of the Mapuche continuing to innovate to resist forced labor. This time it was not Mapuche adaptation in warfare or strategy that stood out but the Mapuche use of dialogue and negotiation to consolidate the advantage gained after armed resistance in 1598.

This chapter details Spanish attempts to punish the Mapuche for the 1598 rebellion and how those efforts failed. I describe the creation of an "Army of Arauco" and how militarizing the frontier actually weakened the Spanish position. The second half of the chapter traces how Spanish failure contributed to the first half of the seventeenth century becoming an "era of great tokis," and I detail how these great tokis used captive taking and parleys to cement their authority and control their territory.

The Failure of the Spanish "Just War" Strategy

Before describing Mapuche diplomatic success, we must understand that this success cannot be attributed to any cessation of violence from the Spanish. To the contrary in fact, as after Curalaba, the Spanish were more determined than ever that the Mapuche must be defeated through force of arms. One keen observer of Spanish attitudes of the time was Alonso González de Nájera. He was a Spanish soldier wounded in the conflict who spoke of "disillusion" being the predominant mood of Spanish colonists in 1601. While he healed, he wrote *Desengaño y reparo de la guerra de Chile* (Disillusion and remedy for the war in Chile), which rather than offering "remedies" for the war instead expressed frustration that neither dialogue or force was making much progress.[1] He was frustrated by what he saw as broken promises and trickery on the part of the Mapuches but also acknowledged that the Spanish gave them two options: resist or be enslaved. The author added that, despite their brutal actions, he "refuse(d) to call them barbarians," impressed with their deftness in negotiating truces to their favor.[2]

Ecclesiastics also tried to find answers behind Spain's fifty years of frustration in Chile. After 1598, members of Chile's most prominent missionary orders wrote extensively about the colony's predicament. A Franciscan named Pedro de Sosa penned *Memorial del peligroso estado espiritual y temporal del Reino de Chile* (Memoir of the perilous spiritual and temporal state of the Kingdom of Chile), where he expressed frustration with the Mapuches and argued that their violence, and their habit of killing missionaries in particular, had much to do with the colony's struggles:

> The Mapuches are rebels, they flee the Spanish and make war on the Christian Indians, wasting the fruit of so many years of hard work. The rebel Indians have been offered peace and good treatment as given to friendly Indians, but as they are barbarians and live without government, republic or law, they do as they please. Being impossible to put them in reducciones, there remains no other solution than to make war on them. Saint Augustine would have approved it, and the Gospel calls a mercenary the pastor that sees the wolf and leaves the sheep.[3]

According to Sosa, the missionaries could not continue to allow these Mapuche "wolves" to prevent the "reduced sheep" from hearing the Word, adding that even Saint Paul asked for army protection.[4]

Even for men of God, the frustration with a lack of solutions quickly turned to thoughts of violent revenge as the best path forward after Curalaba. Melchior Calderón, a priest and treasurer of Santiago's cathedral, had a long career in Chile where he had sought to improve the treatment of encomienda laborers. In 1607, however, his thoughts toward Chile's indigenous population were punitive in nature, as he penned a twenty-seven-page treatise on why those involved in the 1598 rebellion and any future indios rebeldes should be enslaved. He argued that enslaved Indians would work hard and provide a good example for other Indians "outside of the colony" (presumably Peru) to keep them industrious and out of trouble. As a priest (and representative of Lima's Holy Office of the Inquisition), he also argued that slavery could represent a great "spiritual good" when these captives were converted.[5] Viceroy Luis Fernández de Cabrera would later echo Calderón's sentiments, arguing that, once removed from the colony, indios rebeldes could not escape and easily return to torment the Spanish. He added that in Lima the enslaved population could be better "instructed and informed" and prepared for a possible return to Chile as indios amigos.[6] Calderón's treatise eventually made its way to the Council of the Indies and contributed to the Crown's decision to legalize the enslavement of Mapuche prisoners of war in 1608.[7]

It would be up to the lawyers in the Audiencia of Chile to determine which of Chile's Indians were "at war" and eligible for capture and enslavement. In 1609, the Audiencia issued their criteria, deciding that the Indians in and around the provinces of Chiloé, Santiago, and Cuyo were "peaceful" and that the rest were southern *beliches* (indios rebeldes) who had been involved in the 1599 revolt and now threatened Santiago. This last group was eligible to be enslaved, but its definition was much too broad and did not account for the region's complexity or for the thousands of indios amigos who had lived in close proximity to and had frequent contact with indios rebeldes.[8]

With all of these doubts about who was a "rebel" and who was a "friend," some soldiers had already begun to falsify documents regarding illegally taken captives as enslaved people and, much worse, brand those who had never taken up arms against the Spanish. The branding of course would be quite polarizing in the Araucanía, and far from reassuring allied Mapuches, the practice was carried out against Spanish captives out of revenge.[9] Making matters worse was the fact that many captive Mapuches were branded on their faces. The viceroy suggested in 1633 that this practice be discontinued in favor of slightly less inhumane hand branding,[10] but the practice dragged on as any decision on an outright ban was left to the king.[11] Rather than establishing more control over the indigenous population then, branding made matters more difficult for the colonists.

Now that "just war" was official, the quite adversarial Audiencia and governors had to work together to somehow process the export of enslaved Mapuches. Governor Juan Jaraquemada (1611–12) complained that the Audiencia often blocked transport of enslaved people to Peru, potentially to keep them on their own haciendas in Chile. Both governors and oidores sought to profit from slavery, but in diametrically opposed ways. The governor could order and accompany raids against indios rebeldes when he saw fit and seek immediate profit by selling them in Peru. The Audiencia in contrast had no direct access to the enslaved people and was closely tied to encomendero labor. Mapuche indios de guerra were often absorbed into encomiendas but only of course if they did not leave the colony.[12]

After 1608, these debates were starting to cause doubt even among some of Chile's most prominent enslavers. Governor García de Ramón began to worry that the taking of enslaved individuals was hindering the war effort, as Spanish soldiers were inclined to wait for captured enslaved individuals who they could resell. García de Ramón was not motivated to leave the barracks and incur real risk. More and more Spanish soldiers sent indios amigos to capture indios rebeldes. The indios amigos sold at low prices, and the Spanish soldiers who had access to the markets would sell high.[13] There were also concerns that the knowledge that slavery was now legal would make indios rebeldes fight harder.[14]

There was also the role of Santiago merchants to consider. Governor Ribera tried to develop a strategy for the colony's recovery that involved domestic production of supplies for the army.[15] However, Ribera was never able to fully enlist Santiago merchants in this effort as they had a more stable market supplying to the ever-expanding mining town of Potosí and were averse to supporting an army that had repeatedly put their businesses at risk.[16]

Despite this administrative uncertainty, raids to enslave went forward. Governor Laso de Vega boasted that he had captured four hundred Mapuches in three separate raids between 1631 and 1633.[17] By contrast, those who lost ground against indios rebeldes were vilified. In one dispute over the state of the colony, ex-governor Ángel Peredo was accused by Maestre de Campo General Geronimo de Molina of putting his successors in a bind when he returned Mapuche captives to their homes. Molina added that the Mapuche saw Peredo's policy of "tolerance" as a sign of weakness and an opportunity to rebel.[18] Other witnesses in this matter testified that they never received the compensation for the value of the returned enslaved individuals promised by Peredo.[19] Especially among colonists who owned these enslaved people then, the actions of Peredo were regarded as a threat not only to the security of the colony but to their livelihood as well.

After marching energetically to areas in the Araucanía like Curalaba, Yumbel, Elicura, and Purén; burning Mapuche crops; and engaging with Mapuche troops when he did come across them, Laso de la Vega was confident enough to predict that the pacification of Chile was imminent and promised as much to the Crown. However, when Laso de la Vega retired to Peru in 1639, he was no closer to the end of the conquest than his predecessors had been a century before. He did repopulate a number of abandoned Spanish forts including Angól, but with all of the time spent in the field, he should have had much more to show for it. In particular, his inability to repopulate the important port of Valdivia was a significant failure.[20]

The Army of Arauco: The Spanish Retreat to their Barracks

The Flawed Soldiers of the Army of Arauco

The force responsible for waging this "just war" and the Spanish entity most culpable for the "just war's" ultimate failure was the Army of Arauco. For a window into the mood and capabilities of the Spanish army after their defeat at Curalaba, we can again look to González de Nájera and his *Desengaño y reparo*, where he gives his frank assessment that there would be no "just war" waged with 1601 troop levels. The wounded soldier argued that reinforcements were an urgent priority, detailing that Spanish troops were starving in their remaining forts and outnumbered twenty to one.[21] Governor Ribera sought help from the viceroy and Crown, even sending a recruiter to Lima to round up the troops that the viceroy could not deliver.[22] In 1604, Philip III responded in a rather dramatic way, decreeing that Chile would have the only permanently deployed army in the Spanish Americas, an army that would be funded by the treasury of the viceroyalty of Peru. This permanent "Army of Arauco" on the Bío-Bío River was the only exception to Spain's military strategy in its other American territories, which followed the *presidio-fuerte-milicia* (outpost-fort-militia) model, whereby most of the fighting would be done by civilian militias.[23] Chile had never solidified its frontier with a line of presidios or a series of advancing forts. Colonists had already abandoned frontier towns on a number of occasions and the crown felt that a professional army needed to replace the oft-overrun *vecino* (resident) militia.

This Army of Arauco would be a force of two thousand and would receive a yearly *situado* (stipend or payment) of 212,000 ducats. To institute the new strategy, Governor Ribera brought a portion of this new situado with him upon his arrival in Chile and had more than one thousand new troops from Spain and New Spain at his disposal in the year he took office.[24] On paper, two thousand soldiers seemed like a sizeable force that could bring stability to the Bío-Bío frontier. But where would these soldiers come from? The first sign of trouble came when Ribera welcomed the reinforcements but pointed out that he could not pay them. He had only received a portion of the promised situado from Lima and Viceroy García Hurtado de Mendoza had prohibited colonists in Chile from covering the difference.[25] Ribera might have been even more concerned about this salary shortage if he had thought he was getting professional soldiers. Instead, he called his new troops "poorly disciplined" and said that the ranks were marked by "confusion and barbarism" and hardly resembled a Spanish military unit.[26] González de Nájera, who had recently been a part of this "confusion and barbarism," agreed. He argued that if the Spanish were to win the war, royal officials would have to stop punishing Lima's "miscreants" by sending them to serve on the Chilean frontier.[27]

With the legalization of indigenous slavery in 1608, and real doubts about whether they would ever be paid, officers in the Army of Arauco were ideally positioned, not for a strategic victory, but for grift. Embezzling royal funds became a common activity for Spanish frontier soldiers, many running trading posts and *pulperías* (bodegas or bars), where they resold army supplies and alcohol.[28] The Crown was hesitant to send cash to the army, but supplies could easily become specie through sale in Santiago, Concepción, or on the frontier to the Mapuche. There are multiple references to clothes destined for the army appearing in local markets and of soldiers selling army horses.[29] In fact, Spanish soldiers would even try to augment their supply by stealing horses from Spanish haciendas along the frontier.[30] At least one viceroy was fully aware that this was happening but lamented that he had no way to confirm that the situado would arrive safely. He added that all he could do was continue to send it in "good faith."[31] By the end of the seventeenth century, Spanish officials had compiled entire sections of their archives to the "fraud and mismanagement" relating to the situado.[32]

Just as Governor García de Ramón had warned decades earlier, soldiers and officials on the Spanish side were doing more and more trading of enslaved Mapuches and little fighting and governing. According to one 1640 letter from a member of the Audiencia de Chile, there was a vibrant black-market trade in enslaved people between the indios amigos who often captured the Mapuches and the "war ministers" and soldiers who bought them. The loosest of interpretations of Queen Isabella's guidelines would make the sale of these "previously enslaved" Indians legal, but these sales were never reported, nor were required taxes paid. The judge who penned the 1640 letter was also annoyed that in cash-strapped Chile, the indios amigos were both collecting a salary as soldiers and making money in this racket.[33]

Poorly disciplined troops and a lack of resources began to turn the Army of Arauco into something very different from what the Crown had envisioned. While the permanent army was supposed to end the Mapuche threat, what it really did was bring more unscrupulous entrepreneurs to Chile where they could now count on a yearly situado to skim from, and a legitimization of their presence in the Araucanía where they would be in constant contact with potential indigenous captives. Opportunities for dishonest soldiers were unfortunately not limited to Chile. "Frontier captains" in northern Mexico for example took out loans to outfit their slave-taking expeditions and paid them back through the sale of enslaved Chichimecs.[34]

One example of the atypical soldiers who ended up in the ranks of the Army of Arauco was the "Lieutenant Nun," Catalina de Erauso (fig. 3.1). After escaping a convent in her native Basque region, and hiding for two years under the noses of her family and neighbors disguised as a young man, Erauso made her way to Sanlúcar where she paid her way onto a ship bound for Panama.[35] According to her own manuscript, Erauso arrived in Chile with a questionable background, not as a woman in disguise but as a rabble-rouser who had just killed a man in Trujillo.[36] Erauso eventually made her way to Concepción in about 1603 by way of Lima where she and her fellow soldiers were "well received."[37] Erauso served for years along the Bío-Bío and gained the rank of *alférez* (ensign).[38] She led her company for six months after the death of her captain, but any possibilities for her own ascension were lost after she lynched an indio amigo after an alleged betrayal.[39] Later, she participated in a mounted assault on Purén in which she was injured.[40]

Erauso's picaresque tale of a wayward female ecclesiastic engaged in battles, duels, and drunken card games draws the most attention from scholars, but her last days in Chile help us understand how individual Spanish soldiers had the power to derail any strategic gains made by officers. Erauso detailed that the indio amigo she killed had betrayed her, but the fact that she chose to take justice into her own hands certainly indicates that even after they were routed at Curalaba, Spanish soldiers still maintained an arrogance toward treatment of both allied and rebel Mapuches, an arrogance that one author describes as "derecho al despojo" (right to dispossess or enslave).[41] From its beginnings in 1604, the Army of Arauco was both a consumer of and a source of indigenous labor. Free indigenous people, encomienda Mapuches, and enslaved Mapuches moved the army's supplies and munitions

FIGURE 3.1. Doña Catalina de Erauso, a Spanish nun who lived as a male soldier. Lithograph by A. L. Noël, 1833, after F. Pacheco. Wellcome Library no. 282i.

and provided its food. Before the situado arrived regularly (and after), army troops expected and received servants as part of their remuneration.[42] Spanish soldiers regularly levied food, animals, and slaves from the local population, a practice that would not end when they received a stipend.[43] In fact, administrative changes with the introduction of the Army of Arauco assured that this grift would continue.[44] Chile's governor was now to be the capitán general, the head of the Army of Arauco. This military responsibility required every incoming governor to inspect the troops, view conditions on the front, and lead a raid (whether strategically necessary or not) into the Araucanía upon his arrival in the name of *hacer una entrada* or *reconocer tierra* (making an advance or scouting the territory). However, these *entradas* (advances) did not stop after the first months of a governor's term. These raids occurred "day after day," organized by "the highest authorities."[45] These expectations extended to the governor of Chiloé Island as well, which for much of the colonial period was semiautonomous. In January 1610, for example, new Chiloé governor Pedro de Barrera tried to cement his new command by capturing multiple Mapuches in the jurisdiction of cacique Pedro Quintupurai Talcunto.[46]

Many soldiers in the Army of Arauco had fled a difficult past in Peru (the aforementioned "miscreants"), believing that the forced labor and sale of Mapuches was a principal way to improve their economic fortunes. Already in the 1560s, decades before the permanent army was established, the *cronista* (chronicler) Pedro Mariño de Lobera noticed that many soldiers had embraced this *derecho a despojo*. So many soldiers in fact had taken their servants out of the Araucanía that it was becoming hard to maintain a campaign there. Mariño de Lobera added that Spanish soldiers believed the derecho extended to Mapuche women, as he encountered scores of pregnant army auxiliaries during his time on the front.[47]

The Flawed Strategy of the Army of Arauco

The avarice of these army officers and royal officials was left unabated not only because of beliefs about "rights" to labor but also because Spanish strategy literally left them abandoned and with little or no regulation. After the last Spanish towns were abandoned post-Curalaba, Governor Ribera made some efforts to help surviving soldiers recover, constructing a mill near Santiago to provide blankets and other materials. Ribera also had cart-making operations set up in Concepción and Santiago to make sure that these new domestically generated supplies could get to the front.[48] But even if manufacturers could turn out hundreds of carts, the challenge was still how to fill them. After Curalaba, Ribera discovered Santiago vecinos were more than willing to abandon the Araucanía, whether leaving the front to winter in Santiago or by focusing their economic energy toward Potosí rather than Army of Arauco supply. There was also a major flood in Santiago in 1604, further complicating any potential for a supply increase.[49]

After many false starts, Ribera did find an incentive that would motivate vecinos: land. Already establishing a number of successful estancias north of the Bío-Bío to provide for the colonial government, Ribera successfully petitioned the Crown to allow private landowners to do the same. Rather than having agricultural plots with "ambiguous" ownership, divided not-so-elegantly between municipalities, encomenderos, and *indios reducidos*, Ribera was allowed to sell farm plots to individuals. Spaniards and creoles who had fled the Araucanía after 1598 began to buy plots between the Itata and Maule Rivers in communities such as "Chillán, Portezuelo, San Rafael, Cauquenes and Parral."[50] By establishing farms in what today are known as the Maule and Ñuble regions (Chillán's professional soccer team is Ñublense), Chile now had an agricultural colony between the frontier of the Bío-Bío and the "pacified" central region. For much of the seventeenth century, Chile's "Center-South" would provide supplies for Santiago, export wheat and tallow to Potosí and Lima, and supply the soon-to-be formed Army of Arauco.[51]

While these new haciendas and estancias would renew colonization of the Center-South, there would be no new settlement or conquest south of the Bío-Bío. Fifty years earlier, the same Spanish army had attempted to occupy the Araucanía, and one hundred years earlier, the Inka had attempted to do the same. The seventeenth century Army of Arauco, however, was simply there to hold the line. Mapuche resistance had seen to that. Not only had Mapuches scored important victories in strategic battles but their tactical changes would make any future gains more difficult as well. Improved Mapuche horsemanship allowed them to abandon a "fortified war" where the Spanish could count on arquebuses, cannons, and forts, in favor of more mobile, more flexible, and smaller-scale raids called *malones* or malocas.[52] The Spanish responded with more raids of their own, partly because they did not have the resources for a sustained campaign and partly because concern shifted from capturing territory to taking prisoners. Members of a 1626 Spanish expedition exploring the eastern side of the Andes remarked at how fortunate they were to receive funding at all, when most royal military expenditures went toward the 212,000 ducats of the Army of Arauco situado. This expedition even encountered a valley near Villarrica that they wanted to occupy as it seemed to be used frequently by Mapuches rebeldes, but the leaders pressed on as they were en route to Córdoba and not there to "end the Chilean War."[53] These factors would turn the Army of Arauco, which had been designed for a few sustained and decisive campaigns, into "a slave-hunting machine" that would eventually conduct hundreds of smaller raids.[54] Soldiers in the Army of Arauco came to resemble the "frontier captains" of other Spanish-American frontiers for whom "slavery was no sideline to warfare or marginal activity born out of the chaos of conquest, it was first and foremost a business involving investors, soldiers, agents and powerful officials."[55]

The Army of Arauco also failed strategically because it operated less like a conquering military force and more like a trading operation resembling the West India Company or frontier captains in Mexico.[56] After 1598, tax collection and debt payment were suspended in the entire colony, and mortgages (from now-damaged or destroyed buildings) represented significantly less capital.[57] It would be up to the Army of Arauco to provide an internal market for agricultural products to assist with hacienda recovery. The haciendas of the Central Valley and Norte Chico would first provide the army with smoked meats, leather, jerky, grains, and wine and, once recovery was in place, export them again to Lima and Potosí. In the first years after Curalaba, the internal market for these products would have been almost nonexistent. Even after the return of production for export, the Army of Arauco still continued to consume between 5,000 to 8,000 bushels of wheat and 2,500 and 3,000 head of cattle every year.[58] Spanish soldiers themselves were in fact responsible for a wide array of commercial operations, from running trading posts and pulperías, to resupplying ships in less-active colonial ports.[59]

However, the amount of legal commerce on the fringes was at least closely rivaled and likely surpassed by smuggling, embezzlement, and taking of enslaved individuals. The viceroy had learned not to send goods directly from his coffers. Instead, the viceroy would ask suppliers and ship captains from Quito or Lima to submit individual bids. The lowest bidder would then get the contract to take the cloth, nails, shoes, ammunition, horses, hats, and so forth to Chile. Complicating this, however, was the fact that the suppliers themselves operated on credit.[60] A haberdasher might get a loan from a silk merchant who would then charge between 25 to 40 percent interest. After calculating shipping costs, the haberdasher would need to sell these hats in Chile for at least three to four times what they would fetch in Lima. One shipment in 1623 for example counted soap, hats, and shoes for the army as half of its value.[61] Once these goods arrived in Chile, officers and rank and file soldiers were expected to buy the supplies, which they did almost exclusively on credit. A soldier in Fort Boroa could go broke buying soap. This meant that Army of Arauco members needed another source of income, usually the sale of enslaved Mapuches: "Frecuentan este puerto [Concepción] los navios que trahen del Perú el Real situado . . . no sacan carga alguna de consideración, sino de los esclavos que cogen en la guerra"[62] (Ships frequent this port that bring the Royal situado from Peru. . . . They don't take with them any considerable cargo apart from the slaves that they catch in the war). As seen from the Padrón de Lima (see chapter 2), many Mapuches in Peru worked in the garment industry. It was more than likely the same merchants supplying the Army of Arauco were purchasing enslaved Mapuches off ships returning from Chile.

As seen in chapter 2, we know that most viceroys had firsthand knowledge of the enslavement of Mapuches, so it is hard to believe that they did not understand that the Army of Arauco was a distracted operation. Pedro de Toledo, however, was just one of many viceroys who did not understand how taking of enslaved people rendered all other duties of the army impossible. For example, in attempts to drive away Dutch privateers, Viceroy Toledo was frustrated at how difficult it was to get troops already in Chile to rendezvous in Valdivia with the reinforcements that he was sending all the way from Lima.[63] Toledo acerbically remarked that he hoped the incoming governor, Martín de Mujica, would be able to "walk the eight or ten leagues [to Valdivia from the Bío-Bío] . . . that so many Spaniards with fewer troops" had walked. [64] Toledo was also upset when Governor López de Zúñiga argued that a re-fortification of Valdivia would require another situado while the use of the first one had been wasteful and even "pernicious." Toledo correctly observed that the Army of Chile did not want the war to end. An end to the war would mean an end to malocas for enslaving purposes.

Despite gaps in colonial records, we can confidently state that demand for enslaved Mapuches emanating from Lima, La Serena, and Valparaíso assured that the strategic aims of the Army of Arauco would fail and would actually worsen conflict along the Bío-Bío. What is even clearer from dozens of documents detailing the seventeenth-century vida fronteriza is that the Army of Arauco itself was the principal source of those Mapuche captives. Instead of providing a bulwark against Mapuche incursions from the Araucanía, the Army of Arauco was conducting slave raids into the region.

Mapuche Victories after 1608 and the Failure of Raids to Enslave as Policy

Defeating the Spanish at Curalaba, occupying their cities, and dealing with a new group of winkas (see section on Blonde Winkas and Decentralized Resistance in this chapter) emboldened the Mapuche and ushered in an era of the *grandes tokis* who had perfected their resistance strategies against the Spanish.[65] Centuries later, patriot intellectuals would argue that Mapuche tokis had put Chile on an early path to independence by rivaling the power of Spanish governors. While pointing to a bilateral leadership structure might be a bit of an artificial reconstruction of the colonial past, if there was a time that Mapuche tokis operated in the same manner as Spanish governors, it was in this early seventeenth-century period after Curalaba and while the Spanish army fell into very predictable and merely punitive patterns. During this period, the Spanish army fell into a predictable and strictly punitive and ultimately failing "just war" strategy, while Mapuche tokis permanently mobilized and even developed orderly succession patterns like we see with Lientur, Butapichón, and others.

The Curalaba uprising certainly touched off the era of great tokis, but the protagonists of the seventeenth century's first decades are a bit difficult to trace. First of all, even though the Curalaba uprising began in 1598, it really lasted almost eight years, as Fort Boroa was not abandoned until 1606. In 1610, as incoming governor, Luis Merlo de la Fuente led a campaign toward Purén. This *entrada*, led by Maestre de Campo Alvaro Núñez de Pineda, took Mapuche captives and burned fields as previous incursions into Purén had done. This raid stood out only because it prevented an expanding alliance between the purenes and coastal Mapuches and it recovered a Spanish artillery piece that the Mapuche of Paillamachu Island had been using as a decoration/trophy for at least ten years. The Spanish, still smarting from the Curalaba uprising, legalized Mapuche enslavement as punishment in 1608. That decree was suspended, however, four years later, when the Crown gave Jesuit Luis de Valdivia the opportunity to institute a "defensive war." Armed conflict mostly ceased south of the Bío-Bío between 1612 and 1625 when Valdivia left, so tokis really only resumed armed resistance in earnest in the mid-1620s.[66]

Anganamón and Pelantaro were still active as tokis well into the new century and participated in peace parleys with Valdivia. A new generation of tokis, however, emerged in the 1620s, most famous among them the *corsario* (corsair) Lientur. The Spanish referred to Lientur as an indio de paz who had several interactions with Valdivia and, before rebelling, lived in Fort

Cayuguano and led a levo at Pailiguas near Yumbel. Spanish chroniclers do not specify Lientur's prerebellion leadership position, but it was clear that he spoke for hundreds of Mapuches de paz who were performing labor for the Spanish just north of the Bío-Bío. In or around 1620, Lientur witnessed a decline in Mapuche working conditions and began to consider rebellion. In fact, Rosales pinpoints the moment when Lientur understood that rebellion was the most appropriate path for the levo of Pailiguas.

Rosales describes Lientur approaching Sergeant Major Andrés Giménez de Lorca at Fort Yumbel and asking him to free one of his female relatives into his custody as it was "his right" since she was a single mother. When Giménez de Lorca rejected the idea, Lientur began to suspect that the Spaniard wanted to enslave his relatives for his personal use, not just as temporary workers fulfilling their personal service obligations. Lientur said, "Why don't you go to Purén instead to *maloquear*, as it is *tierra de guerra*, and not to Pailigua, where we are in peace. These things cause the Indians to rise up and you the Spanish don't want peace through your deeds even though you claim it in your words." With that, Lientur "left for enemy lands," taking with him his levo of nearly one hundred Mapuches.[67]

The toki Lientur would appear again multiple times in colonial accounts. The *corsario* led a 1626 attack on Chillán, where he allied with Pehuenche or Puelches to enter the town from "behind the mountains."[68] Lientur led another attack on Chillán in 1628 where the corregidor (mayor) and his son were killed. In response, soldiers from Yumbel attacked Lientur's troops in the Battle of Cangrejeras, a Mapuche victory that yielded Spanish captives, arms, clothes, and rations.[69] Lientur would eventually retire as toki and turn his troops over to his lieutenant Butapichón. This act was significant in that these grandes tokis of the seventeenth century had a clear process of succession, as permanent mobilization was becoming the preferred mode of resistance. With the ascension of Butapichón, the Mapuche continued to demonstrate a preference for tokis who were familiar with the customs of Spanish colonists and had intimate knowledge of the enemy. Butapichón had been enslaved by a colonist named Diego Trujillo as an adolescent and as toki was not shy about using Spanish symbols of authority, wearing the "deep red cape" of Spanish governors in several battles. Butapichón was killed in an assault on Fort Arauco known as the Battle of La Albarrada, but only after demonstrating how organized the permanently mobilized Mapuche resistance had become. Butapichón's troops were described as decorated with "attractive plumage on their heads, and as content [on the field of battle] as if they were attending a celebration or banquet." The troops were divided into multiple battalions and attacked in unison when Quepuantu, the vice toki gave the order. The next toki was Loncomilla, who was killed in battle and succeeded by Cusimilla. Lincopichón replaced Cusimilla in 1639.[70]

Ethnogenesis through Captive Taking

The steady pattern of Spanish punitive raids after the end of Valdivia's Defensive War still afforded Mapuches the opportunity to assassinate or capture Spanish officials as they had done in the sixteenth century, but under permanent mobilization, this strategy seems to have changed. Ritual murder or captive taking were not necessarily acts that meant a call to initiate resistance but instead played a part in establishing toki hierarchy. The permanently mobilized Mapuche of the early seventeenth century began to use Spanish captives as pawns, selling them to other groups to cement alliances, to better define levos and ayllarehue, and to use the very reputation of their captives to announce their own largesse. The most famous of these luminary captives was Núñez de Pineda, the author of *Cautiverio feliz* (Joyful captivity).

Núñez de Pineda's account is one of the most well-known captivity narratives in the colonial Americas, rivaled only by those penned by Mary Rowlandson, Alvar Núñez Cabeza de Vaca, John Smith, or Hans Staden.[71] Núñez de Pineda's father, Alvaro, was the well-known Spanish officer mentioned earlier, who had helped repel Cayencura's attack on Angól in 1585. Francisco too was a young officer in 1629 when he was knocked off his horse in the Battle of Cangrejeras. In his own account, he said he hoped not to be recognized as Alvaro's son but was soon identified and subjected to kicks and punches. His attackers shouted, "Die, die already, . . . this is the son of Alvaro Maltincampo [maestre de campo] who had our lands destroyed." Soon, however, Lientur, the toki responsible for the Cangrejeras victory, also recognized Francisco and stopped the beating. Lientur respected Alvaro as a fellow worthy war chief and believed quite rightly that his son would be a valuable captive.[72] Francisco would be held by Lientur and his father, Maulicán, for six months.

Later in life, in response to rumors and a fictionalized Lima play about his captivity, Francisco wrote the "joyful" account of his captivity. In 1634, the Lima theater company Los Conformes had a hit on its hands with its original comedy about "the supposedly true adventures of a Spanish soldier captured by the Araucanian Indians." In the context of explaining "what had gone wrong" with the conquest in Chile, the actors poked fun at "interracial romance" and methods of religious conversion.[73] Francisco had tired of these mischaracterizations of the Mapuche, and *Cautiverio feliz* partly remedied this by offering the most complete Spanish depiction of Mapuche life in the early seventeenth century. Francisco's account reflected on what he learned during his six months as a captive and delved into themes of religion, politics, violence, sex, and morality. As a prominent creole, Francisco called out the shortcomings of public servants in Chile, arguing that they pursued profit above all else and that the colony's administration was laden with peninsular appointees. There were too few Chilean-born officials who understood and appreciated colonial society.[74] Francisco also spoke out against the enslavement of Mapuche captives even while admitting he had participated in the trade. He argued that his time in Lima helped form his stance against it, as he discovered that there was a robust abolition movement in Peru that never made it to Chile.[75]

Francisco's narrative certainly holds up as a coming of age story full of tragedy and triumph for a twenty-two-year-old man. But more important for our purposes is how his description of the Mapuche use of both violence and revelry to organize their capacity for resistance. In the first days of his captivity, Francisco was brought before a circle of people that included other Spanish captives and prominent Mapuches. Butapichón announced that he wanted to purchase Francisco and sacrifice him to Pillán and various tokis offered to contribute jewelry, *guanacos* (camelids, relatives of alpacas), sheep, and horses toward a potential purchase.[76] Butapichón also offered his daughter in exchange, proclaiming "our goal is none other than to exalt our names, and affix the toquis and ancient insignias of our dear nation with the blood of opinionated Spaniards, and solicit an effort to expel them from our lands."[77] Fortunately for Francisco, at some point during the cahuín (meeting of the clan), Butapichón was pulled aside and convinced to sacrifice another captive Spaniard.[78]

Francisco's comrade was brought before the tokis, where one held a lance with three knives (each representing a different *butanmapu* [region]) tied to the point in the form of a trident, and another had a toki (club). Butapichón commanded the unfortunate Spaniard to start gathering sticks from the ground, and with each one that he picked up, he repeated the name of a "brave" Spaniard or indio amigo who had fought against Butapichón and Lientur. When the captive had collected a number of sticks, Butapichón had him drop the sticks into a hole one by one, again repeating the names of "brave" Spaniards. When he had dropped all twelve of his sticks into the hole, Butapichón told him to cover it with dirt and struck the captive in the head with his toki, killing him. Núñez de Pineda witnessed that "right away the acolytes that were with knives in their hands, opened the chest and took out the beating heart and delivered it to my master [Maulicán]; and after having sucked the blood, they brought him a *quita* of tobacco, and taking smoke into his mouth, he blew it here and there, like incense for the demon to whom they had offered that sacrifice. The heart passed from hand to hand, and with it made a ceremony for my master." Meanwhile, others were "running around the poor deceased, shouting in their manner, while the rest made the earth shake with their feet. When this barbarous and evil right had finished, the heart was returned to my master's hands, and he proceeded to cut it into little pieces, and each began to eat his piece with great speed."[79]

Although Butapichón was persuaded not to kill Núñez de Pineda, Maulicán was determined to use his captive, the valuable son of a high-ranking Spanish officer, in other ways. Francisco describes another cahuín, where he was toasted, feasted, and invited to what best can be described as a party in his honor. When he arrived, "the youngsters were dancing and singing with the rest of the people, in all there were about 2,000 people dancing, including married and single women." "They sat us down on some [rugs] that they had prepared for us and as soon as we arrived there were women upon women who, with everyone else were anxious to meet 'the son of Alvaro,' they came and went, toasting us with quite delicious liquors, that they make from all kinds of fruits and legumes."[80] The food, much of it prepared by Spanish female captives included "stews from different kinds of birds, fresh fish and shellfish, well-seasoned and other gifts of little cakes and fried empanadas, with abundant bee honey; foods that we are accustomed to in our banquets." At the same banquet, Francisco made his way to the dance platform where his hosts announced, "Here comes Alvaro's son, everyone come and greet him." Francisco continued, "We arrived at the platform, where the single women were . . . singing and dancing in a circle . . . and upon seeing us toasted us with many delicious pitchers of chicha. Among them was beautiful young woman with a decorative crown on her head . . . adorned with precious stones. After toasting me the young woman told me she was to put the crown on my head, and . . . insisted that we dance hand in hand."[81]

By having the Spanish cook for them, and by incorporating Francisco into Mapuche ceremonies, the Mapuche resistance co-opted or captured symbols of Spanish dominance. Ritual murder might be a political tool, but the Mapuche could not "kill" Spanish society. During the seventeenth century and with the advent of great tokis, the Mapuche dressed like the enemy as Butapichón did; they used iron, let their beards grow, and incorporated horses into their warfare and ceremonies. All of these steps were designed to "assimilate the qualities" of the Spanish in the name of cultural resistance.[82]

The First Parleys of the Seventeenth Century: Anganamón and Luis de Valdivia

Núñez de Pineda's account demonstrates how these cahuínes were not only about sharing effective "sensuous symbols."[83] Cahuínes were also effective at establishing political hierarchies, not only among the different levos, but also between the Spanish and rebel Mapuche. For the rest of the seventeenth century, any progress made between the Spanish and rebel Mapuche would come through cahuínes or "parleys" where the Mapuche made demands of the Spanish. Any conflict between the Spanish and Mapuche during this period was frequently due to the Europeans ignoring or breaking agreements established at those same parleys.

For most of the sixteenth century, the Spanish usually described any agreement with a levo as a *dando la paz* (peace treaty). But in the 1590s, Spanish scribes began to describe meetings between Mapuche and Spanish officials as *parlamentos* (parleys).[84] This change makes sense both semantically and politically. These were more than simple peace treaties. These agreements would often involve weeks of negotiation, gift exchanges, ceremony, consultation, conversations, feasting, and occasional violence. Politically, calling them parleys makes more sense because by the 1590s, most of the groups involved had already "given the peace" at some point, and these gatherings were a way for new governors to symbolically take command of a group already allied with the Spanish. In fact, as Mapuche resistance continued throughout the century, the location of these parleys moved farther and farther north. Eventually, Spanish officials recognized the futility of having a new governor trying to claim sovereignty over rebel provinces like Purén or Villarrica. Instead, new governors would parley with frontier amigos or Mapuches de paz and claim victory in their communications with the viceroy. What the viceroy should have observed from descriptions of these parleys was that he was wasting his money. He was spending 212,000 ducats every year on the Army of Arauco, a force that was losing territory and status year by year. These parleys were a form of Mapuche resistance through negotiation, in that they were really cahuínes in which the Spanish were only guests and signposts to reinforce the fact that the Mapuche were setting the terms of daily life in the Araucanía.

The first meetings widely known as parleys by chroniclers and historians alike were the Parleys of Quilicoya, Rere, Taruchina, and Imperial in 1593. Not all parleys were identical, as agreements made with brand-new governors were often vague and short-lived. Such was the case with these 1593 meetings involving Óñez de Loyola. These meetings all took place between September and November 1593, and the agreements mostly involved personal service obligations and treatment. Many of the levos represented at Quilacoya, Rere, and Taruchina were encomendados, already in the service of particular Spaniards. But despite their position in the colonial hierarchy, tokis like Cayupillán, Curinechico, and Manquetur still communicated that they expected to be treated fairly. The tokis petitioned the Spanish to stay out of their homes and away from their women and daughters, that they be allowed to meet in cahuínes (the Spanish called them *bebederos* [drunken feasts]), that they not be taxed for labor performed for encomenderos (which amounted to a double tax), that they not be forced to work in the mines during prime hunting and planting seasons, and that they be protected from indios de guerra.[85] The parley at Imperial, however, was held farther into the Araucanía and seems to have included former indios de guerra. The attendees from Maquegua Island and environs asked that they be pardoned for the killings of Spanish captain Pedro de Maluenda and soldier Cristobal de Aranda. In exchange, the tokis agreed that they would pardon those responsible for the Spanish malocas that saw Mapuches "killed, taken and exiled" (presumably sold into slavery).[86] Even before the Mapuche victory at Curalaba, then, rebellion was explicitly tied to enslavement, and peace was only possible if enslavement ceased.

After Curalaba, the first Mapuche-Spanish meetings were led by Luis de Valdivia in 1605. As one of a handful of Jesuit missionaries in the Americas in 1605, Valdivia's goal was not to establish a permanent dialogue with the Mapuche but to convert them to Christianity. (By the latter half of the century however, most dialogue at these parleys was not about religion but rather specific Mapuche demands.) After leaving his native Spain for Peru in 1589, Valdivia was among the first group of Jesuits to arrive in Chile, reaching Santiago in 1593. He returned to Peru from 1602 to 1605 when his Jesuit brothers in Santiago complained that he was too "melancholy." Back in Chile in 1605, he bypassed his testy Jesuit colleagues in Santiago and sailed with governor-elect Alonso García de Ramón to Concepción.[87] Valdivia traveled with García de Ramón to Paicaví, where they met up with outgoing governor Ribera.[88] Despite the presence of the colony's highest political authorities, it was Valdivia that negotiated the release of Anganamón's lieutenant Tereulipi at Paicaví.[89] According to the chronicler Rosales, Anganamón was envious of Pelantaro's prominence and believed that a parley with the Spanish could boost his reputation.[90] Anganamón and Valdivia eventually discussed the abolishment of personal service and other themes like monotheism and polygamy.[91] Anganamón did not reach any agreements or have any constructive dialogue with García de Ramón after the latter made no assurances that he would suspend Spanish malocas.[92] Lacking the support of the governor, Valdivia once again returned to Peru in 1606.[93] His dispute with García de Ramón left doubt as to whether any agreements made with the Mapuche at Paicaví would be honored by either side.[94] Whether or not the agreement stood up, however, simply meeting with Chile's Jesuit rector meant further legitimation of Anganamón's status as toki or gentoki and also helped define the boundaries of Mapuche reguas. The actions of tokis like Anganamón demonstrated a belief that the early seventeenth century would be a time to consolidate the gains of violent resistance through further diplomacy. The era of grandes tokis then, while ushered in by Curalaba, would be cemented by negotiation with winkas. This negotiation took the form of multiple Mapuche-Spanish parleys between 1605 and 1692.

Despite the lack of success with the 1605 parleys, García de Ramón did meet with a number of tokis in 1608 at the Parley of Conuco, near Fort Nacimiento. This meeting had modest outcomes, but there was an agreement by the Spanish to cease the destruction of Mapuche fields in the area, and in return, the cacique Colaguen agreed to move some of his people closer to Fort Nacimiento. One of the attendees is described as "Enetur," which could be a poor transcription of "Lientur" and would fit with the corsair's biography.[95] In 1612, Valdivia was back in Chile for a third time. Alonso de Ribera, who would be starting his second stint as governor, accompanied him. Valdivia also brought with him an order from Viceroy Juan de Mendoza, "order[ing] the cessation of offensive warfare," and a new title as visitor general of Chile. His title meant that, even though he accompanied Ribera on the return trip to Chile, Valdivia would not be subject to Ribera's authority or to that of the Audiencia. Viceroy Mendoza also decreed that under no circumstances were any Spanish infantryman to wander south of the Bío-Bío, a decree punishable by death. This new approach or "Defensive War" also meant forbidding nonviolent contact, particularly trade, and sexual relationships between Spanish soldiers and Mapuche women. Finally, the polemical and quite recent 1608 "slavery decree" was suspended.[96] Valdivia also traveled to Chile with a cédula addressed to the "Chiefs of Araucanía" where King Philip III wrote, "I have been informed that the occasion and causes that you have had for rebelling and continuing the war for so many years have been some humiliations and poor treatments that you received from the Spanish during which time you were living peacefully." The king added that such abuses were against his will and that of his predecessors, who all had wished that the Indians be treated, "like free men, as you are no lesser than the rest of my Spanish vassals." Philip III assured the Mapuche they could trust Valdivia and go to him for what they needed.[97]

Valdivia's previous conversations with tokis caused him to believe that the key to peace this time would be the Ilicura regua, led by the elderly toki Untablame. Valdivia arranged to meet with Untablame at a second Parley of Paicaví, the toki arriving along with seventy-three other tokis and lonkos.[98] In the 1617 Parley of Nacimiento, Butapichón and Catinahuel (Caguanaguel) freed a Spanish captive and again talked with Valdivia about living closer to the Spanish. This time they proposed leaving the safety of the mountains for the valleys. In a revealing conversation, Valdivia explained to the tokis that the Spanish were "ready for war" constantly while the Mapuche had to hold cahuínes and waste large quantities of chicha and food to get neighboring levos to rebel.[99] While Valdivia's assessment is fairly accurate, from the Mapuche perspective the Spanish were wasting their chicha and food (the situado) every year while the Army of Arauco stood idle, and Mapuche alliances could grow temporarily as a need arose.

In 1619, Valdivia returned to Spain, and the Defensive War was abandoned as a Spanish strategy in 1625. Again, despite enthusiasm from some colonists, the return to "offensive war" would bring Spain no closer to control of the Araucanía. The 1630s especially saw very little progress for Spain in the region, given that strategy was crafted by a governor who tried to simultaneously end Mapuche personal service and expand Mapuche enslavement. With little consistent Spanish presence in the Araucanía during the 1630s, ethnographic information about Mapuche activities is sparse. What we do know is that upon the return of parleys in the 1640s, the Mapuche were no less confident in their negotiations than they had been immediately after Curalaba and that their successful resistance continued.

The Parley of Quillín

While abuse by ecclesiastics was not unheard of in Chile, very rarely were the Jesuits or other orders involved in the particular crime of capturing or selling enslaved Mapuches.[100] In fact, Jesuits like Rosales returned hundreds of captive Mapuches to their communities. Rosales was born in Madrid in 1601 and, upon his arrival in Chile, maintained a fervor for "spiritual conquest." He lived in the Araucanía on several occasions and for ten consecutive years at one point (1629–39). Well into his seventies, Rosales rejected a promotion to Jesuit provincial, instead preferring to continue his mission work in the south.[101] With the absence of any real outreach from Governor Laso de la Vega in the 1630s, it fell to Rosales to initiate discussions with Lincopichón, a gentoki who led Mapuche negotiations at the Parley of Paicaví in 1612.[102]

The efforts of Rosales meant that Lincopichón would agree to meet governor Francisco López de Zúñiga in 1641 near the Imperial River, where Lincopichón and his sons shared a meal of bird stew with the Spanish as a sign that they were ready to negotiate (fig. 3.2).[103] The next step of this process was typical of these mid-seventeenth-century meetings and would provide nineteenth-century patriot leaders with names and actions of great tokis to emulate and use in the construction of their mythical version an indigenous representative government. After the stew was gone, López de Zúñiga returned to Concepción, while Lincopichón stayed behind to see whether he could build a coalition among rival *rehues* (levos/reguas). These rivalries were often deep, in some cases between Mapuches amigos and Mapuches rebeldes who had been at odds for decades. Lincopichón had the tall task of convincing rehues from the rebel province of Elicura that they should ally with the Mapuche amigos who had killed their famous toki Querepoante.[104] Lacking direct communication with the rehues not in attendance at the parley, Lincopichón could not proceed as he had no consensus. (In fact, any hope for gains from a second parley of Quillín in 1647 would be dashed when a group of only three tokis, led by Curiguante of La Mariquina, broke from negotiations, instead using the occasion to plot a potential revolt.)[105]

The amigos meeting with Lincopichón in 1641 did consider an alliance but made their position clear. Amigo representative Catumalo expressed that it would be impossible to defeat the Spanish Empire, which one scholar speculates might have been the argument that drove him and his people to live near Spanish forts and become a capitán de amigos: "What has war brought you: if not death, enslavement, the loss of your farms, and exile from your lands?

FIGURE 3.2. Parlamento de Quilín, 1641, "The Marquis of Baides López de Zúñiga meets an Indian Cacique," in Alonso de Ovalle, *Histórica Relación de Chile*, 1646.

How can you end, as some poor Indians, the Spanish Empire, that extends all around the world, and governs all of our actions? From four thousand miles away, the King sends Spaniards, arms and reinforcements. Who will help us to make war?" If Lincopichón was skeptical of Catumalo's "defeatist" position, it did not prevent an alliance. The two groups proceeded to sacrifice a chilihueque (a now extinct camelid) to celebrate the partnership, and Lincopichón proceeded to receive another group of amigos.[106]

As word got out that Lincopichón was putting together alliances in preparation for another meeting with the governor, the "gallantly cut" mestizo and indio amigo Antonio de Chicagüala arranged a meeting with Lincopichón near Fort Nacimiento. Chicagüala was intimately familiar with both Mapuche and Spanish worlds as he was the son of toki Gualarán of Maquegua and raised Mapuche. Chicagüala's mother, Aldonsa de Aguilera y Castro, however, was Spanish. He had been baptized by Spanish captives and had a cousin who was a captain in the Army of Arauco.[107] Chicagüala was bilingual and explained his desire to join Lincopichón's alliance as "returning to his roots."[108] With this broad coalition in hand, Lincopichón was again ready to meet the governor and "hacer las paces" (make peace).

In 1641 then, hundreds of representatives led by Lincopichón, Catumalo, and Chicagüala met with hundreds of Spanish soldiers, priests, and auxiliaries on the banks of the Quillín River (now Quellén), a tributary of the Cholchol. A number of seventeenth-century luminaries attended, including Butapichón, Lientur, and Rosales.[109] Rosales described some of the tokis arriving as "dressed in painted *guanaco* and colorful tiger hides, with long hair, quivers on their shoulders, and crowns or multicolored wool halos on their heads, crisscrossed with many arrows."[110]

The decorative ceremonies, the food and drink, and the number of attendees certainly made this an event full of "sensuous symbols," but the agreement signed by both parties was by far the most impressive part of this parley. After an exchange of prisoners, and a promise by the Spanish to again abandon Fort Angól, the Mapuche agreed to allow the Spanish to rebuild the cities they had lost after Curalaba, if the Spanish recognized that the Mapuche present were to serve the king and only the king. This service would take the form of military support, but there would be no more personal service nor tribute of any kind. "Not one kernel of corn, not one bean" would be turned over to the Spanish.[111] This was an extraordinary agreement that is really mislabeled as a "peace treaty" and is more accurately described as coalition building. For months after Rosales's conversation with Lincopichón, the Mapuche had been building alliances and drafting terms of peace. In the end, the Mapuche gave nothing up and had achieved a position in the Spanish kingdom legally equal to that of Spanish vecinos.

Blonde Winkas and Decentralized Resistance

In a development that enraged the Spanish but revealed much about the nature of Mapuche politics, a separate Mapuche region would have their own opportunity to negotiate with Europeans in 1643. This time it was not Governor López de Zúñiga who would sit down with tokis, but the Dutch privateer Elias Herckmans (fig. 3.3). The first "blonde winkas" that the Mapuche encountered had the misfortune to arrive in the midst of the Curalaba uprising. In 1600, the remnants of a Dutch five-vessel expedition commanded by Jacob Mahu entered the Magellan Straits and promptly became stuck. Mahu's goal had been to explore and trade in the Pacific, but his ships were blown back by strong headwinds, were embarrassingly overtaken by the famous Olivier Van Noort voyage and would eventually become scattered along the coast of Chile.[112] One of the Dutch ships landed at Lavapie on the Bay of Arauco, in the immediate aftermath of the Curalaba revolt. After

FIGURE 3.3. Dutch explorers and a *chilihueque* (camelid). "Expedición Holandesa de Hendrick Brouwer y Elías Herckmans en la ciudad de Valdivia, Chile en el año de 1643."

initially welcoming the winka and offering them copious amounts of chicha, the Mapuche clubbed the landing party to death. The expedition was now to be led by the nephew of one of the Lavapie victims, a twenty-two-year-old mariner named Baltasar Cordes.[113]

Cordes would command the remaining Dutch ship *Fidelity*, which dropped anchor at Carelmapu near Chiloé. Most of the Huilliche of Chiloé had been "reduced" earlier in the century, but just before the Dutch arrived, they had become involved in the Curalaba uprising. The *Fidelity* needed provisions and after negotiations, the Spanish agreed to provide gunpowder and ammunition, an odd choice considering these two nations were at war.[114] Things predictably went sideways however, when Cordes sprung a trap and killed the Spanish envoys. Joined by a group of Huilliche, Cordes and his men then advanced on Castro, sacked it, and killed a number of Spanish men and a priest who had sought refuge in a church.[115] Spanish reinforcements fleeing Mapuche-held Osorno eventually drove the Dutch out of Castro and killed thirty Huilliche leaders who had assisted them.[116]

This attack on Castro presented a post-Curalaba conundrum for royal officials. The Dutch did not yet have major territorial aspirations in Chile, so the Spanish did not envision the Dutch stepping in to rebuild the cities destroyed in 1598. The Spanish had an opportunity to confirm Dutch intentions when they interrogated Rodrigo Giraldo, the captain of one of Mahu's ships that had become stuck in the Strait of Magellan. Giraldo claimed that he himself had no designs on South American territories as he was a friend to the Spanish having been raised on the Iberian Peninsula. He was aware of Dutch desires to settle in the Indies, but his particular expedition was there only to trade and then move on to China, Japan, or the Moluccan Sea.[117] The Spanish were also pleased that the stormy Magellan Strait was still providing a bulwark against European enemies.[118] However, with the abandonment of the Araucanía, a Mapuche–Dutch or Mapuche–English alliance could more easily develop, opening up all sorts of geopolitical possibilities, none of which were good for Spain. Would indios amigos and indios fronterizos maintain some level of loyalty to the Spanish and fend off or at least warn the Spanish of the arrival of their European rivals? Or would the victorious tokis of Curalaba meet all of Spain's enemies with open arms, making alliances with all their European rivals? Or would they drive off all winkas now that they had vanquished the Spanish? Future European arrivals could be Puritans or pirates or anything in between.

The Spanish would have to wait fifteen years to understand the potential of Mapuche–Dutch alliances, , but sure enough in 1615, the mere sight of Europeans off the coast would give post-Curalaba tokis an immediate upper hand. In that year, the Dutch privateer Joris Von Spielbergen's *Great Sun, Great Moon, Morning Star, Aeolus,* and *Hunstsman* anchored in Concepción's harbor but did not disembark.[119] The Spanish had advanced news of their arrival and prepared a defense of the city in full view of the Dutch. The Spanish forces were of course also in full view of the Mapuches rebeldes. Taking advantage of the troop concentration in Concepción, a group of Mapuches raided the now relatively defenseless reducción of Picúl, taking captive twelve Mapuches de paz. A month later the rebeldes returned but, finding Picúl defended, hurled only insults, yelling out to the Spanish, "What are you doing, Spaniards? Don't fall asleep, there are Moors on the coast."[120] The exact insults may have been an embellishment by the chronicler Rosales, but this episode reveals that the tokis were aware that keeping one eye on the Pacific weakened Spanish defenses. Colonists noted that although the Spielbergen expedition was in Chile only briefly, the Dutch brought carpenters along.[121] Carpenters were of course commonplace on any long voyage, but to skittish Chilean authorities, their presence meant plans for settlement.

Any intelligence the Spanish could glean about European movements in the Pacific was analyzed and reanalyzed. In 1624, the much larger Nassau Fleet commanded by Jacques l'Hermite's sailed past Chile on the way to a raid of Lima and Guayaquil. The initial pass did not even occur within view of the Araucanía, but once the fleet had scattered, a number of Dutch stragglers seem to have made their way ashore near the Itata River. Ten crewmen were taken prisoner by the Spanish and interrogated extensively about their intentions, especially when it came to the potential for settlement and alliance with the Mapuche. Among the ten was a "great mathematician and experienced pilot" who provided the most detail. The prisoner described how the group had pillaged metals like silver, iron, and copper, taken samples of white ash and pepper trees, and captured an "Indian boy." The pillaged items were destined for Europe, but the Spanish also discovered that the Dutch had brought supplies to the Americas with plans to settle on Mocha or Juan Fernández Islands, after sacking all they could from Lima. Taking plant samples and bringing hammers meant a potential settlement and alliance with the Mapuche.[122] What authorities in Chile did not know was that Dutch pretensions actually extended far beyond farming. For the Dutch, embroiled in their own war of independence against Spain, Curalaba was not a "disaster" but a revolt led by "valiant" Mapuche warriors who had destroyed "popish idols." Dutch authors warned that if the United Provinces, a predecessor to the Netherlands in rebellion against Spain, were defeated by the Spanish, the Dutch would soon replace the Indians as laborers in the mines of Potosí. Other Dutch authors contributed to renewed hostilities by arguing that a Dutch victory in the Americas would drive the Spanish out of the Low Countries.[123]

This admiration began from two oceans away, but at least in the Dutch imagination, the Mapuche soon materialized into a very real potential "American ally."[124] The backers of the Nassau Fleet shared this belief in potential cooperation, and aboard the ships arriving in 1624 were "letters of alliance" to convince Mapuches to rebel and help the Dutch ignite a full-scale revolt in the Americas that would "oust the Spanish decisively from the New World."[125] The "lure of Peru" would prove too much for the Nassau Fleet to stop in Chile and present these letters of alliance to the Mapuche,[126] but the Henrik Brouwer expedition of 1643 came ashore and actively sought an alliance with tokis in the Araucanía. By this time, the Dutch West India Company had expanded its influence in Brazil to conduct raids on Spanish ships and territory in the Caribbean. As a takeover of silver-rich Peru was the company's next plan, they outfitted Brouwer, hoping he could "establish a foothold on the coast of Chile" and "launch attacks on the mineral-rich interior."[127] Brouwer himself added that he wanted to ally with the "freedom-loving and Spanish-loathing warriors" depicted in *La Araucana*.[128]

Brouwer's expedition took on provisions at Recife and landed just north of Chiloé in May 1643, where their two hundred musketeers defeated Spanish resistance and took on some provisions, but they lost their element of surprise.[129] The desperate and outnumbered Spanish called local Huilliches to their aid, but the Dutch soon advanced on Castro, sacking it and partially destroying a Jesuit church. There they left a message in Latin that accused the Spanish of being cowards for fleeing and signed it, "Victor (olandii), cola España" (Holland is the victor, Spain is the vanquished).[130] Brouwer took ill during the voyage and died aboard one of the ships, but the expedition's new leader Elias Herckmans pushed on, "landing [in Valdivia] with two companies of troops, delivering 'an excellent harangue and oration' to a crowd of about three hundred" Mapuches. Herckmans explained the Dutch purpose in the South Pacific, presented a new batch of "Letters of Credentia" from the Prince of Orange, and distributed gifts. In another speech to an audience of 1,200, Herckmans reminded the Mapuche that the Dutch had also fought the Spanish for eighty years, and agreements were made about exchanges of provisions for merchandise.[131] Herckmans also addressed the toki Manqueante in writing, a letter that was copied by the Spanish and made its way into the Archive of the Indies in Spain:

> Valdivia, 14 October 1643.
>
> Sir,
>
> With pleasure and desire, we have received the message that Your Grace sent us via your three messengers. We respond (only) now because we are very busy supervising the maintenance that the locals have promised us but not completed, and considering that we are on the verge of starvation here, we have decided to set sail for Santa María Island or Concepción to see if we can find new information about our Spanish enemies. The lack of food has greatly affected our soldiers, some of whom have fled, some of them arriving in the lands of Your Grace. Don't let them stay, but rather do us the favor of killing all those that you find, and tell your neighboring caciques to do the same because they will go to Concepción and undoubtedly tell the Spanish of our situation since Your Grace and other caciques have cooperated with us[.] Because

> of that we must insist again that you not leave any of ours alive because we will not send anyone to meet with you other than me or our lawyer. Every other detail I will send verbally with your three messengers. With that I desire you health and a good life. Friend of Your Grace, Elias Harquemans.[132]

After all the speeches and gift exchanges, Manqueante confirmed Spain's fears by promising to ally with the Dutch against the Spanish and offered "his lands, people, arms, rich gold mines and women." Manqueante also even sent his son to live among the Dutch as proof of his trustworthiness,[133] a common practice when the Spanish were cementing alliances with Mapuches de paz. A Dutch deserter, Antonio Juan, confirmed the worst Spanish fears by testifying before the governor of Chile that the Dutch had brought carpenters, ironsmiths, and a multitude of tools useful in construction and farming. They also brought a number of small arms, which Antonio Juan believed were "to arm the Indians that befriended [us] to fight against the Spanish and drive them out of the Kingdom" of Chile.[134] According to other interogees, the Dutch had told caciques in Valdivia that they would soon return with twelve to fourteen ships, "two thousand soldiers and a thousand African slaves, to relieve the Indians" of any forced labor.[135] The Dutch had also expressed that next time they would not only settle Valdivia but would try to take Concepción as well.[136]

Panicked Spanish officials scrambled (with seventeenth-century speed, it should be said) to respond, with Governor López de Zúñiga claiming that the presence of the Dutch was a watershed moment for indigenous people in the region. Brouwer's arrival came at a very interesting time for Chile's governor. López de Zúñiga had just made peace with Lincopichón, which meant that he had an ally near the strategically important Imperial River. However, attempts to repopulate nearby Valdivia in the 1630s had failed, and he feared that the rebel Mapuche near the port would become "extremely bold" and perhaps even provoke those in reducciones to rise up against encomenderos. López de Zúñiga argued that the only way to prevent the Dutch from "infesting" Chile was for Spain to send one thousand men.[137] But while he waited (probably months) for reinforcements, he sought to convince the coastal Mapuche (as he had done with Lincopichón) that the Dutch were not to be trusted and that the Mapuche should defend Chile. (The viceroy eventually sent a twenty-two ship fleet to take back Valdivia, but the Dutch had been gone for two years by the time it arrived in 1645.[138]) López de Zúñiga sent both Spanish and Mapuche messengers to spread the word that the Dutch were there for gold and that the Mapuche would soon be forced to work in Dutch mines.[139] These messengers were sent with instructions to give the Mapuche whatever they wanted to keep them in "obedience to His Majesty."[140] Ironically, of course, the Mapuche who received the messages were being asked to trust the Spanish who had already forced them to work, rather than the Dutch, who only might do so.

By the 1640s, it was clear that the Mapuche were in control of the Araucanía. This control was a function of some violent resistance but more and more a function of coalition building through negotiation. If the Spanish wanted to know the contents of letters brought by European enemies, wanted to rebuild long-abandoned towns, or wanted to know about Mapuche rebelde movements, they could do so, but not through force. They would have to meet, trade with, and appeal to the Mapuche tokis for help. Above all, the Spanish could not backslide into abusing encomienda Mapuche or conducting malocas to capture and export Mapuches. The punitive 1608 policy of "just war" had not worked, and, moving forward, progress could only be had through dialogue.

Quillín was the pinnacle of Mapuche resistance through negotiation, but there would be more parleys in subsequent years as well as more informal meetings between Spanish officials and Mapuche tokis that reinforce just how essential dialogue had become in asserting Mapuche hegemony. In a 1645 letter, for example, López de Zúñiga wrote to Viceroy Pedro de Toledo about an unnamed parley he had with toki Guentecoli near Toltén. Guentecoli had been a Spanish captive as a boy but returned to Lavapie as an adult. Like Chicagüala, apparently, Guentecoli's time among the Spanish as a youth caused him to still hold them in esteem, and he decided to warn the Spanish about areas where it was too dangerous for their limited forces to go. Guentecoli and Uchamalal had both warned the Spanish that the recently founded Fort Boroa was in danger of being abandoned but that the Spanish should be careful with any resupply attempts as some of the access points were narrow and could be prone to ambush. Guentecoli also warned that Spanish forces near Arauco were stuck since there were *enemigos* on the coast and enemigos near the mountains who would attack indio amigo reduciones if the Spanish attempted to redistribute their troops.[141] If there was any doubt that the Mapuche resistance was working, this letter reveals just how few places the Spanish controlled in the Araucanía fifty years after Curalaba.

López de Zúñiga was still well regarded when he retired in 1646, his contemporaries viewing him as fair, efficient with the colony's funds, and having no personal economic interest in expanding the trade in enslaved Mapuches.[142] Building on this momentum, Governor Martín de Mujíca continued to seek peace between Spaniards and Mapuches but also tried to repair fractured interindigenous feuds among allied groups and bring in mountain dwellers who had not previously been involved in these parleys. In 1650, peace was signed at Fort Boroa with Mapuches from the provinces of Osorno, Cunco, Ranco, and Villarrica as well as Puelches of the cordillera. The Puelche attendees informed the Spanish of many additional communities of Puelches and Pehuenches within the cordillera who were not aware of the peace and were anxious to keep them from being caught by Spanish malocas.[143] Boroa sat much deeper in the Araucanía and was accessible by nomadic Puelches and Pehuenches as well as Mapuches. The Spanish presence there had to be handled very carefully. In 1650, new governor Antonio de Acuña y Cabrera declared that war was not to be made upon the Puelches. Rosales was sent to meet with Puelche leaders to help cement an alliance with the Spanish and help prevent disruption caused by the new fort. Unfortunately, and predicably, the Spanish presence revived old feuds and created new ones. Rosales observed that when one group, led by Puelche chief Chaclaye, left their lands to meet to offer an alliance with the Spanish, Millacuga, a Pehuenche chief and longtime rival, killed Chaclaye.[144] These hostilities around Boroa provided a new opportunity for the Army of Arauco to *maloquear* (raid) and renew the enslaving that was so important to their bottom line. In fact, it was the very family members of Governor Acuña who would be the most active captive takers, their actions leading directly to a Mapuche uprising in 1655 and endangering the diplomatic progress made in midcentury parleys.

4

Indios Amigos and the 1655 Mapuche Uprising

As parleys of the mid-seventeenth century yielded more alliances, the Spanish slowly made their way back into the Araucanía. But soon after they arrived, the greed of the mal incurable saw the Spanish turn on their indigenous allies and provoke another general Mapuche rebellion. This chapter details the importance of indios amigos to the seventeenth-century Spanish presence in the Araucanía and how a particular group of Spanish officers chipped away at this alliance in the 1650s. It also details how these indios amigos saw a general rebellion as the only way to reject increasing Spanish abuse and how this uprising was different from what took place at Tucapél and Curalaba in the sixteenth century.

Indios Amigos: Whose Friends Are They?

Indios amigos and more informal indigenous allies were instrumental to Spanish attempts to control several of their American frontiers. Even in Chile, where a permanent army with professional European soldiers had been established for more than fifty years, 75 percent of the rank and file were still indios amigos.[1] Over time, Chile's indios amigos had proved extremely valuable as "auxiliaries" and later soldiers in campaigns against indios rebeldes, and the colony still had not recovered from the loss of five thousand indios amigos in the 1598 assault. Indios amigos were just as trustworthy if not more so than the Spanish soldiers who accompanied them, as they were usually assured of spoils from their campaigns, could not flee to the lands of the indios rebeldes who branded them traitors, and usually lived within a stone's throw of Spanish settlements.

As seen in chapter 3, parleys, although not producing ironclad agreements, did further cooperation between the Army of Arauco and the all-important indios amigos. Allied indios amigos aided the Spanish army in all sorts of engineering tasks like building bridges, widening roads, fortifying barracks, and chopping wood. The indios amigos also had an equally important combat role in Spanish campaigns against indios rebeldes or indios de guerra, often enslaving indigenous people themselves. In fact, the Spanish argued that enslaving indios de guerra was actually designed to help indios amigos, in that their combat role would expand if the indigenous enslaved population could perform more support tasks.[2]

Allied natives of course had helped the Spanish defeat the Aztec and Inka Empires, and Diego de Almagro had indigenous help with his foray into Chile.[3] The Inka Empire would count on yanaconas, vassals who had lost their connection to a specific community, with a number of tasks, including soldiering. This meant that there was already something of a mercenary caste for the Spanish to incorporate upon their arrival.[4] In the 1570s, Chilean creoles began to speak of indios amigos as a unique set of allies, separate from yanaconas or mitae laborers. In this decade, the role of these allies also expanded to include the capture of indigenous enslaved individuals, like it did during a 1578 expedition to the Andean region of Pudoa.[5] In the last two decades of the century, most indios encomendados were required to work in mines or haciendas and leave their homes for months at a time. But when indios encomendados near the Bío-Bío frontier left their communities to fulfill labor obligations, these same communities became more vulnerable to *malones* (malocas/raids) from indios de guerra. Recognizing this risk, colonial authorities on the frontier began to allow some indios encomendados to fulfill their labor obligations through military service on the frontier as amigos.[6]

But from the moment Spain decided to establish the permanent Army of Arauco presence in Chile, the indios amigos were more than indispensable. In the sixteenth century, it was often indios encomendados who would travel with their encomenderos from Santiago or Concepción to serve for a few months in the militia along the Bío-Bío.[7] By the seventeenth century in turn, it was "newly reducidos" Mapuches who made up the allied troops that accompanied the now permanent Army of Arauco.[8] Army of Arauco payments to indios amigos and *indios jornaleros* (temporary workers) made up a major part of their annual budgets, as much or more than the army was spending on ammunition, ship repairs, and fort maintenance.[9] These arrangements were further clarified in meetings like the Parley of Arauco in 1612 where Governor Alonso de Ribera both attempted to establish a "Defensive War and the role of indios amigos within it. Out of this parley came a Spanish promise that none of the Mapuches who had agreed to peace and to be protected by Spanish forts would be asked to mine gold or be asked to move to perform labor elsewhere. The parley also established that the protected Mapuches would be paid for their labor. In return, the amigos were to restrict the movements of the enemy, provide troops to the army, allow visits from missionaries, and remain in the strategic areas where they had agreed to settle. From this moment on as, Andrea Ruíz-Esquide explains, "los amigos . . . ostentaron una condición juridical especial" (indios amigos held a special judicial condition).[10]

Although the frontier could often be characterized by its instability, it seems that the Army of Arauco could indeed count on aid from indios amigos. According to albeit incomplete army records, such indios amigos were regularly paid to serve as armed escorts, sailors, or hacienda guards.[11] Specie and goods were also offered to indigenous allies for intelligence about indios de guerra. In the province of Cuyo just east of Santiago, indios amigos were rewarded with clothing after informing Governor Cristóbal de la Cerda that the indios de guerra from the "other part of the cordillera" had carried out two large *juntas* (meetings) and were preparing to fall upon certain Spanish lands.[12]

In a 1603 letter, Governor Ribera lauded indio amigos for their bravery and efficiency, claiming that each allied Indian was worth two Spanish soldiers.[13] Especially after the 1608 legalization of enslavement, the indios amigos participated in thousands of raids to enslave, making up a much larger proportional percentage of Spanish forces than Spanish or creole troops. For example, in a 1634 attack on the always difficult territory of Purén, four hundred indios amigos were joined by "some [Spanish] harquebusiers."[14] In the early seventeenth century, Alonso González de Nájera estimated that among the "Coyunches, Gualques, Quilacoyas, Reres, Quechureguas, Talcahuanos, Andalicanes and Araucanos there were a total of 6,000 *indio amigo* soldiers."[15]

Santiago de Tesillo, a close associate of future Governor Laso de la Vega, wrote of the battle exploits of indios amigos in great detail. During a 1630 campaign, captain and future governor Alonso de Figueroa sent indio amigo commander Remulta to occupy the strategic coastal mountains near Quidico. Spanish troops eventually relieved Remulta and his troops, but three days later, they were called into action again after an attack by an unidentified group of Mapuches on another Spanish column. In response to being caught off guard, the maestre de campo (field marshal) reassigned Remulta to intelligence gathering. Remulta was to watch the territory of the

FIGURE 4.1. Game of *chueca* (*palín*), from Alonso de Ovalle's *Historica Relación*, 1646.

suspected attackers so closely that they were to even show up as spectators at their *chueca* (Mapuche sport similar to field hockey) contests (fig. 4.1).[16] Remulta and his troops maintained their scouting mission until the Spanish showed up with reinforcements in the form of four hundred infantrymen and cavalry.[17]

Tesillo also described both the quantity and quality of amigos, detailing how they performed bravely in rescuing captives held by indios de guerra, while also adding that they made up the bulk of the Army of Arauco. In one particular campaign, only thirty Spanish harquebusiers accompanied a column of two hundred indio amigo cavalrymen.[18] In a battle against Querepoante the following year, five hundred indios amigos accompanied the Spanish against an estimated seven thousand indios de guerra. Obviously outnumbered, the Spanish and indios amigos could not prevent the counterattack where Querepoante's troops burned the "ranches" belonging to indio amigo leader Catumalo.[19]

Indios amigos also served the Spanish in their conflict with European enemies. Chile never was able to do much to prevent Dutch or English incursions into the Spanish Pacific, but they did try to solicit help from indios amigos in protecting their coast. For example, Cristobal Talgui Pillán, an indio amigo scout in the 1670s, had reported that the English had populated two islands 160 leagues from Chiloé, "toward the Magellan Strait." Talgui Pillán added that the English had two forts, artillery, sheep, and goats; had planted wheat; and were building "a large ship whose wood was brought by Indians loyal to them."[20] On one island, the English were said to have built a stone wall and on the other a mill.[21]

Thus, there would be no Army of Arauco without indios amigos. By allying with the Spanish, indios amigos risked banishment by their own Mapuche neighbors, counterattacks by Mapuche indios de guerra, and displacement from their families as they accompanied the Spanish on campaigns. An important question therefore becomes: how did the indios amigos benefit? For the most part, the answer seems to be a sense of stability. In many of the peace agreements creating their indio amigo status, the Spanish promised that they would not *repartir* (resettle) the amigos.[22] For their part, the indios amigos would be required to move closer to Spanish forts and serve as a buffer against the indios de guerra. So this was a resettlement of sorts, but with the Mapuche and Huilliche deciding whether and when to approach Spanish forts.

This settlement of allies near forts represented "frontier policy on the cheap" and was successful enough in Chile for the Spanish to try it in other colonies. Sending indios amigos to make raids or trade missions farther into the Araucanía would prevent the need for expensive major offensives that had proved unsuccessful or even counterproductive.[23] This settlement policy represented an important post-1598 change, as now forts would not be isolated outposts well south of the Bío-Bío; instead, a new fort would only go up if adjacent territory had been pacified. Viceroy Francisco de Borja y Aragón expressed the strategy as way to *estrechar* (stretch out, put pressure on) indios de guerra by adding new settlements south of the Bío-Bío:[24]: "It wasn't the fort that sheltered the *amigos*, but the amigos who came to protect the fort."[25] Forts would be centers of indio amigo activity and settlement, not necessarily bulwarks against them. Figure 4.2 shows a 1637 map of the Spanish fort of Angól where the *alojamiento del exercito* (soldier barracks) were outside of the fort's walls. The Spanish would later abandon Angól as part of the Peace of Quillín in 1641 when indios amigos argued that it had been founded too far into Mapuche territory.[26]

The amigos led Spanish campaigns, they married into Spanish families,

FIGURE 4.2. Map of Angól, by Alonso Villanueva Soberal, 1637. Original in Archivo General de Indias.

and they asked the Crown for rewards for their service to the empire. Ignacio Chuecas Saldías has explored the purchase of indigenous enslaved people in seventeenth-century family budgets and details the case of the family Sotomayor. He describes Captain Tomás de Sotomayor as a "Lengua General del Reino [chief translator for the colony] and a first cousin of the *indio amigo* [Antonio] Chicagüala.[27] Intermarriage certainly could create alliances between Spaniards and Mapuches, but often, it simply furthered an already strong connection. For example, in 1613, Catalina de Morales and Antonio de Payba were a married couple living in Lima. Payba was a Spanish blacksmith who had married into Morales's Chilean indigenous family. Morales identified her cacique as her father Pedro de Moraga, and her encomendero as Hernando de Moraga Galindo, *vecino de Santiago*. It was quite common for allied aborigines to take Spanish last names, but marrying the daughter of a Chilean cacique may have greatly improved the status of Payba the Spanish artisan.[28] By midcentury then, prominent indios amigos were a part of landed colonial families.

Not only did indios amigos capture most of the piezas sent to Peru; they also maintained an important link in the export itself, especially in the aforementioned pampa circuit.[29] Pehuenche amigos like Bartolo Yoyari were vital to this circuit, as they knew of and navigated Andean passes still unfamiliar to the Spanish. Yoyari was baptized, raised in Concepción among creole colonists, and moved by them as part of a reducción to Talcahuano. He eventually escaped to the cordillera and hid for years near "Pehuenche Pass," where he interacted with Puelches, eventually becoming fluent in three languages. Despite being on the lamb, Yoyari maintained a relationship with the Spanish and would travel to Chillán every few years. Some observers even suggested he sent information to the Spanish about movement around the front, making him a double agent of sorts.[30]

As amigos were the most valuable soldiers to the Spanish cause in the Araucanía, a number of them began to request the pensions that their Spanish contemporaries had already begun to receive. Cacique Martín de Cuevas Palán served in Fort Valdivia for many years, and in 1696, Governor Joseph de Garro forwarded his petition for twenty *escudos* (Spanish gold or silver coins) a month to Madrid. Cuevas Palán was born in Toltén, captured by the Spanish, and converted to Catholicism. He "defended His Majesty's standard" for years, leading his own troops in a victory over cacique Ampallantos. Later, Cuevas Palán assisted Spanish missionaries in his native Toltén by converting other caciques and by helping build a church. Cuevas Palán's son even followed him in the family business, reaching the rank of infantry captain.[31]

Meanwhile at Boroa: Fifty Years After Curalaba

Generations of indios amigos joined the Spanish army and took on increasingly important roles as settlers. But by the mid-seventeenth century, indio amigo communities had their loyalty tested. In 1639, the Audiencia wrote that a measles and smallpox epidemic of the previous year had severely affected indio amigo communities. All told, the Spanish could only count on a force of six hundred indio amigo infantrymen when they were accustomed to having several thousand at their disposal. Without the indios amigos at full strength, the Audiencia recommended that the Spanish suspend or at least severely restrict incursions into the Araucanía.[32]

Already weakened by a lack of amigo infantry, the Spanish army was further debilitated by an earthquake that leveled much of Santiago in 1647. In 1651, Governor Acuña wrote that the earthquake, subsequent floods, and an epidemic had left the cattle industry in particular in shambles.

Slaughterhouses had been damaged and lost many of their employees to illness, meaning that there was very little beef or tallow getting to soldiers in Valdivia.[33] Without resupply, the Audiencia worried that Spanish soldiers would increase their participation in the sale and export of captive Mapuches. Acuña warned that there would be "grave consequences" for those selling enslaved Mapuches out of the Araucanía, as this practice would cause "great difficulties" for the colony.[34]

With embezzlement from their superiors, postearthquake decline, and mountains of personal debt, pressure was on creole soldiers and indios amigos to produce war captives for sale. However, the increasing tendency to conduct raids simply to "increase the number of 'salables'" was hurting the overall health of the army just as it had immediately before the Curalaba uprising.[35] The bishop of Concepción, Dionisio Cimbrón, observed that Spanish raids did little more than tire horses and soldiers, especially when led by governors who traveled with more resources. The bishop added that the army was also lacking in supplies, as many yanaconas who ordinarily would help provide bread, wine, meat, and legumes were exported out of the Araucanía. Finally, he perceived that the situado never covered even half of the needs of the army "from marshal to drummer" and that many deserted despite facing hanging if caught.[36] At least one viceroy acknowledged this shortfall. In 1651, Viceroy García Sarmiento de Sotomayor wrote that the "Caja de Potosí" (Potosí treasury) would need to send at least 60,000 pesos more every year, especially considering that troops in Valdivia were supposed to somehow share intelligence and resources with the ninety soldiers defending Buenos Aires.[37] (It is unclear whether the viceroy thought potential threats would come from sea or by land, but he likely meant both.) The morale of the Army of Arauco was "hanging by a thread" as new governor Acuña arrived in 1650.[38] One could even argue that morale was so low that soldiers began to turn on their allies.

The Friendship Unravels

Usanza

As seen, the Spanish fort of Boroa was of great strategic importance in the seventeenth century. At Boroa, the Jesuit Rosales had negotiated the release of more than forty Puelches illegally enslaved by a Spanish raid in 1650. The captive exchange led to a larger peace treaty in which the nearby indios amigos agreed to become Christians and live and farm near the fort.[39] Peace had been achieved but only as a quickly cobbled and risky response to enslaving indigenous people. The Spanish had to stop enslaving the indigenous people around Boroa in the future as Boroa stood much farther south than even the abandoned Angól. The fort was precarious and both Mapuches rebeldes and amigos knew it.[40]

It seems that the Spanish knew that Boroa could not be a base from which to launch malocas. Concepción was too far away to provide winter breaks and resupply and not nearly enough Mapuches had signed peace treaties in the Purén/La Imperial region to achieve a comfortable base of indio amigo infantrymen. In leaner times then, like those after the 1647 earthquake, the Spanish continued to expand their labor search by introducing new tactics like the practice of *usanza* (renting out of the services of an indigenous servant).[41] Most common during times of scarcity, Mapuches had begun to take the extreme step of "renting" a son or daughter to feed the rest of the family.[42] Usanza was declared illegal on several occasions and even made punishable by death, but these bans did not stop the practice. In fact, usanza transactions not only appeared in court cases denouncing the practice but were recorded by notaries to distinguish usanza Indians from war captives. For example, in 1652 Isabel de Villagra was accused of violating royal prohibitions by selling twenty Indians, many of whom she had come to possess through usanza.[43] In the same year, Gaspar Mayo, the captain of *San Francisco de Milagro*, sold two "indias aucaes de la usanza" named Llanqueguetar and Casilda to Violante de Ulloa in Valparaíso.[44]

Any slippery Spanish official could also hide these transactions and avoid legal actions like the ones described. Unfortunately, one such official, Juan de Salazar y Enríquez, happened to take charge of Fort Boroa in 1651 after being named to the position by his brother-in-law, Governor Acuña. Salazar abused his authority to convert usanza agreements into licenses for enslaved people, falsely claiming that usanza Mapuches were actually war captives and having them forced aboard ships leaving Concepción.[45]

Salazar's expansion of enslavement did not stop with the misuse of usanza, as he quite openly facilitated the sale of Mapuches and Huilliches de paz. Rosales observed an occasion where an unnamed cacique approached Spanish lieutenant Méndez with twenty-five of his people offering peace and agreeing to live avecindados (neighboring/next to) to the Spanish. The cacique wanted assurances that his people would be fairly treated to which Lieutenant Méndez replied that the "royal word" was sufficient. (As seen in chapter 3, in formal parleys, there was usually the slaughtering of animals and an exchange of gifts to mark the occasion and to cement the agreement. This appeal to the "royal word" was a breach of protocol). Without a formal agreement, it comes as no surprise that Méndez eventually imprisoned the cacique and his people. When Méndez's superior, Sergeant Major Geronimo de Molina, got wind of the lieutenant's activities, instead of sanctioning him, Molina took the enslaved Huilliche himself, giving twelve others to Governor Acuña and six to Salazar. Some of the Huilliche were destined for sale in Lima; others were given to the governor's wife, María de Salazar. Beyond being appalled by these activities, Rosales recognized their larger implications when he testified that the Huilliche had begun to mistrust the "royal word."[46] Bishop Cimbrón wrote that many enslaved Mapuches had complained to him about their treatment, arguing that they had never been "rebels" and did not understand why they had been deprived of their freedom.[47]

Instead of heeding these warnings, however, Acuña sent his wife's brother to the most strategically delicate part of the frontier. Once he arrived at Boroa, Salazar ordered another raid on the same Puelche group Rosales had just freed.[48] In a matter of months, Boroa went from the site of a peace treaty and captive exchange to a slave market.[49] In one case, an officer under Salazar's command, Captain Luis Pónce de León, brought seventy Puelche captives to Boroa. When ordered to return these Puelches to their homes, Salazar instead kept a number of them hidden and subsequently sold them into slavery.[50] Another witness claimed that junior officers gave the enslaved individuals to Salazar in exchange for promotions.[51] The illegal trade in enslaved individuals was brisk enough at Boroa for Salazar and his brother José to share the profits with a handful of others, principally their sister. According to Rosales, María bought enslaved indigenous people and sent them to be sold in Lima. María paid for the enslaved individuals with goods from a stash she kept at Boroa, goods that were undoubtedly meant for the army. Rosales listed other officers outside of the Salazar family like Captains Domingo de Solto and Pedro de Torres and Alférez Simón de Solto, who were also involved in the illegal trade at Boroa.[52]

Withholding Payment

Selling allies into slavery was obviously the most egregious of Salazar's immoral acts, but Salazar also decided to profit from his position by withholding payment from amigos that he hired for his other schemes. As mentioned, amigos were essential to Spanish malocas, but they were often underpaid for their service or any bounties they were promised. Despite the underpayment however, maloca spoils were a principal source of income for the indios amigos. But with Salazar this practice was so common that he received personal and direct instructions from the King's Council of the Indies to "NOT take anything from them" (indios amigos) that they had seized in these malocas or raids.[53] Undeterred, Salazar was said to have "violently" taken captive Mapuches from indios amigos like Tinaqueupu and the principal cacique Quilaturi.[54] If the indios amigos complained about this, Salazar berated them.[55] Consequences could also be grave for Spanish soldiers who balked at these arrangements with Salazar. One witness claimed that Salazar beat the soldier Andrés Martín to death when the latter refused to testify that he had taken an Indian girl in war, when in fact Salazar had ordered her stolen from a group of indios amigos.[56]

Salazar and his brother José also directed indios amigos to projects that had little to do with the business of erecting and maintaining a fort, instead obligating them to transport the wine and other items they sold in their pulperias or trading posts where many items destined for the army (not the officers' profit) were sold. This transport took six weeks on average to complete, and not only did the amigos not receive payment when the goods were delivered but the Salazars did not feed them at any point during the journey. At some point, the king found out about this embezzlement and sent a cédula ordering that all soldiers be paid before the quartermaster released any supplies. Rosales testified that instead of kissing the royal order as a sign of honor, José crumpled up the order and, to paraphrase, "wiped his rear end with it."[57]

Amigo *Complaints and Spanish Response*

Spanish allies of course protested these abuses, but the Spanish response was to blame the victims. Amigo complaints prompted the Spanish to assign an arbitrary border between "rebel" and "peaceful" Indians, thereby declaring more of them eligible for enslavement. The Spanish stated that anyone on the wrong side of the Vanegue River in shared Puelche-rebelde territory could be enslaved. (The Vanegue River does not appear in future documents, but Rosales appears to be referring to an area south of Lonquimay Volcano.) However, as this border was slapdash, on the "friendly" side there was nothing to eat. Predictably then, two indio amigo caciques, Pichunlab and Quichenecul, complained that their people had been enslaved for crossing the river in search of food.[58] As Salazar saw no consequences after the enslavement of amigos, he began to make this common practice at Boroa. These actions created a feud with the aforementioned toki Antonio de Chicagüala.

As noted, Chicagüala was bilingual and respected by both the Mapuche and the Spanish. His levo also happened to be at Maquehue, very close to Boroa. All this put him in direct conflict with the arrogant Salazar, and a feud developed, at one point leading to violence. Salazar was accused of breaking the arm of Antonio's brother during an argument over "an Indian servant."[59]

The Real "Disaster": The Spanish Rio Bueno Campaign

The Salazar brothers present perhaps the most egregious example of abuse and embezzlement within the Army of Arauco, but the institution was in a bind because of continued Mapuche resistance. The 1641 earthquake had temporarily interrupted the army's supplies from Santiago, but they still needed to demonstrate their worth as a fighting force or the viceroy of Peru would cut off yearly contributions. Perhaps more importantly, if the Army of Arauco was not conducting malocas, they also could not count on their most direct source of funding: the sale of Mapuche captives. In 1651, this conundrum reached crisis proportions when the ship carrying the situado wrecked in a storm near Valdivia. Some of those aboard survived, but most drowned or were killed by a local Huilliche group known as the Cuncos, who also made off with most of the supplies not swallowed up by the Pacific. At this point, Acuña probably should have cut his losses. There were other years where the situado had been lost or not sent, and a weakened army would have little hope of recovering any of the supplies, especially since it would take them weeks to arrive at the site of the wreck. But he did not take the most prudent course of action and, in provoking resistance among his Mapuche allies, would make things much, much worse.

Acuña would obstinately organize an expedition to recover the situado and more importantly for him, to punish the Huilliches responsible. Never missing an opportunity for nepotism, Acuña tasked his brother-in-law with leading the excursion of 900 Spanish soldiers and 1,500 Mapuche amigos.[60] Even before it left Concepción, the expedition was beset by problems. Still smarting from their run-ins with Salazar in and around Boroa, many of the indios amigos slated to aid him in the campaign refused to join, even when threatened with hanging for desertion.[61] Also problematic were the instructions for the mission sent by Governor Acuña, which gave carte blanche to his brother-in-law who had showed no capacity for restraint:

> Look for the enemy on the plains of Osorno or the Cunco highlands or wherever they may be hiding, and even if they have withdrawn into the most hidden forests, you must look for them and fight them until their surrender, and wherever you pass you must plow under their seeds, and burn their ranches and seize all of the cattle that you can, destroying everything you come across, so that they may feel the punishment with everything they own, and you must not leave until the Field Marshall orders it and that all captured Indians over ten be put to the sword, and without doing anything else, and bring the women and young children prisoner to serve in perpetual slavery.[62]

Predictably, Salazar wasted no time proving that his intentions were not pacification of the Cunco or recovery of the situado but more enslavement as sanctioned by his brother-in-law. When Salazar and his troops arrived at the Bueno River, his war council urged him to wait, as they feared the Spanish and indios amigos would be too vulnerable to ambush during the crossing (fig. 4.3). The captains were further hesitant when they saw that a number of Cunco children were swimming on the opposite bank of the river in full view of the Spanish troops. The Cunco apparently knew that Salazar relished capturing valuable children and had sent them to the river to entice him into an ambush.[63] Despite these warnings, Salazar took the bait and ordered his troops to ford the river, calling them "chickens" for being so reluctant.[64]

To no one's surprise, Salazar's troops were quickly ambushed and scattered. A pontoon bridge they constructed broke apart drowning dozens, and the campaign was abandoned. Somewhere from 150 to 250 Spaniards were killed in this ambush,[65] and during the fighting, three thousand horses were lost, killed, or, much worse, stolen by the Cunco.[66] Referring to Salazar's previous goading, one of his soldiers is said to have shouted to Salazar "oh how you let your chicks be killed, mother hen."[67] Rather than assisting the ill-fated members of the assault he so insisted on leading, Salazar left them behind, calling out "save yourselves." Salazar's wife, whom he had clandestinely brought to the front, exhorted him to stay and appealed to his sense of honor. Salazar is to have replied, "I have plenty of honor, what I need is to live." The maestre de campo's wife responded to this act of cowardice by taking his sword and declaring that she would lead the army. Unimpressed, Salazar fled anyway.[68]

Rather than taking responsibility for the catastrophe of Río Bueno, Salazar quickly began to put together a defense of his actions. Salazar claimed

FIGURE 4.3. Carlos Ibáñez del Campo Bridge across the Bueno River, 2019. Photograph by Carlos Figueroa Rojas, CC-BY-SA 4.0.

that only between 70 and 80 Spanish soldiers were killed, and not the 120 that other witnesses had estimated. Salazar added that very few were actually killed in combat, the majority perishing in the bridge collapse. Furthermore, added Salazar, very few indios amigos were killed, as they were very strong swimmers. This last argument is a bit of an indictment of the campaign, of course, as none of the soldiers were supposed to be in the water. Salazar perhaps realized this, and at the end of his testimony, he added that fellow officer Molina never arrived with the boats he was expecting.[69] Salazar also argued that even though the initial assault was a failure, his retreating troops did manage to burn several enemy ranchos, destroy tons of corn, and kill 150 Indians.[70] Salazar had recognized that the odds were probably against him when he launched the attack, but he thought that not going through with the order to cross the Bueno River would have shown weakness and brought discredit to the Spanish army.[71] Further blaming his subordinates, Salazar added that Molina also failed to secure passage across the river and ignored his written orders to meet up. Salazar also claimed that this lack of escort meant the assault was doomed, as hundreds of indios amigos abandoned the assault when they recognized they were sitting ducks. Salazar said that Molina also never brought the two thousand indios amigos from Chiloé that he was expecting. Not just Molina was to blame, however, said Salazar. Lieutenant Manuel Méndez and Captain Juan Catalán were among Salazar's subordinates who he said disobeyed orders and had their own agendas in the campaign.[72] Even in Salazar's own version of his actions, we see that at the very least he was guilty of being poorly prepared and a weak leader.

Not one to give up easily, when Salazar got wind the following year that he was to be left out of another planned push across the Bueno River, he left Fort Arauco where he was temporarily stationed to try and convince Governor Acuña to let him lead a second attempt. As he was supposed to remain in Arauco, Salazar stole away in disguise to Concepción, where, through the intervention of his sister, Acuña awarded him the command of a second offensive.

The Mapuche Uprising of 1655

This second attempt to punish the situado thieves boasted of an even larger force of 2,400 men, who Salazar proceeded to march toward the Bueno. Building such a large contingent of course required pulling Spanish troops and indios amigos from other areas. The Spanish were vulnerable not only in the Araucanía but also on the *frontera de arriba* in Valdivia and Chiloé.[73] Huilliches and Mapuches from both regions attacked their Spanish creole neighbors and employers on February 14, 1655, cutting short Salazar's march to the Bueno River.

The 1655 uprising did not have a single spark like Tucapél and Curalaba, but similarly it was clearly the result of Mapuches being forced to work and work without compensation. Also, fifty years of resistance after Curalaba meant that Spanish abuse would be exponentially less tolerated by the Mapuche. The Council of the Indies sent specific instructions to Governor Acuña in 1654, detailing how the indios amigos were to be given the "largest gift possible" to join Salazar's second punitive expedition. Once convinced to participate, the amigo tokis Chicagüala, Tinaquecepu (Tinaquepu), and Catinaguel (Catanahuel) would be ordered to meet up with tokis from a *butanmapu* near Lake Riñihue and all travel together to the Calle-Calle River. There they would meet up with Captain Molina who would have boats ready for this amigo army to cross. The author of the order also specified that under no circumstances were Spanish soldiers on the way to or on the way back from Valdivia to *maloquear* (raid) in lands where they were given the right-of-way by indios de paz.[74]

These instructions were probably the best that could be expected from a group of royal advisors half a world away, but for anyone with knowledge of the situation in Chile, the instructions contained critical errors. First of all, the Army of Arauco could not be expected to avoid malocas. As mentioned, the capture and sale of Mapuches, Puelches, and Huilliches were a principal source of the army's income. The council had now given Spanish soldiers license to cross territories where residents may not have known to be wary of such raids. Another important oversight contained within the instructions, however, was how little they understood parleys. As seen in chapter 3, it took months of negotiation between Lincopichón and other tokis before they could even be convinced to show up to a meeting with the Spanish. Chicagüala, Tinaquepu, and Catanaguel had all been at Quillín and understood that the terms of the agreement were set by them not the Spanish. For the Spanish to show up ten years later at Boroa and try to bribe them into joining a hastily crafted punitive expedition was insulting. The above-mentioned tokis were also not indios fronterizos. Villarrica, the closest Spanish town to their territory, had been abandoned after the Tucapél and Curalaba uprisings and would not be reedified again until the nineteenth century. These Mapuches were not accustomed to making concessions to the Spanish. Tom Dillehay's work has also identified isolated kueles to the north and kuel clusters to the south of Lake Villarrica, meaning that this had become an area with concentrated leadership and organized resistance.[75] For the Spanish to treat these tokis the same way they treated *amigos auxiliaries* along the Bío-Bío was a mistake that would lead directly to the 1655 uprising. Last, the fact that the Salazars would lead the punitive expedition to Valdivia after their history of captive taking was also unacceptable, and soon, former amigos like Catanaguel and Bartolo Yoyari were leading attacks within the rebellion.[76] The 1655 uprising was chaotic, of course, so not all of the protagonists were named. We do know, however, that the Salazars had a bounty on their heads, and so at least dozens of tokis were looking for them during the rebellion, many of whom knew them personally.

The Governor of Chile Is Ousted Once More by a Mapuche Uprising

Ultimately, the Mapuche, Huilliche, and Puelche led an army of eight thousand against the Spanish in February 1655.[77] The assault forced the evacuation of the governor's estancia, its more than two thousand residents forced to walk dozens of miles under the cover of darkness to Concepción. Witnesses recounted that the stress of the journey caused a number of stillbirths and the deaths of adults due to heat exhaustion or fatigue.[78] By the time they reached Concepción, the refugees' anger with Governor Acuña had reached a boiling point, so much so that the authors of one account preferred not to record the "offensive language" being used toward the governor. The refugees from the estancia joined four thousand other residents of Concepción, and together hunkered down in the city center to fend off the assault.[79] On the night of February 20, an angry mob gathered outside the Acuñas' residence. The mob overpowered Acuña's guards, shouting, "Long live the King, death to the bad governor," and entered the residence with swords drawn. Acuña escaped through a back door and into the nearby Jesuit monastery, taking refuge among the missionaries until an announcement of his resignation placated the mob.[80]

Hiding among the refugees in Concepción was also Salazar. Despite the aforementioned bounty that had tokis stopping boats on the Bío-Bío to search for him,[81] he managed to escape from Valdivia, escape Concepción, and eventually make it to Peru before he was arrested for his responsibility in the uprising.[82] If his conduct before 1655 was wrong, his actions during the revolt were beyond reprehensible for an army officer. His column of troops was scattered by the Mapuche, and he took refuge in Fort Mariquina, which he eventually destroyed, jettisoning artillery in the river during his retreat. He then made his way to Valdivia, where another officer unsuccessfully tried to talk him into a counterattack.[83] Instead, Salazar prepared an escape by sea, ordering thousands of Spanish horses killed to keep them from the encroaching enemy.[84]

His biggest failure might have been as a brother, as among the troops left behind was José, who was wounded and eventually drowned. The Council of the Indies concluded that through his negligence and greed, Salazar "originated the destruction and loss of (Chile) . . . and of costing His Majesty what he had conquered and built from the beginning [of the conquest], more than twenty million [pesos], and the death and spilling of blood of 22,000 Spaniards."[85] One witness claimed that Salazar actually welcomed the prospect of a rebellion because it would provide more enslaved people to sell.[86] Essentially, he was blamed for losing all that had been gained in the one hundred years since the conquest of Chile.[87] His brother-in-law, the deposed Governor Acuña, was eventually released, the beneficiary of a power struggle between the king and the viceroy. Acuña would die a free man in Lima.[88]

The Parleys of the 1660s: All Style, No Substance

After 1655, Spanish colonists were in a situation even more troubling than what they saw after Curalaba. Not only was Concepción now threatened, but Chillán had been abandoned, and Mapuches had begun to shift fighting into the Maule region, north of the Bío-Bío. A Spanish army deserter, El Mestizo Alejo, led Mapuches to a number of victories near Concepción in early 1657 with the Spanish putting up little resistance from Forts Conuco and Yumbel. Things for all parties around Concepción would change dramatically in March 1657 when a devastating earthquake (above eight on the Mercalli scale)[89] and tsunami flattened Concepción.[90]

With the South's economy gutted, Spanish governors made no plans to try and retake territory lost in 1655. Instead, governors turned to the Mapuche to restore their own credibility with parleys organized beginning in 1662 at Forts Santa María de Guadalupe and San Felipe de Austria. On the surface, the 1655 uprising seems not to have done too much damage to the credibility of these parleys. Having Spanish authorities stand trial after the 1655 uprising was a step that was not seen after Tucapél or Curalaba and undoubtedly helped the colony recover some of the broken trust. Toki general Quelantaro greeted Spanish officials with a warm embrace in one 1664 meeting, and so much wine and chicha were imbibed that the first day's agenda was scrapped. On the second day, the Spanish officers informed the tokis that Governor Francisco de Meneses had agreed to pull out of Boroa and to cease all *campeadas* (campaigns) and malocas. Meneses had also sent word that it was safe for the Mapuche to "come out of the mountains and farm in the plains." After the discussion of specifics, the attendees proceeded with the ceremonial planting of a winter's bark and the sacrifice of a sheep at the foot of a tree. The rest of the day consisted of yet another feast with lamb, wine, and chicha.[91]

At first glance then, this parley seems to have restored the relationship that Rosales and others had built with Lincopichón, and now that Salazar and Acuña were gone, the Spanish could once again be comfortable settling in the Araucanía. But looking at the agreed-upon terms coming out of these meetings, as well as who attended, it is clear that these 1660 parleys were smoke screens to protect governors who were doing little more than treading water or, worse, embezzling and enslaving. First, all of these 1660s parleys were conducted on or around the Bío-Bío. None of them were near Boroa, Purén, or the Imperial River, which were lands of the Mapuches responsible for the 1655 uprising. A casual observer would remark that the Spanish seemed afraid to venture into the Araucanía. Second, the process of the Santa María Parley was very different from what occurred in Quillín. The terms were not the product of a negotiation but were drafted by Governor Ángel Peredo's war council and agreed upon by the Mapuche Clentaru who represented nearby indios amigos, indios reducidos (already pacified), and indios rebeldes. Including indios reducidos in a peace parley was an absurd move for the Spanish and demonstrated how desperate they were to restore credibility. The specific terms of the parley also bordered on the absurd and included promises by Clentaru (drafted by the Spanish war council) to free any Spanish captive they encountered and to "return all *indios* or *indias de servicio* whether enslaved or of any other quality or condition that were in possession of the Spanish . . . before the uprising." Essentially the Spanish war council said to Mapuche allies, "Can you get our slaves back for us, please?"[92] Finally, an unnamed toki meekly asked that the governor do what he could to stop a smallpox outbreak. The Spanish responded that it was not them but God who had sent smallpox, but that they would hold mass and ask God to stop the outbreak.[93] Such a response shows a lack of agency among these particular Mapuches, as on previous occasions Spanish incursions were repelled because of disease outbreaks. The fact that Spanish governors were essentially using these parleys as smokescreens meant that officials were not taking seriously the lessons of 1655. The Mapuche would need to consolidate their power further and continue to resist attempts to enslave them in the 1660s and 1670s.

5

Toward a Ban of Mapuche Enslavement

Midcentury Resistance and Outrageously Corrupt Governors

After the 1655 rebellion, viceregal authorities imprisoned Salazar in Lima, but he escaped during a nightly furlough. The viceroy explained that he "took measures" to find the prisoner but to no avail. Salazar would surface again in Spain some ten years later and set about trying to rehabilitate a reputation that seemed irrecoverable.[1] This unlikely image rehabilitation was actually a resounding success, as the officer who left Chile in disgrace was now a newly knighted member of the Order of Calatrava. His journey from enslaver to knight reveals much about the relationship between the empire and its colonies and about how the betrayal of indios amigos and other frontier protagonists went on completely unnoticed by Spain.

This chapter details how little the Spanish did to stop the corruption that both contributed to and was generated by illegal raids to enslave. The Crown banned the enslavement of Mapuches in 1667, but the ban had little effect, as by then several consecutive governors of Chile were operating more like crime bosses than representatives of the empire. I describe the extensive corruption of these governors, a corruption that often actually helped some Mapuche levos. Parleys continued but only as a means to show the Crown that these late-century governors were "doing something" about growing Mapuche autonomy in the Araucanía. Spanish malocas into the Araucanía were essentially suspended, and instead, late-century governors leaned more heavily on the labor of Mapuches fronterizos.

From Enslaver to Knight

It may seem astonishing that someone who was by all accounts a war criminal and bad commander would be knighted upon his return to Spain, but Salazar did not defend or even reference his actions in his petition for knighthood, only his title of maestre de campo. There were plenty of examples of enslavers being shunned by Spanish society, like in the case of Luis de Carvajal y de la Cueva who became an infamous enslaver on the Chichimec frontier in the 1580s. Carvajal had parleyed his experience in West Africa and against English pirates in the Caribbean into the governorship of Nuevo León, where he "exploited the availability of human slaves to create wealth."[2] However, Carvajal's ostracism did not come about because he "killed, maimed and sold into bondage innumerable Africans and Indians" but because of rumors about his Jewish ancestry.[3] After these accusations, Carvajal was "banished from Mexico for six years."[4] Salazar was on his way to suffering the same fate as Carvajal and may have faced further sanctions in Spain had he not so vigorously pursued Calatrava membership by hanging his hat on his family's reputation.

Salazar's contemporaries in Chile would often take a similar approach. They did not attack political enemies through evidence of their misdeeds but by personal scandal. For example, in 1657 the incoming governor Pedro Porter Casanate took revenge against a rival member of Chile's Audiencia by accusing him of allowing his daughter to marry without a license.[5] In another seventeenth-century case, encomenderos and soldiers buttressed themselves against accusations of mistreatment not by finding witnesses or evidence to prove their innocence but instead by accusing Antonio Ramírez de Laguna, Chile's protector general de indios, of womanizing, bribery, and running an illegal pulpería. All the charges against Ramírez de Laguna were eventually rescinded, but they prevented the protector from doing his job.[6]

These accusations were more damaging than facts because colonists in Chile were merely reflecting a seventeenth-century Spanish double standard. Documents of the era present the conquest as a series of "individual achievements from generous and heroic men," but in reality, it was conducted by "presumptuous individuals" who put their lives and fortunes at risk to become part of the Spanish elite and "enjoy the privileges of nobility."[7] No clearer is this than in the case of Salazar's petition to join the Order of Calatrava.

Much of the first one hundred pages of his petition is the response of friends and acquaintances to a standard thirteen-point questionnaire. The questions range from whether the witness knows the applicant or his family to whether the applicant is healthy or has any "infectious diseases." The most interesting question for our purposes in his case is number eight, where the witness is to respond with whether they know if the applicant "esta infamado de caso grave y feo" (infamous for any grave or ugly episode). At first glance this question would obviously disqualify someone who had caused a massive rebellion in one of His Majesty's colonies. However, the question continues with "de tal manera que su opinión este cargada entre hombres Hijos de algo . . ." (in such a way as to weigh upon noblemen). This question is not asking whether the applicant did anything wrong; it is asking whether the applicant has a bad reputation. Any detail about service in Chile is limited to Salazar's familial relationship to the governor of Chile, essentially saying, "since his sister was married to a good guy, he must be a good guy."[8]

It is not too surprising that, in the context of midcentury Hapsburg decline any true consequences for Hispano-creole wrongdoing were more likely felt in the colonies rather than in Spain. Peninsular authorities issued decrees and prohibitions against the mal incurable, but it was all too rare to see a colonist face accusation of such actions in Spain. Instead, it was colonists on the frontier trying to regulate the behavior of army officers. Salazar's example is yet another, albeit fascinating, example of what Richard Slatta describes as "Eurocentric ideologies, not frontier social realities, generally set[ting] the parameters of [Spanish] military strategy" on the fringes of their American empire.[9]

Repatriation and Reversal

Admittedly, Salazar and other Army of Arauco officers were actually enslaving indios amigos and ruining decades of alliances, but the idea seemed to come from Governor Acuña. Despite all evidence to the contrary then, Acuña persisted in his belief that indios amigos were useless as allies, but as enemies, they would help him and his cohorts "make themselves very rich."[10] His strategy was to pocket indio amigo salaries allocated in the situado. When indios amigos tired of the mistreatment and rebelled, he could collect again when they were captured and sold as enslaved people. To get them to turn against the Spanish, Acuña left a number of companies of indios amigos without supplies or payment for their service.[11] The governor's brothers-in-law also were party to his strategy. Salazar angered the indios amigos in the first months of his command by leading them into the Río Bueno ambush, threatening those who balked with the gallows.[12]

With all of this agitation then, there was little doubt that the 1655 rebellion was a product of "natural loathing" that the indios amigos had for the governor. Not only did Acuña start the revolt but also did little to stop it once it had begun. A letter from the Jesuit *provincial* Father Vicente Modele detailed that the rebellion had run the Spanish out of most of the territory from Chiloé to Maule, an area he estimated to be 150 leagues in length. Modele added that Acuña was in such a hurry to abandon his estancia that he left Jesuits in adjacent missions defenseless. Modele wrote of barefoot women, exhausted and distraught over the loss of their homes and possessions. He added that there was so much anger directed at Acuña by this multitude that it was "a wonder he wasn't killed" and described how Acuña sought refuge among the Jesuits until another governor was named. Modele praised the Audiencia for taking over the government in this tense time for the colony.[13]

Even after Acuña and Salazar were long gone, however, ecclesiastics and lawyers from Chile continued to send letters denouncing poor treatment and enslavement of Mapuches, prompting King Philip IV to take the extraordinary step of ordering that all Mapuches sold to Peru be returned to Chile. In his 1662 cédula, Philip IV argued that these repatriated Mapuche could be divided among encomenderos in Chile and return abundance to the colony.[14]

This uncommon decision by the king brought no shortage of protestations from Chile and Peru. The viceroy of Peru, Diego de Benavides, asked for more time so that the king might hear more from Chile and Peru. The viceroy provided the king with a summary of the wide range of arguments he had gathered. Some officials were against freeing the enslaved population because they saw them as too valuable in prisoner exchanges and as laborers. Many argued that the Indians killed and captured colonists and that without punishment these Indians *sin fe ni ley ni palabra* (without faith or law or word) were sure to attack again. Others argued that Chile's indigenous population outnumbered Spanish colonists, and, therefore, selling enslaved Indians to other colonies would limit the possibilities of revolt. Some officials argued that Mapuches had behaved badly in Peru, and if returned among their own people, they would present an even greater threat. Finally, there were those who argued that enslavement was justified because those captured would be baptized.[15]

Other voices supported the repatriation of Mapuches by arguing that sending enslaved people to Lima was an excessive punishment, which none of the Spanish subjects of the "rebel provinces of Europe" had endured. Still others thought that Philip IV had not gone far enough and should have banned enslavement in Chile altogether. Abolitionists reminded the Crown that multiple raids had been conducted unjustly against indios amigos and had led to an Indian "conspiracy" in 1655.[16] Ultimately, however, the viceroy suspended the 1662 decree because the enslaved Mapuches were too valuable in Peru. He justified this move partly on religious grounds, arguing that Mapuches in Lima could be catechized.[17] More important than any spiritual need, however, was the fact that any reversal or even an interruption in the supply of the enslaved people from Chile would have caused a "serious economic crisis" in Peru.[18]

Francisco de Meneses: The Mal Incurable and a Governor Turned Crime Boss

The viceroy's decision to protect Lima holders of enslaved people was welcome for exporters of enslaved people, but they also knew that Viceroy Benavides had only bought them time. The Crown would not take kindly to Lima's stalling, and more restrictions or even a complete ban on indigenous slavery was probably on the horizon. Therefore, despite the lessons of 1655, and still suffering its effects, governors hurried to take advantage of the potential rewards from enslaving raids while they were still legal.

Whether or not Acuña had designed it as such or whether he was simply doing the bidding of influential relatives, the governorship of Chile had undeniably become a privileged post. New *capitanes generals* boasted absolute power, revenue from the slave trade, and a quick exit to a plum appointment elsewhere in the empire. These men wanted to come to Chile because they knew it meant they could personally direct and profit from the capture and sale of enslaved Mapuches.

In the months immediately after the 1655 rebellion, the Spanish were of course on their heels and in no position to capture anyone. Several haciendas were destroyed in the uprising, greatly complicating supply to the Army of Arauco.[19] Interim Governor Porter Casanate's immediate priority was to break the Mapuche siege of Fort Boroa, tasking former captive and now Maestre de Campo Núñez de Pineda with leading the Spanish forces. In April 1656, Porter Casanate was comfortable enough with the progress along the frontier to travel to Santiago. However, the Spanish would soon suffer more setbacks with a Mapuche attack led by El Mestizo Alejo near fort Conuco, an uprising by the Pehuenche against several estancias, and an attack on a Spanish ship by Indians on Santa María Island that took twenty Spanish prisoners.[20] The colony was still in crisis when the massive earthquake of 1657 destroyed Concepción.

In early 1664, Chile may have thought they finally had some stability with the arrival of the first royally designated governor since Acuña. Francisco de Meneses was to be the new executive, but, unfortunately, he managed to find conflict wherever he set foot. On his way out of Spain, he arrived in Cádiz on Good Friday and expected to leave for South America at once. Not surprisingly, however, his ship would not be ready on a holiday, and there were arguments about whether it was even appropriate to leave before Easter Sunday. Once that controversy was resolved, the expedition stopped in the Canary Islands to load supplies. There, the journey experienced more difficulties as many of the supplies they were counting on had gone bad. Much of the wine had turned to vinegar, their pickled cod had spoiled, and instead of bacon, they found only beef.[21]

According to Meneses, this was not simply a matter of expired goods but part of a pattern of mismanagement by Ignacio de Maleo. Maleo was the owner of at least two ships and funded much if not all of Meneses's journey to South America. Meneses even went so far as to accuse Maleo of defrauding him and to demand that he return the 2,000 pesos that Meneses gave him in Cádiz.[22]

Meneses complained that most of the characters accompanying him to South America were "greedy, selfish," and out to get him. He was especially wary of members of the expedition who he said stole medicine and, once in Buenos Aires, persuaded a number of soldiers to flee. Meneses also denounced a practice that he would later commit dozens of times himself in Chile: the sale of goods destined for the army. According to the future governor, the stolen medicine ended up in the hands of Maleo for him to sell.[23]

Ready to set sail for Chile, Meneses encountered even more embezzlement, this time by force. Meneses claimed that Spanish defenders of Buenos Aires had turned against him and would not let him leave until he surrendered more of the goods destined for Chile. As he set sail, the *porteño* thievery turned violent when his ship received canon fire from the fort, causing it to run aground. A boarding party approached, sailors with Meneses fired upon them, splinters flew everywhere, and one of Meneses's pages was killed. Eventually the ship was boarded, the sailors were disarmed, and the booty was taken ashore. Meneses detailed that the expedition's three ships had license to carry twenty total tons of goods. But instead of authorized cargo, they were loaded (much to his surprise according to him) with contraband. Below deck during the entire transatlantic journey were "1,200 tons of 'noble cloths' [perhaps silk, as it was frequently smuggled into the Spanish

Americas] and contraband most of which was from Holland, France, England and Portugal." Meneses added that "against Your Majesty's orders, a large number of Dutchmen were living in Buenos Aires, who maintain public stores and warehouses and live the same carefree existence that they would in Amsterdam."[24]

Still stuck in Buenos Aires days later, Meneses claimed that "minions" of Buenos Aires governor José Martínez began to spread leaflets encouraging members of the expedition to not continue on to Chile. Meanwhile, on August 24 a *pingue* (smaller cargo ship) that had separated from the rest of the expedition appeared in Buenos Aires, full of "negros de las costas de Brasil" (Black people from the coast of Brazil).[25]

Toward the end of his letter, Meneses, a rampant smuggler in Chile, gave his thoughts on how to curb rampant smuggling in Buenos Aires. He first went to ecclesiastics and judges about this criminal activity. The oidores did little and the ecclesiastics did next to nothing, except to denounce smuggling at mass.[26] Meneses then called for a special prosecutor to look into the case of enslaved Africans smuggled from Brazil. While all involved in this shipment claimed that it was legal, Meneses said he knew better. He added that there was even a second ship on the way from Brazil with "near one thousand negroes, . . . tobacco, sugar and other drugs." Meneses opined that the smugglers of these goods made little attempt to cover their tracks since they were so far from Spain.[27] Meneses detailed that the smuggling was so brazen that Governor Martínez was even planning to conscript up to one hundred men, including deserters from Chile, and start an autonomous trading post. Meneses rightfully argued that a more appropriate outcome for these deserters would be their forced return to Chile, but instead, they stayed in Buenos Aires, were recruited by smugglers, and paid up to 300 pesos (apparently as a signing bonus). Meanwhile, said Meneses, soldiers loyal to the Crown were starving due to a lack of provisions. When Meneses informed oidor Pedro García de Ovalle about this rampant desertion, nothing came of it. Meneses added that, ultimately, he wasted three months dealing with all of this misconduct in Buenos Aires, but in the end, he had to move on to Chile and throw up his hands, saying, "What can one man do, when those that are to help him are the ones that hinder him in so many ways?"[28] Not surprising, especially to scholars of colonial Latin America, was Meneses's last claim in the letter: that he defended Spanish bureaucracy with his life. He called accusations that he lost the royal seal in all the chaos "mental" (imaginary) and argued that he defended it against *cañanazos* (canon blasts).[29]

If he was not aware already, Meneses learned in Buenos Aires that soldiers in the viceroyalty of Peru were not using supplies from Sevilla or Lima to end threats or make their posts more secure. They were using them as a source (sometimes their only one) of income. Meeting His Majesty's geopolitical aims was far from the top priority of defenders of forts in Buenos Aires or Boroa. Once profiteering became the priority, the Mapuche trade in enslaved people became yet another way that greed interfered with strategic victories.

After his much-delayed voyage to Chile, Meneses proved to be in no hurry to get to the Araucanía, staying in Santiago for a full year after his January 1664 arrival, an eternity for most governors in charge of the only standing army in Spain's American colonies. Once convinced to travel to Concepción, Meneses's first military act was to replace the most knowledgeable officer in the field, Maestre de Campo Ignacio Carrera, with an inexperienced loyalist, Tomás Calderón.[30] This preference for loyalists had also touched off a feud between Meneses and the Audiencia. There were a series of accusations leveled by the Audiencia against Meneses in their intense 1660's feud, including the claim that Meneses ordered enslaving raids against groups of indios amigos, selling many of them himself for at least 400 pesos each. The oidores feared that this practice would provoke "a second general uprising," which they would have considered "not unjustified." The judges added that the governor's right-hand man, Melchór de Cárdenas, had suddenly become quite wealthy, acquiring riches that included a number of illegally enslaved Mapuches.[31]

While Meneses was still on the other side of the Andes, interim governor Ángel Peredo had directed the construction of a few "small forts" along the Laja River,[32] which aided the organization of the March 1664 parley mentioned in chapter 4. Captain Augustín Quejada represented the Spanish at the meeting near Carelao, and Augustín Quelantaro, Lientur, and Neguiante all attended for the Mapuche and Pehuenche. Toki general Quelantaro gave a speech during the meeting's second day, warning that despite the friendly dialogue, the Mapuche had not forgotten the 1655 uprising nor the reasons for it:

> You have all seen the changes over time; not many years ago we had a satisfactory relationship with the Spanish. You were obligated to treat us well until the tyrannies and wrongs of the Salazars, in-laws of Governor Acuña . . . whose names you didn't want to mention, but who

> broke the peace, bringing war back to our lands and those of our neighbors. This war brought trials to all of you and to our own children and women. Even though we (here today) are many, with different opinions about making peace, and from many different provinces, (we hope) the winter's bark and the slaughtered sheep will mean that none of us lack the fortitude to keep to our word. If we do, we will again enjoy peace in our land, and once again harvest freely on our plains without having to hide in the mountains like beasts.

Ten years later then, former and potential Mapuche allies still remembered how the Salazars were such "friends to slave-taking" and how their greed had seen so many allies drown in the Bueno River.[33]

The next year, Meneses did conduct his own parley and began to brag about the founding of new forts. Critics, however, claimed that these new forts were nothing more than surveying stakes that Meneses ordered placed at sites Peredo actually established.[34] There was also concern that, for Meneses, a parley where several Mapuche communities gathered would mean an opportunity to enslave.

Meneses conducted his parley in April 1665, and speaking for the Mapuche was Chicagüala, the same man attacked by the Salazars ten years before.[35] Despite this demonstration of incredible patience by former and future allies, Audiencia members wrote that these Meneses peace parleys were not attempts to build alliances but instead designed to bring to him potential people to enslave. The judges also claimed that many Mapuches that made war on the Spanish at this time did so because their family members had been enslaved and that Meneses had cut off any possibility of a peaceful resolution by politically persecuting the protector general de Indios.[36] Meneses did not deny that raids to enslave closely followed his parleys, but he tried to give the impression that he was "pacifying" previously unallied groups in the Araucanía. However, the Audiencia countered with the claim that most of the Mapuches taken in recent malocas had been sold by Governor Meneses himself, making it more likely that the motive of these parleys was profit, not peace. Critics also observed that the agreements at Meneses's parleys lasted only as long as it took for the Mapuches to return to their homes. Just as Acuña had done, Meneses began to enslave the same Mapuches who had just made peace. Meneses had even less of an excuse for this behavior, as according to the aforementioned 1662 cédula, he was supposed to be returning enslaved people to the Araucanía.[37] The Audiencia judges added that even the *indios más amigos* (strongest Indian allies) were unsafe and opined that Meneses's greed would lead to the "destruction of the kingdom" of Chile.[38]

Undeterred by this criticism, Meneses actually introduced new ways to profit from forced labor. Meneses ordered that all encomenderos in Chile turn over their titles to him, declared these encomiendas "vacant," and then held the titles hostage until the encomenderos could come up with a bribe. In only six months, Meneses made 40,000 pesos through this scheme and all-told close to 100,000.[39] This was especially infuriating to the oidores, who, along with their colleagues, would have to hand over hundreds of pesos to keep their servants, Meneses would use that money to attend festivals dressed in garments lined with gold and silver and sport an "ostrich-feathered" (most likely *ñandú*) hat.[40] The encomienda Indians themselves were of course also at risk with such uncertain legal status. The bishop of Santiago observed that encomenderos continued to "enslave" their Indians, despite his constant admonitions, including the reading of prohibitions of "personal service" from the pulpit. The bishop added that no religious or secular authority had been able to stop Meneses and the encomenderos, and he feared that they would die "excommunicated."[41]

Meneses only became bolder with this lack of oversight, further enriching himself by hoarding tallow, wheat, and clothing meant for the army and for export. With the artificial scarcity created, Meneses could more easily profit. When his spending habits outstripped his embezzlement efforts, Meneses would simply take a "loan" from a fund of unclaimed santiaguino property (*bienes de difuntos*). However, as capitán general, Meneses was not opposed to using the army to silence critics, even removing soldiers from the Araucanía to use as muscle in his Santiago disputes.[42] The gall and ostentatious displays from Meneses infuriated most, but one individual was so incensed that he was driven to violence, shooting at Meneses on a Santiago street. In October 1667, the *veedor general* (general counsel) of the army (who would know of Meneses's corruption perhaps better than anyone), Manuel de Mendoza, shot at the governor as he left a meeting at San Juan de Dios Hospital. Meneses was not hit but was injured in the ensuing scuffle. Two days later, Meneses was at the head of a mob that dragged Mendoza out of jail, stabbed him, shot him, and hung his body on a pole in a nearby plaza until he expired.[43]

Another wrinkle in Meneses's seemingly endless tale of malfeasance was an accusation that he was in fact a spy for the English or perhaps some sort of agent provocateur. Meneses certainly caused enough damage to give rise to such theories, but there was some evidence to support such rumors. For example, an officer captured from an English expedition to Valdivia, Carlos Henríquez Clerque, claimed that he had met Meneses in Flanders and that the king of England was fond of him.[44] Another captive testified that Henríquez had not made plans to meet up with anyone in Chile but that he had heard him say during the voyage that he had a powerful brother-in-law in Peru and that with all his connections he and his men would be showered with gifts upon his arrival in Chile.[45] Henríquez later declared that he did not know whether Meneses was a spy or even if he had corresponded with the king of England. However, Henríquez did confirm the presence of English spies in the viceroyalty.[46]

After years of slave taking enabled by generalized corruption, Mariana de Austria fired Meneses in 1668, replacing him with Juan Henríquez. With the arrival of a new governor, would the mal incurable continue to attract executives anxious to profit from the Army of Arauco's access to enslaved people? It did not take long to see that the mal incurable would indeed persist. Rosales, who witnessed Governor Acuña's abuses twenty years earlier, wrote in 1672 to the Crown about enslaving. Rosales detailed that under Governor Henríquez the Spanish continued to call "peace parleys," whose sole purpose was actually to enslave more people. Rosales also claimed that Spanish officers continued to enslave indios de paz. In one of the most dramatic of these cases, the indio amigo Mtumpillán had three hundred of his people illegally enslaved. When he threatened to go to the governor about it, "that very night four masked men entered his house and killed him as he slept in his bed."[47] When Rosales's accusations reached Lima, the viceroy of Peru tried to curb Henríquez's enslaving by reminding him that he had no authority to declare a "just war" against the Mapuche.[48]

While staggeringly corrupt, these governors of Chile did not act alone and certainly would not have seen a path to their ill-gotten wealth without a market for the Mapuches they were ordering taken and sold. Some of these captives were exported to Peru, others stayed with the Army of Arauco, but most served Chile's encomenderos. The most prominent encomenderos all had at least one estancia or hacienda near Santiago and used their presence in the capital not to hobnob with the governor, priests, the Audiencia, and vecinos but to carefully cultivate their status as feudal lords or *señores*. The "lord/vassal binary" was extensively applied in the Americas but was particularly intense in Chile, a colony whose urban core was far enough away from

Lima or Madrid to make it a frontier within the empire and a colony where there was no pre-Hispanic indigenous nobility to contend with. The first legalization of enslavement of Mapuches in 1608 meant that these señores or *latifundistas* had an even more stable source of rural laborers, and it was rural production that gave these latifundistas their power.[49]

One of these señores was Gonzalo de los Ríos, son of one of Chile's original encomenderos who owned two massive estates near Santiago, which included 20,000 grapevines producing 1,500 barrels of wine per year. De los Ríos also possessed cattle, pigs, wheat fields (producing 20,000 bushels per year), and, as of the 1570s, the only sugar plantation in the colony at La Ligua. La Ligua's two mills ran ten months of the year.[50] The 1580 Tasa (assessment) de Gamboa revealed the labor required for such vast holdings. Forty two Indians were working at the de los Ríos hacienda of Putaendo, forty six at the sugar mill of La Ligua, and sixty seven at the placer mines and farms of Codegua. The dowry de los Ríos prepared for his daughter's 1576 wedding included 14,000 pesos in gold.[51]

Maintaining a workforce of over 150 required a constant influx of new laborers, and after the post-Curalaba redistribution of encomiendas, this workforce was composed more and more of enslaved Mapuches. As seen, the Army of Arauco was more than capable of providing those enslaved people, but an accompanying phenomenon was the cooperation of governors like Acuña. As the 1655 uprising approached, the Army of Arauco was not only enslaving Mapuches and trading them throughout the Araucanía and to Peru but were specifically meeting the demands of estancieros and hacendados around Santiago. The governor of Chile became the factor in this trade because he could send the Army of Arauco to raid Mapuches, falsely certify that these were enslaved in just war, and reassign those enslaved as encomienda laborers to work haciendas like La Ligua. The governor's reward was support by encomenderos and hacendados in the Audiencia and the cabildo of Santiago, especially against accusations coming from Peru of fraud and mistreatment of Mapuches.[52] By the time Meneses arrived, Mapuche enslavement meant an unprecedented level of colonial corruption, contributing to the further moral decline of colonial society.

This material wealth helped support a societal lord/vassal relationship that proved stronger even than the economic one. Even as encomiendas became more widely distributed and families like the de los Riós possessed relatively less land, their power as plantation owners never waned and in fact increased. Santiago encomenderos were not only able to manage mostly illicit commerce involving the governor and the situado but also brought oidores into their orbit. In an attempt to preserve their neutrality, the Crown prohibited members of the Audiencia from owning land or having separate businesses. In Chile, however, this did not stop judges from bestowing "political support, . . . and a majestic aura" upon self-conscious encomenderos in exchange for "riches, lands and local prestige."[53] Many of the aforementioned disputes between the Audiencia and governors of Chile seem in fact to involve jealousy over the others' close relationship to encomenderos.

Catalina de los Ríos, "La Quintrala," was the daughter of Gonzalo and part of the powerful the Flores-Lisperguer family that had been accused of using nefarious means to achieve and maintain status. Authorities accused her mother, Catalina, of attempting to poison Governor Ribera, and La Quintrala herself was accused of murdering a number of her enslaved indigenous and African laborers. Meneses actually defended La Quintrala when the Audiencia accused her of the murder. Meneses showed the limits of his loyalty, however, when he tried to take over the family estate upon Catalina's death, citing the charges against her.[54]

Governor Henríquez Expands the Grift

The fact that Henríquez did not take royal prohibitions seriously should be unsurprising, as he had essentially turned his position into a crime syndicate by 1674. To be fair, Henríquez faced an uphill battle upon his arrival in 1670, as most members of the Audiencia were still emboldened over their role in Meneses's ouster, and they were unwilling to cede any of their newfound power to Henríquez. He recognized this and tried to have one of the most powerful oidores fired, even soliciting the help of Meneses's father-in-law to do so.[55] The Audiencia responded by spreading gossip about a Henríquez ally whose relationship with a young woman caused her family to "get her to a nunnery." When Henríquez tried to intervene, the Audiencia removed him from his functions, mere months after he arrived in the colony.[56]

As had become the tradition, the ouster of Henríquez was backed by rumors and false accusations thrown at him by prominent santiaguinos but also some very serious charges substantiated by multiple witnesses. As part of the Audiencia's first petition for his removal, Henríquez did have a chance to defend himself. Former bishop of Concepción, Dionisio Cimbrón wrote in 1672 that among other things Henríquez had "reduced" (conquered) eight thousand Indians (obviously an exaggeration since Henríquez had just arrived). Cimbrón also tried to discredit Henríquez's accusers, labeling oidor Joseph de Meneses as being "el mas escandaloso de todos" (the most scandalous of all). "He is not erudite, nor has he tried to be. . . . Since he has arrived in Chile he has dedicated himself to nothing more than satisfying his carnal urges, and since dishonesty is a venereal dropsy, there is no counting the number of women he has abused."[57]

Henríquez also included his own defense in the file sent to Lima, arguing that he pushed farther into the "craggy mountains" than any previous governor and had captured ten thousand Indians who had been hiding there. The incoming governor was able to do all of this despite, he claimed, the sorry state of the munitions and soldiers in Chile. He also asserted he had interrupted a Mapuche revolt as it was just beginning, imprisoning twenty two of the caciques involved in Concepción. He added that one thousand of the rebels were killed, and those who survived were sent to Santiago to "rebuild the temples and convents" damaged by recent earthquakes, and others would build a new bridge over the Mapocho River. He bragged that all this would be accomplished with no cost to the royal treasury.[58]

Most likely perturbed that a new governor had only lasted months before being relieved of his duties by Chile's judges, the viceroy of Peru, Pedro Fernández de Castro, ordered a series of depositions to find the underlying cause of the conflict. Testifying were merchants, army officers, and royal officials, who, despite their tendency to gossip, managed to present a damning portrait of a governor who found profit through illegal malocas and decided to expand his crimes to all sorts of fraud and abuse. It is evident from the detail involved in these accusations that these were not schemes hatched by Henríquez alone. For several years, it seems, Chilean governors both hoarded supplies meant for the Araucanía and forced free and encomienda Mapuches to work without paying them. The governors also diversified their exports to Peru, forcing Mapuches to work in unsafe conditions in new and unregulated industries. When Mapuches rebelled because they had no food to buy or money to spend, the governors would wage war against them.

This process began with Henríquez hoarding the situado and supplementing it with private shipments of cloth from Lima. Many of the witnesses were ship captains to whom he owed money after they had brought thousands of bolts of cloth for him to sell alongside the situado supplies. This was quite easy for him to get away with, as the governor of Chile had a dedicated ship for official business that he instead used for profiteering. These shippers in Lima were patient with him and extended him credit and ignored the fact that he rarely paid their shipping costs, all because he promised to bring them piezas in return. He even gave one of his servants a military rank so that he could be "stationed" in Valparaíso and watch for merchants willing to make a deal advantageous to the governor.[59] Henríquez was even known to pocket the salary due junior officers in the Araucanía, and instead, "pay" them with a promotion.[60]

Clothes bought from Lima were not sold right away or given to the army, rather they were usually distributed to corregidores for them to sell or trade for tallow, cordovan (horse leather), and jerky.[61] If residents of these towns did not have cash or items to trade, Henríquez forced many of them to buy the clothes on credit.[62] These were large quantities of fabric. In one case, he took nine thousand yards (*varas*) of *ruanes florets* (Rouen fabric with flower patterns) from the situado and sent it back to Santiago where he had his own store run by Francisco de Argomedo.[63]

The price gouging went beyond clothes. Captain Pedro de Valenzuela, the corregidor of Maule, forced soldiers to buy honey on credit and at elevated prices.[64] One witness testified that Henríquez also seized "grains" from the situado and sold them through the same corregidores for ten times what they usually cost outside of Concepción. Most of the witnesses interviewed in Lima also spoke of the scandal caused when Henríquez helped himself to three hundred head of cattle destined for the army, had them butchered, and then sold the tallow and cordovan back to his contacts in Peru. So, essentially, he made the viceroy buy back his stolen cattle. This price gouging made him a significant amount of money, and it directly affected creoles and indios amigos in the Army of Arauco: soldiers went hungry or had to buy their food on credit. The only way the soldiers could dig their way out of this debt was by conducting raids and selling the Mapuche captives.[65] Indios amigos could also pay off debt through raids, or they could indenture family members through usanza agreements that would promptly be ripped up and converted to sales for enslaved people. Indios de paz and Mapuches on reducciones also saw their supply of beef dry up with Henríquez's hoarding, forcing many to choose between personal service and resistance.

As more and more Lima textile merchants were recruited into this price-gouging scheme, Henríquez needed a corresponding export increase to keep them involved and keep creditors from hounding him. Part of this imbalance was made up through Chile's increasingly important timber export, with Henríquez arranging for the export of two pounds of amber and two

FIGURE 5.1. Nalca (*Gunnera tinctoria*), Parque Nacional Chiloé, Chile, 2014. Photograph by Natalia Reyes Escobar, CC BY-SA 4.0.

thousand boards from Chiloé. He vertically integrated the cattle industry, by hoarding supply and monopolizing manufacturing. He commandeered reducción or encomienda Indians to work for his pangue or nalca plantations, a close cousin of rhubarb used in the tanning process. These nalca plantations required Mapuches to work in dense and humid forests and wade in frigid water for hours at a time (fig. 5.1).[66]

All of this described activity was only possible with Mapuche labor, but the most lucrative of Henríquez's illicit business activities was the sale of the laborers themselves. Aside from essentially seizing encomienda Indians and not paying them, he also used the practice of usanza as de facto enslavement. He assigned Sargent Major Figueroa to the Army of Arauco, with explicit instructions that Figueroa send him Mapuches via usanza arrangements. Once in Concepción, several groups of these usanza Mapuches were sold to Henríquez's co-conspirators (Veedor General Jorge Lorenzo de Olivar and Sargent Major Juan de Narbaez) for 350 pesos each. Figueroa purchased Mapuches via usanza and also led raids for Henríquez against indios de paz and indios amigos. One witness also talked to another group of Mapuche piezas after they were captured. One of them was a *china* (young girl) purchased by Father Juan Izquierdo for one 120 pesos. The witness added that while

Henríquez officially ordered that no piezas be sold, he saw piezas being led into the governor's house by Henríquez's brother Blas and his nephew Antonio de Córdova.

This brazen display of enslaving ended with Mapuches in the hands of the governor and his family but began with a series of raids denounced by multiple officials in Concepción. One raid captured the caciques Dunquiguala, Yclentaro, and Lepitaro all of whom were interviewed in prison by Auditor General Diego Velazquez. Neither Velazquez nor the Jesuit Juan de Ulloa found any evidence that these caciques had ever planned or even talked about rebelling and sent letters of protest to the Crown and to the viceroy. An Army of Arauco commander, Tomás de Sotomayor, also resisted carrying out raids with no strategic purpose. When he objected to taking more enslaved people, Henríquez publicly berated Sotomayor and removed him from his command. In fact, Figueroa and his accomplices had so little interest in parsing Mapuche ally from Mapuche foe that they actually imprisoned a group near Arauco that was approaching them with chicha to toast these Spanish "visitors." Undeterred by all of the objections, Figueroa captured hundreds of Mapuches, 192 of whom were personally sold by Henríquez.[67]

For both the aforementioned Acuña family and the Henríquez family, the trade of enslaved indigenous people was part of the family business. The Henríquez family also acted with extreme arrogance, shirking their official responsibilities and spending most of their time in extralegal pursuits. Henríquez neglected to meet with his war council, preferring to insulate himself with family members and close allies. He brought his brother Blas to Santiago with him when he took the job, apparently to help him intimidate his political opponents. Blas was invited to several peace parleys during Henríquez's governorship, despite the fact that he was best known for threatening to beat to death anyone who dared talk back to him. Henríquez also sent seven hundred head of cattle destined for the army to his wife's first cousin in Concepción.[68]

Even colonists not directly connected to power imitated the beastly behavior inspired by enslavement. For example, hundreds of Spanish soldiers who were supposed to be in the Araucanía were instead in Santiago trying to sell Mapuches they had captured. These AWOL soldiers would often engage in petty theft or would serve as professional bullies working for the governor in his multiple disputes.[69] Governor Henríquez blocked the arrest of another officer, Lorenzo Laso de la Vega (who may have been a relative), who undoubtedly had advanced knowledge that the governor would protect him. Upon receiving his arrest order, Laso de la Vega loudly announced that he was going to use it to clean his "dirty parts."[70] This conduct evokes images of the same kind of disruptive presence slave hunters brought to the US South,[71] a presence that of course begat years of violence and tension culminating in the Civil War.

Individual servants, enslaved people, and free Indians could petition the protector de indios on their own behalf. Jaime Valenzuela describes how, in an increasingly urbanized Santiago, there were more opportunities for enslaved Mapuches to earn a wage, learn to read, and petition for better treatment or freedom.[72] Rural enslaved Mapuches did not often have these opportunities, however, and with this increasing corruption, even well-meaning *protectores* were rendered less and less effective by infighting. As a result, very few advocates for the enslaved population maintained an unblemished reputation, and it became difficult to distinguish real crimes from rumor. This was an especially troubling development when enslaved Mapuches were subject to the very real crimes of murder, kidnapping, torture, child abuse, and sexual assault. In perhaps the most infamous case of latifundia excess gone awry, abuses committed by La Quintrala and the Lisperguer family went unpunished when rumors of witchcraft, sexual deviance, and secret poisonings distracted investigators.

Justice for enslaved Mapuches became even more elusive as concern shifted from the illegality of the trade to the societal effects of an increasing Mapuche population in Santiago. As the number of encomienda Indians declined, the Spanish worried about how their dominance would be affected. After generations of living with the Spanish, the native population trended toward mestizaje and assimilation and many could "pass" in colonial urban spaces. New sumptuary laws in the seventeenth century were designed to prevent more homogeneity and to avoid "confusion," limiting the use of capes and long hair to Spaniards.[73] If as it seemed, by the 1670s, santiaguinos had simply accepted forced labor without regard to provenance of their workers, any further regulation or prohibition would have to come from outside of the colony.

A New Ban with Few Results

The Valladolid Debates of 1550 represent a fascinating and essential part of understanding Spanish-indigenous relationships in Chile and the rest of the Americas. However, scholars and students of the colonial period alike tend to lose track of any further debates about indigenous rights or slavery until postindependence abolition movements of the nineteenth century. There was quite a bit of history between those years, of course. This history included new and equally vigorous debates about slavery and in our case specific to a particular colony. The aforementioned debates after the Curalaba uprising were renewed and adjusted after the Río Bueno disaster. After Tucapél, Curalaba, and now Río Bueno, the latifundia understood that their primary task would be to "find permanent labor." After 1655, encomenderos defiantly moved their laborers, others traded in Mapuche prisoners of war, and estancieros began to create an *inquilino* (serf) class composed of "poor Spaniards, mestizos, mulatos and Indians."[74]

Especially after the destitution and trial of Governor Acuña, residents of Chile realized that the Río Bueno disaster was not just another maloca gone wrong. This was a governor commandeering troops for "slave catchers," troops who had been sent by the viceroy to mete out punishment for the theft of the situado. In other words, the indios amigos were right not to trust Acuña or any of the subsequent *capitanes generales* of his generation. Acuña was gone by 1662, but his ability to personally profit from the slave trade was not lost on his successors. The Council of the Indies would have to react.

As early as 1662, the council called upon military, religious, and political leaders in Chile to discuss the indigenous slavery question. In a 1667 cédula, the king banned all "personal service" and slavery in Chile. However, despite its detour into the slaving business, the Army of Arauco remained in Chile. If anything, after the 1655 rebellion it became more difficult for officials in Chile to curb abuse by soldiers and encomenderos. Neither military tactics nor demand for labor changed after 1655, and political bullying of slavery's opponents increased. Not long after Acuña left, vindictive encomenderos leveled spurious charges against the protector general de Indios, Antonio Ramírez de Laguna. His real crime was that he was doing his job too well, as he had rebuked at least three of his accusers for having their Indians work "as slaves." One encomendero even stopped by to "provoke" him while he was under house arrest and to inform him that he would be testifying against him.[75] His tormentors called him a womanizer and accused him of bribery and of profiting from the management of an illegal pulpería to augment an imagined hidden fortune.[76]

Only seven years after Spanish soldiers and indios amigos drowned in pursuit of captives, the viceroy was again writing to Philip IV that these raids were a distraction to the overall war effort and that soldier greed was again causing the Spanish to lose battles.[77] The veedor Francisco de la Fuente Villalobos warned that illegal raids to enslave were spreading to cordillera Indians who once captured were shipped out from Valdivia. He warned that such practices threatened to turn back the conquest, provoke an Indian rebellion, and render meaningless the deaths of twenty-six thousand in the War of Arauco's one hundred years. He added that parleys, like those conducted by the Governor Marques de Baides (Francisco López de Zúñiga), were more effective, "reducing" 18,900 Indians over the years.

Rosales, who again had witnessed Governor Acuña's abuses added details about cases of illegal enslavement in 1672 and asked the king to put a stop to it. He said that a captain, Pedro de Ripete, invited a number of caciques to a parley in 1672 and subsequently killed them and imprisoned their subjects. Three caciques were killed and eighty-seven Indians were captured. In Pacaví and Cayucupil, the Spanish captured four hundred piezas de paz and killed a group of Indians who stumbled upon the scene. Another captain took three hundred indios de paz and killed nine caciques who complained about it.[78] Finally, also in 1672, Capitán Bartholome de Villagrán killed twelve caciques who came to him in peace, while others escaped with lance wounds. Two hundred and forty-five Indians were taken in this campaign (*campeada*).[79]

1674: The Crown Bans the Enslavement of Mapuches

The Crown did eventually take action after two decades of complaints and debate when Mariana de Austria abolished enslavement of Chilean Indians in December 1674.[80] Since past royal prohibitions did little to end the practice (in fact, Governor Henríquez tried to overturn the ban in 1676), both the council and the Crown tried to make their instructions clear by comparing Chile's case to that of other American colonies. The council specified that "the Indians of Chile and Tucumán, shall not be slaves, nor be obligated under personal service." The council also added that this decision would put Chile and Tucumán in line with the rest of Spanish America where "generally . . . [indigenous] slavery is prohibited."[81] The "generally" in this case is of course very revealing, and the *obedezco pero no cumplo* (I obey but I do not comply) approach of the colonists enabled the trade in the indigenous enslaved population to continue.[82]

The Crown shifted tactics in 1676, trying to shame the members of Chile's Audiencia into enforcing the ban on slavery. Charles II remanded the judges to follow the example of their counterparts in the Audiencia of Guadalajara. These justices in New Spain had obeyed the king's orders, freeing enslaved Chichimecs in various provinces along the colony's northern frontier in 1672.[83] The next month, Charles II went into even more specifics, saying that it was his mother's wish that Chile be rid of the enslavement of war captives, the enslavement of children and usanza.[84]

In 1679, Charles II tried yet another tactic: removing formerly enslaved Mapuches from Chile altogether, not trusting local officials to obey the new ban. Charles II ordered that all enslaved Mapuches be loaded onto the situado ships that had arrived in Chile, and taken back to Peru as freedmen. This was nothing if not an odd decision, as for decades Lima kept Mapuche slavery profitable. But Governor Henríquez objected for a different reason, arguing that a major loss of Mapuche labor would ruin Chile's economy. One author claims that this action revealed the governor to be the "spokesperson for *encomenderos*," another example of their aforementioned interdependence. In 1683, realizing the folly of the export plan, Charles II rescinded the 1679 order but again declared the Mapuches free.[85]

What Charles II did not eliminate with his orders, however, was demand. If demand for forced labor did not stop after a half century of regulation and attempts to ban it, if it did not stop after a massive rebellion with hundreds of Spanish casualties, then there was no stopping it. Slavery had blighted every part of colonial Chile. This blight would rot both everyday colonial society and any strategy for achieving détente with the Mapuche, a failure that continues to have ramifications today. It may have seemed to many along the frontier that it would require an act of God to slow raids to enslave, and they were exactly right.

As conditions in Lima had much to do with Chilean attempts to prolong the War of Arauco and continue to export enslaved people, it is appropriate that events in Peru would interrupt this trend. A massive earthquake in October 1687 heavily damaged Lima, flattening "all of its churches and most of the houses."[86] Witnesses describe survivors as "crying and covered with dust, asking for God's forgiveness" while they looked for injured relatives.[87] Fear and subsequent disease outbreaks caused an exodus from the city and caused its population to drop from eighty to forty thousand residents in only five years.[88] The earthquake also damaged or destroyed many aqueducts in this arid part of the continent, and to make matters worse, a wheat blight followed immediately after. These two developments rendered the Peruvian wheat harvest insignificant for several years and weakened the economic and political influence of coastal haciendas.[89] As a result, wheat prices in Chile almost immediately tripled in response to the new demand. Although the colony struggled to retool its agriculture, Chile eventually would become "Peru's Sicily," providing the viceregal capital with its wheat for much of the eighteenth century.[90]

Conclusion

An Act of God and an End to the Trade?

After years of prohibitions, investigations, interventions from dozens of different authorities, and even uprisings, export of enslaved Mapuches finally slowed on its own when wheat began to fetch higher prices than human bodies. The Lima earthquake signaled the end of Chile's "tallow century." Fat, beef, and hides exported to the mines of Potosí would give way in the eighteenth century to wheat and cereals to Lima.[1] Sedentary haciendas and their hacendado families became more prominent than the more mobile ranching latifundistas of estancias. Decreasing mobility meant a decrease in all kinds of raiding, including raids designed to capture and enslave the indigenous. An increased need for Mapuche labor in Chile provided colonists with an economic motivation to obey the various prohibitions on sale and export of Chile's indigenous people. In some cases, hacendados could even afford to pay free Mapuches to work their wheat fields.

As infrastructure and productivity improved, wheat proved to be a more lucrative product than did cattle,[2] meaning that profits for wheat export now approached those made in the trade in indigenous peoples and with much less risk (and much less immorality) involved.

Meanwhile, another late seventeenth-century shift was occurring on Chile's southern frontier. Missionary activity had been scant in Chile since the end of the Defensive War in the 1620s. Franciscans and Jesuits worked mostly with indios reducidos and stayed close to or within Spanish settlements or forts. The missionaries lacked the funds and support required to establish new and independent missions, and secular and religious authorities alike were hesitant to send missionaries far into the Araucanía after three Italian Jesuits were murdered there in 1612.[3] After decades of failed military attempts to end the conquest including the disaster of 1655, Charles II was ready to make another attempt at a "spiritual conquest" of Chile. In 1692, the king instructed new governor Tomás Marín de Poveda to establish new missions. In the next twenty years, the Jesuits alone founded six, and the Franciscans were not far behind.[4]

The missions were not immediately successful and suffered from the same lack of resources that Chile had seen for years. However, for the first time since a permanent army was established in Chile in 1600, significant military cutbacks were made to fund mission activity and provide wheat to Lima.[5] The War of Arauco was no longer Chile's top priority.

This new landscape also brought changes to frontier political relationships. While the seventeenth century saw important yet sporadic parleys, it was really defined by raids. In contrast, parleys and trade dominated the eighteenth-century frontier.[6] This is not to say that there was no conflict in the next century. Some colonists took advantage of the new relative calm to enslave more people, while some indigenous groups used it to gather strength for attacks. Overall, however, a more sedentary frontier meant that new energy could be dedicated to cultivating stable relationships, while economically more energy was dedicated to maintaining local labor pools. In the seventeenth century, Chile's indigenous laborers were lucrative exports, while in the eighteenth the laborers produced them.

However, despite the fact that Mapuche workers were now more valuable in Chile than outside of it, this did not eliminate Araucanía conflict.[7] In response to a 1696 "attempted uprising" by a group of mountain indigenous people, Governor Marín de Poveda decided to permit raids to "take piezas" belonging to this group. More specifically, the governor asked volunteers to conduct these raids. Those who took captives could determine what to do with them, a step that had not seen before and that contrasted the previous pattern of gubernatorial micromanagement. The Audiencia of Chile quickly ordered Marín de Poveda to retract this decision as it was contrary to the orders of His Majesty and infringed upon "the liberty of the Indians." When Viceroy Melchór Portocarrero got wind of this, he also condemned it and added that Marín de Poveda was not the first governor of Chile to permit such raids in a blatant challenge of vice regal authority. Portocarrero claimed that in previous years Governors Marín de Poveda and Henríquez would often call impromptu war councils in Concepción and declare such raids part of a "just war" against the Mapuche, despite the fact that they had no authority to do so. Portocarrero added that the governors never consulted him or the Audiencia of Chile and still regularly practiced usanza.[8] In a 1690 letter, Maestre de Campo Geronimo de Quiroga added his observations about the turmoil that raids to enslave had brought to Chile's recent history. Quiroga had just returned from the frontier and expressed his chagrin at the lack of missionaries among the Indians and the lack of religious fervor from soldiers and colonists serving "His Most Catholic Majesty."[9]

Part of this may be explained by the fact that even though the wheat trade made export of laborers less profitable, it did not eliminate a general and growing need for labor. In a 1692 letter, a number of officials in the town of Mendoza complained that they already had a shortage of laborers when the population suffered a smallpox epidemic. These Mendoza residents claimed that the nearby indigenous population had been reduced to 175 people, some of whom were sent to work in the mines of San Lorenzo. In response, Mendoza vecinos asked for special permission to have enslaved Africans sent through Buenos Aires. The authors also requested that the Crown lift the prohibition on moving enslaved Africans from Buenos Aires to Peru and "the other side of the cordillera" so that Mendoza might survive this crisis.[10] Demand for indigenous labor remained, and populations continued to decline through abuse and disease. Overall, however, a more sedentary frontier meant that new energy could be dedicated to cultivating stable relationships, cultivating wheat, and cultivating local labor pools to harvest it.

The persistence and profitability of enslavement of Mapuches well into the eighteenth century raises some important questions about the historiography of the colonial period. For example, many historians still reference Valdivia's concept of the poverty and sacrifice of the frontier. Today, the idea not only applies to the Araucanía and its unique history but has become important as a tool for establishing Chile's sense of nationhood. In a 2002 article, historian Cristián Gazmuri calls poverty one of the most important historical antecedents of the modern "Chilean mentality." Gazmuri claims that Chile was the poorest Iberian-American colony and that the Crown maintained an interest in the colony only because it was "wealthy Peru's southern door, that had to be defended against corsairs and against the ambition of European powers." Gazmuri adds that this poverty not only contributed to Chile's mentality but continues to be reflected in a national architecture that maintains a "rustic" quality in both cities and farmhouses.[11]

However, we must remember that the "southern door" opened in both directions, with Chile always managing to find markets for their exports even with their relative isolation. In the seventeenth century, it was enslaved Mapuches and tallow. In the eighteenth, it was wheat. In the nineteenth, it was gold and nitrates. Even today, Chile remains one of the world's largest exporters of copper. The relatively constant price of copper has helped Chile earn praise as an "island of stability" in Latin America.

With all this in mind, perhaps we should take a closer look at Chile's early national period and the historiography that still influences it today. While Vicuña Mackenna's postindependence Chile was Sarmiento's "civilization" and the colonial past its "barbarism,"[12] we must remember that Sarmiento was exiled from Argentina by a quite barbarous postindependence *caudillo*, Juan Manuel de Rosas. *Caudillismo* also persisted in Chile, with *caudillo* autonomy bolstered by access to enslaved Mapuches in the seventeenth century, expanding with access to land in the eighteenth, and continuing through control of export in the nineteenth. We can draw a clear line between Henríquez dominating colonial politics through control of captives and *sebo* (tallow) and Diego Portales, *caudillo* of the early republic. Portales used "strong-arm methods" to enforce his *estanco* (tobacco monopoly) as a private citizen, even becoming minister of the interior to get his monopoly back after a dispute.[13] Portales's belief in a "strong, centralizing government," open to only "families of rank,"[14] is more than just casually evocative of the insulated governors of the late seventeenth century made wealthy through the export of enslaved Mapuches. But for the time being, the successful parley format of the seventeenth century remained in place, a format that the Spanish were forced to accept through the efforts of seventeenth-century gentokis. We see hints of this in the 1692 Parley of Yumbel, where the Spanish agreed that there would be no future usanza and that the only Mapuches turned over to the Spanish were those that the Mapuche themselves wished to exile for specific crimes. We also see the fruit of seventeenth-century gentoki efforts in the 1712 Parley of Tapihue. Tokis from Purén, Arauco, Yumbel, and Valdivia all attended the parley and agreed that, with a reduced Spanish military presence, their communities were at peace and had not spoken of or made plans for a general rebellion in years.[15]

Glossary

adelantado: Military governor
almagrist: Spanish soldier loyal to Diego de Almagro who accompanied him on his travels to Chile and in his feud with the Pizarro brothers in Peru
asiento: License
alzado: In rebellion
Araucanía: Region of Chile extending from the Bío-Bío River to the Island of Chiloé, considered the Mapuche "heartland"
Audiencia: Court system in Spanish Americas
ayllarehue: Group of several Mapuche levos, rehues, or reguas (communities)
ayllu: Community or family group
bozal: Enslaved person in the Americas born in Africa
butunmapu: Mapuche confederation
cabildo: Town council in the colonial Americas
cacique: Indigenous chieftain
cahuín: Gathering or meeting of several Mapuche family clans
carrera: Silver fleet
cédula: Royal order
chueca: Mapuche sport similar to field hockey
chicha: Alcoholic beverage made from fermented corn or fruit
consejo: Council
cordillera: Mountain range
corregidor: Local Spanish official, often equivalent to a mayor or judge
corsario: Corsair
creole: Person of African or European descent born in the Americas
encomendado: Indigenous servant within the encomienda system
encomienda: System of labor obligations the Spanish applied to conquered indigenous groups in the Americas

entrada: Raid
escudo: Gold or silver coin used in Spain's American colonies
estado fronterizo: Frontier community
estancia: Cattle ranch
Flota de Indias: Spanish Treasure Fleet
fronterizo: Living on the frontier
gentoki: Toki in charge of an allyarehue
hacendado: Owner of a hacienda
hacienda: Large estate usually producing wheat or grain for export
harquebusier: Soldier armed with harquebuses, an early type of portable gun
indio amigo: Indigenous soldier allied with the Spanish
indio de guerra: Indigenous resident of Chile whom the Spanish labeled as resistant to colonization
indio de paz: Indigenous resident of Chile living near and or cooperating with Spanish colonists
inquilino: Tenant farmer
junta: Meeting
kuel: Mapuche mound
ladino: Enslaved person of African descent born or raised in Europe
latifundia: Large estate modeled after those in the Roman Empire
latifundista: Owner of a latifundia estate
lavadero: Buddle (container) for gold mining
levo: Mapuche family clan or community (seventeenth century); meeting of Mapuche family clan or community (sixteenth century)
lonko: Leader of a Mapuche levo, usually a descendent of previous leader
maestre de campo: Field marshal
mal incurable: Incurable evil of slavery
maloca: Pillaging raid of Spanish or Mapuche communities, which often obtained captives
Mapuche: Indigenous group of south-central Chile and western Argentina
Mapuzugún or Mapudungún: Language of the Mapuche
mayorazgo: Entailed estate
merced de tierra: Land grant
minga/minka: Reciprocal labor system similar to mitae, used more commonly to refer to specific infrastructure projects
mitae: Reciprocal labor system used by both the Inka and Spanish Empires
oidor: Judge

oro: Gold
padrón: Census
parlamento: Parley/meeting
parley: Mapuche-Spanish diplomatic meeting in the colonial period
paulista: Raider from São Paulo seeking indigenous captives
pieza: Enslaved African or indigenous person
personal service: Labor performed by indigenous Americans in lieu of royal tribute in specie
Pillán: Mapuche deity sometimes described as "spirits" or "the god of fire"
pueblo reducido: Reducción (community) of conquered indigenous residents obligated to live near Spanish settlements
pulpería: Informal grocery store or commissary
puren: Mapuche from the Purén region, who offered the strongest resistance to Spanish colonization
Real Audiencia: Superior court
rebelde: Rebel
reche: True people
Reconquista: Spanish reconquest of the Iberian Peninsula after occupation by Islamic caliphates
reducción: See "pueblos reducidos"
regua, rehue: See "levo"
repartimiento: System of forced labor similar to encomienda
requerimiento: Sixteenth-century Spanish document used to justify the enslavement of indigenous groups in the Americas
santiaguino: Resident of Santiago
señor: Feudal lord
situado: Annual outlay for the Army of Arauco, usually received in goods and specie
toki: Mapuche warrior chieftain
ülmen: Mapuche elder
usanza: Practice of "renting" the services of an indigenous servant from another Spaniard or from an indigenous family member, often returned and sold into slavery
vecino: Ordinary citizen, a social category falling below Spaniards with titles, but above servants, slaves or outsiders
veedor: Special counsel
viceroy: One of two "vice-kings" in the Americas (New Spain and Peru); in Peru, the ruler of all of Spanish South America

vida fronteriza: Frontier life
visitador: Investigator
winka: Mapuzugún for "outsider" or "foreigner"
yanacona: Inka term, later adopted by the Spanish, for an indigenous servant or vassal in colonial Chile

Notes

Introduction

1. January 20, 1630, El Obispo de Santiago de Chile a SM, Archivo General de Indias (hereafter AGI), Chile, 60.

2. Recent estimates put pre-Columbian population of Chile at one million, with five hundred thousand living to the south of the Bío-Bío River. José Bengoa, *Historia del pueblo Mapuche* (Santiago: Ediciones Sur, 1985), 15.

3. Mapuche means "people of the earth" in Mapudungun, but the term only sporadically appears in sixteenth- and seventeenth-century sources. The Spanish had various terms to refer to the Mapuche, usually based on the region from whence they sent representatives in peace talks, but the most universal term was Araucano or Auca. (Araucanian) Guillaume Boccara correctly points out that both Mapuche and Araucano are flawed and instead uses the term *reche* meaning "true people" to refer to the inhabitants of this area. Guillaume Boccara, "Etnogénesis Mapuche: Resistencia y Restructuración Entre los Indígenas del Centro-Sur de Chile (Siglos XVI–XVIII)," *Hispanic American Historical Review* 79, no. 3 (August 1999). *Reche* was used and understood by the Spanish, but it too is imperfect as it refers to the masses or individuals and does not include this region's political or religious leaders. Tomás Guevara, *Historia de la civilización de Araucanía*, vol. 1 (Santiago: Imprenta Cervantes, 1898), 186. *Reche* is becoming more widely used among Chilean historians, but Mapuche remains more universal. Promoaucae is also commonly used by anthropologists and has its origins in the Quechua *purum auca* or "indomitable."

4. Salvador Canals Frau, *Las poblaciones indígenas de la Argentina: Su origen—su pasado—su presente* (Buenos Aires: Editorial Sudamericana, 1953), 357. The plains peoples include the Mapuches, the Huilliche, and the Pikunche. Raul Molina, *Territorio y comunidades Pehuenches del Alto Bío-Bío* (Santiago: Corporación Nacional de Desarrollo Indígena, 1996), 11.

5. Jerry D. Moore, *A Prehistory of South America: Ancient Cultural Diversity on the Least Known Continent* (Boulder: University Press of Colorado, 2014), 84–86.

6. Carlos Aldunate del Solar, *Cultura Mapuche* (Santiago: Editorial Gabriela Mistral, 1978), 9.

7. Mario A. Rivera, "Prehistory of the Southern Cone," in The Cambridge History of the Native Peoples of the Americas: Vol 3: South America, Part I, ed. Frank Salomon, and Stuart B. Schwartz (Cambridge: Cambridge University Press, 2008), 752.

8. Rivera, "Prehistory of the Southern Cone," 752.

9. Tom D. Dillehay and Carlos Aldunate del Solar, *Araucanía: Presente y Pasado* (Santiago: Editorial Andrés Bello, 1990), 42–43

10. Tom D. Dillehay, *Monuments, Empires and Resistance* (Cambridge: Cambridge University Press, 2012), 96.

11. Dillehay, *Monuments, Empires and Resistance,* 103.

12. Bengoa, *Historia del pueblo Mapuche,* 39–40.

13. Bengoa, *Historia del pueblo Mapuche,* 42–43.

14. Carlos Aldunate del Solar, *Mapuche, Seeds of the Chilean Soul: An Exhibit at the Port of History Museum at Penn's Landing, Philadelphia, Pennsylvania, March 27–June 30, 1992,* trans. Richard C. Baker and Peter W. Kendall (Santiago: Museo Chileno de Arte Precolombiano, 1992), 43.

15. Dillehay and Aldunate del Solar, *Araucanía,* 44.

16. Horacio Zapater, *La búsqueda de la paz en la Guerra de Arauco: Padre Luis de Valdivia* (Santiago: Editorial Andrés Bello, 1992), 89–90.

17. Guevara, *Historia de la civilización de Araucanía,* 9–10. Aldunate del Solar, *Cultura Mapuche,* 13.

18. Rivera, "Prehistory of the Southern Cone," 752.

19. Roque Esteban Scarpa, *Prologo breve,* in *La Araucana,* by Alonso de Ercilla (Santiago: Editorial Andrés Bello, 1983), 7–8.

20. Alonso de Ercilla, *The Araucaniad: A Version in English Poetry of Alonso de Ercilla Zúñiga's La Araucanca,* trans. Charles M. Lancaster and Paul T. Manchester (Nashville, Vanderbilt University Press, 2013), 15.

21. Eduardo Solar Correa, *Semblanzas literarias de la colonia* (Santiago: Editorial Difusion Chilena S.A., 1945), 50–52.

22. Simon Collier, *Ideas and Politics of Chilean Independence: 1808–1833* (Cambridge: Cambridge University Press, 1967), 212–13.

23. Collier, *Ideas and Politics,* 214.

24. Collier, *Ideas and Politics,* 213.

25. Collier, *Ideas and Politics,* 369.

26. Nathan Wachtel, *The Vision of the Vanquished: The Spanish Conquest of Peru through Indian Eyes,* trans. Ben Reynolds and Siân Reynolds (Hassocks, Sussex: Harvester Press, 1977). Alvaro Jara, *Guerra y sociedad en Chile y otros temas,* 3rd ed. (Santiago: Editorial Universitaria, 1984). Alfred J. Tapson, "Indian Warfare on the Pampa during the Colonial Period" *Hispanic American Historical Review* 42, no. 1 (February 1962): 1–28.

27. Rolf G. Foerster, *Jesuitas y Mapuches 1593–1767* (Santiago: Editorial Universitaria, S.A., 1996); Eugene H. Korth, *Spanish Policy in Colonial Chile. The Struggle for Social Justice, 1535–1700.* (Stanford, CA: Stanford University Press, 1968).

28. Dillehay and Aldunate del Solar, *Araucanía.*

29. Sergio R. Villalobos, *Los Pehuenches en la vida fronteriza* (Santiago: Ediciones Universidad Católica de Chile, 1989).

30. Edmund S. Morgan, *American Slavery, American Freedom: The Ordeal of Colonial Virginia* (New York: Norton, 1975), 386.

31. Morgan, *American Slavery, American Freedom,* 380.

32. Morgan, *American Slavery, American Freedom,* 387.

33. Ira Berlin, *Many Thousands Gone: The First Two Centuries of Slavery in North America* (Cambridge, MA: Harvard University Press, 1998), 8.

34. Berlin, *Many Thousands Gone,* 96–97.

35. Berlin, *Many Thousands Gone,* 4.

36. Allan Gallay, *The Formation of a Planter Elite: Jonathan Bryan and the Southern Colonial Frontier* (Athens: University of Georgia Press, 2007), xii.

37. Alan Gallay, *The Indian Slave Trade: The Rise of the English Empire in the American South, 1670–1717* (New Haven, CT: Yale University Press, 2002), 135–36.

38. Gallay, *Formation of a Planter Elite*, xiii.

39. Gallay, *Formation of a Planter Elite*, 15–16.

40. Gallay, *Formation of a Planter Elite*, 7.

41. Gallay, *Indian Slave Trade*, 3.

42. Matthew Mulcahy, *Hubs of Empire: The Southeastern Lowcountry and British Caribbean* (Baltimore: Johns Hopkins University Press, 2014).

43. Christina Snyder, *Slavery in Indian Country: The Changing Face of Captivity in Early America* (Cambridge, MA: Harvard University Press, 2012).

44. Ruben Thwaites, "France in America: 1497–1763," in "Rescuing Early America from Nationalist Narratives: An Intra-Imperial Approach to Colonial Canada and Louisiana," by Daniel H. Usner, *Historical Reflections/Réflexions Histoirques* 40, no. 3 (Winter 2014): 5–6.

45. William Deverell, *Whitewashed Adobe: The Rise of Los Angeles and the Remaking of Its Mexican Past* (Berkeley: University of California Press, 2005).

46. Herbert Eugene Bolton, *The Spanish Borderlands: A Chronicle of Old Florida and the Southwest* (Whitefish, MT: Kessinger Publishing, 1921).

47. Brett Rushforth, *Bonds of Alliance: Indigenous and Atlantic Slaveries in New France* (Chapel Hill: University of North Carolina Press, 2014).

48. Andrés Reséndez, *The Other Slavery: The Uncovered Story of Indian Enslavement in America* (Boston: Mariner Books, Houghton Mifflin, 2016), 185.

49. Reséndez, *Other Slavery*, 195.

50. John M. Monteiro, *Blacks of the Land: Indian Slavery, Settler Society, and the Portuguese Colonial Enterprise in South America,* trans. and ed. James Woodard and Barbara Weinstein (Cambridge: Cambridge University Press, 2018), 204.

51. Ronda Ward, "A Colonial Woman in a Republican's Chilean History: Benjamín Vicuña Mackenna and La Quintrala," *Journal of Women's History* 13, no. 1 (2001).

52. Guillermo Feliú Cruz, *Las encomiendas según tasas y ordenanzas* (Buenos Aires: Talleres Jacobo Peuser, 1941), 218.

53. Frederick Douglass, "The Constitution of the United States: Is It Pro-Slavery or Anti-Slavery," March 26, 1860, Teaching American History.

54. Della M. Flusche, *Two Families in Colonial Chile* (Lewiston, NY: Edwin Mellen Press, 1989), 88.

55. Mario Góngora, *Orígen de los inquilinos de Chile central* (Santiago: Instituto de Capacitación e Investigación en Reforma Agraria, 1974). In most of the Spanish-speaking world, *inquilino* means "renter." A person with an apartment in modern Madrid, for example, would be an inquilino. But, in Chile, modern renters are *arrendatarios,* while *inquilino* almost exclusively refers to tenant farmers.

56. Alvaro Jara, *Fuentes para la historia del trabajo en el Reino de Chile,* vol. 3: *Alquileres y ventas de indios, 1599–1620* (Santiago: Editorial Universidad Católica, 1958). Rolando Mellafe, *La introducción de la esclavitud negra en Chile: Tráfico y rutas* (Santiago: Universidad de Chile, 1959).

57. Macarena Sánchez Pérez, "De cautivos a esclavos: Algunos problemas metodológicos para el Estudio de los indios cautivos en la Guerra de Arauco," in Valenzuela Márquez,

América en diásporas. Jimena Obregón Iturra, "'Indios en collera,' Deportaciones coloniales de trabajadores Huarpes y Aucaes razón de estado e intereses particulares. Chile, 1598–1658," *Revista Tiempo Historico* Año 9, no. 16 (Enero–Junio 2018): 15–38.

Chapter 1

1. *Novio* or *novia,* which is "boyfriend" or "girlfriend" in most of Latin America and Spain, usually means "fiancé" in Chile. This has been known to cause some embarrassment for foreigners navigating the dating world in Chile.

2. José Bengoa, *Historia de los antiguos Mapuches del Sur* (Santiago: Catalonia, 2003), 39–40.

3. Simon Collier and William F. Sater, *A History of Chile, 1808–1994* (Cambridge: Cambridge University Press, 1996), 4.

4. Bengoa, *Historia de los antiguos Mapuches,* 38.

5. Garcilaso de la Vega, *Los comentarios reales de los Inkas,* vol. 2 (Lima: Imprenta y Librería Sanmarti y Ca., 1918).

6. Osvaldo Silva Galdames, "¿Detuvo la batalla del Maule la expansión Inka hacía el sur de Chile?," *Cuadernos de Historia* 3 (Julio 1983).

7. Leonardo León Solís, "Expansión Inka y resistencia indígena en Chile, 1470–1536." *Chungara: Revista de Antropología Chilena* 10 (1983): 98.

8. Dillehay, *Monuments, Empires and Resistance,* 103.

9. Inka Garcilaso de la Vega, *Historia general del Peru: Segunda parte de los Comentarios Reales,* vol. 1 (Lima: Editorial Universo S.A, 1970), 175.

10. *Conquista y población del Perú* in J. T. Medina, ed., *Colección de documentos inéditos para la historia de Chile: Desde el viaje de Magallanes hasta la batalla de Maipo: 1518–1818: Tomo 7* (Santiago: Imprenta y Encuardernación Barcelona, 1895), 467.

11. Giovanni Ignazio Molina, *The Geographical, Natural and Civil History of Chili,* vol 2 (Middletown, CT: I. Riley, 1808), 29. Korth, *Spanish Policy in Colonial Chile,* 24.

12. Vicente Carvallo Goyeneche, *Descripción-histórico-jeográfica del reino de Chile,* in *Colección de historiadores de Chile y documentos relativos a la historia nacional,* vol. 8 (Santiago: Imprenta del Ferrocarril, 1875), 10. Disponible en Memoria Chilena, Biblioteca Nacional de Chile (hereafter BN).

13. Alonso de Góngora Marmolejo, *Historia de Chile desde su descubrimiento hasta el año de 1575,* in *Colección de historiadores de Chile y Documentos Relativos a la historia Nacional,* vol. 2 (Santiago: Imprenta del Ferrocarril, 1862), 5. Disponible en Memoria Chilena, BN.

14. León Solís, "Expansión Inka y Resistencia Indígena," 108.

15. Bengoa, *Historia de los Antiguos Mapuches,* 38.

16. Carlos González Vargas and Hugo Rosati Aguerre, "Métodos y Formas de Resistencia Indígena en la Crónica de Gerónimo de Bibar," *Diálogo Andino* 38 (2011): 47.

17. González Vargas and Rosati Aguerre, "Métodos y Formas," 50–51.

18. H. R. S. Pocock, *The Conquest of Chile* (New York: Stein and Day, 1967), 84–85. Diego Barros Arana estimated that Chile had no more than five hundred Spanish residents in 1550. Tracing population numbers for the rest of the century becomes a difficult task with miscegenation and the abandonment of Spanish settlements. Barros Arana, *Historia general de Chile,* vol. 1 (Santiago: Editorial Universitaria, 1999), 263. The next significant arrival of Europeans did not come until 1605 when one thousand reinforcements arrived for the Army of Arauco (see chapter 3). AGI, Chile, 4, Consultas de la Junta de Guerra. 1602–1699, letter from *junta,* Madrid, October 4, 1606.

19. González Vargas and Rosati Aguerre, "Métodos y Formas," 53.

20. Pocock, *Conquest of Chile*, 94. This act has been embellished quite a bit with some authors claiming that the chiefs were decapitated and had their bodies flung toward the attackers. However, most sixteenth-century chroniclers refer to only "an impaling." González Vargas and Rosati Aguerre, "Métodos y Formas," 53.

21. Lucía Invernizzi Santa Cruz, "'Los trabajos de la guerra' y 'Los trabajos del hambre': Dos ejes del discurso narrativo de la Conquista de Chile (Valdivia, Vivar, Góngora Marmolejo)," *Revista Chilena de Literatura* 36 (1990): 7–9.

22. See Tomás Thayer Ojeda and Carlos Larraín de Castro, *Valdivia y sus compañeros* (Santiago: Academia Chilena de la Historia, 1950), for brief biographies of the 150.

23. Jerónimo de Vivar, *Crónica de los Reinos de Chile* (Madrid: Dastin, 2001), 160.

24. Gregorio Álvarez, *Neuquén, su historia, su geografía, su toponimia* (Neuqén, Argentina: Universidad de Neuquén, 1972), 27–28.

25. Diego de Rosales, *Historia general del Reyno de Chile: Flandes indiano*, vol. 1. (Valparaíso, Chile: Imprenta del Mercurio, 1878), 501.

26. Boccara, "Etnogénesis Mapuche," 439. Clifford Geertz, *Negara: The Theatre and State in Nineteenth Century Bali* (Princeton, NJ: Princeton University Press, 1980), 103.

27. Boccara, "Etnogénisis Mapuche," 437.

28. Boccara, "Etnogénisis Mapuche," 437.

29. Boccara, "Etnogénesis Mapuche," 438.

30. René León Echaiz, *El Toki Lautaro* (Santiago: Talleres de Ricardo Neupert, 1971), 40.

31. J. H. Elliot explains that Mapuche decentralization ipso facto slowed very early attempts at Spanish conquest. With no Mapuche capital to attack or emperor to capture, things started very differently in Chile. "The very absence in other parts of mainland America of the conditions prevailing in the civilizations of the Andes and central Mexico" had much to do with the slowing of conquest in peripheral areas like the Yucatán and the Araucanía. Elliot, "The Spanish Conquest and Settlement of America," in *The Cambridge History of Latin America*, vol. 1, ed. by Leslie Bethell (Cambridge: Cambridge University Press, 1984), 186–87. Bengoa, *Historia del pueblo Mapuche*, 24.

32. Dillehay, *Monuments, Empires and Resistance*, 93.

33. Zapater, *La búsqueda de paz*, 89–90.

34. Dillehay, *Monuments, Empires and Resistance*, 116.

35. Tom D. Dillehay, "Reflections on Araucanian/Mapuche Resilience, Independence, and Ethnomorphosis in Colonial (and Present-Day) Chile," *Chungara, Revista de Antropología Chilena* 48, no. 4 (2016): 694–95.

36. Bengoa, *Historia de los antiguos Mapuches*, 468

37. Dillehay, *Monuments, Empires and Resistance*, 118.

38. Pillán has been described as "spirits," "the Devil," or "the god of fire." While Pillán's nature is not universally understood, we do know that the Mapuche both feared and respected Pillán and would consult with the spiritual entity when conducting specific ceremonies or going to war.

39. Robert Charles Padden, "Cultural Adaptation and Militant Autonomy among the Mapuches of Chile," in *The Indian in Latin American History: Resistance, Resilience and Acculturation*, ed. John E. Kicza (Wilmington, DE: Scholarly Resources, 1993), 78.

40. Boccara, "Etnogénesis Mapuche," 435.

41. Boccara, "Etnogénesis Mapuche," 435.

42. Louis de Armond, "Frontier Warfare in Colonial Chile," in Where Cultures Meet.

Frontiers in Latin American History, 2nd ed., ed. David J. Weber and Jane M. Rausch (Wilmington, DE: Jaguar Books, 1994). Alonso González de Nájera, *Desengaño y reparo de la Guerra de Chile* (Santiago: Editorial Universitaria, 1970), 26–28.

43. Villalobos, Tres siglos de vida fronteriza, 25–26.

44. Bengoa, *Historia de los antiguos Mapuches*, 48, 59.

45. José Manuel Zavala Cepeda and Tom Dillehay, "El 'Estado de Arauco' frente a la conquista Española: Estructuración sociopolítica y ritual de los Araucano-Mapuches en los valles Nahuelbutanos durante los Siglos XVI y XVII," *Chungara, Revista de Antropología Chilena* 42, no. 2 (2010): 439.

46. In chapter 4, I discuss how in the seventeenth century Spanish soldiers were angered that indios amigos were both profiting from the sale of Indian prisoners and collecting a salary.

47. Juan de Torralba, Carta ... al Rey indicando las causas que han influído en el alzamiento general de los indios, June 13, 1569, in José Toribio Medina, *Colección de documentos inéditos para la historia de Chile. Segunda serie*, vol. 2: *1558–1572* (Santiago: Fondo Histórico y Bibliográfico J. T. Medina, 1956), 230.

48. James F. Brooks, *Captives and Cousins: Slavery, Kinship and Community in the Southwest Borderlands* (Chapel Hill: University of North Carolina Press, 2002), 36.

49. Richard White, *The Middle Ground: Indians, Empires and Republics in the Great Lakes Region, 1650–1815* (Cambridge: Cambridge University Press, 1991), 75.

50. Armond, "Frontier Warfare in Colonial Chile," 120.

51. For more on ethnogenisis and Spanish captives in indigenous societies, see Boccara, "Etnogénesis Mapuche." Susan Migden Socolow, "Spanish Captives in Indian Societies: Cultural Contact along the Argentine Frontier, 1600–1835," *Hispanic American Historical Review* 72, no. 1 (February 1992): 73–99.

52. Especially during the summer months, the Spanish often established temporary encampments deep within Araucanian territory from which they conducted raids. Toki Anganamón claimed that his murder of three Jesuits in 1612 was revenge for the flight of a handful of Mapuche women to a Spanish fort and their subsequent baptism. Francisco de Núñez de Pineda y Bascuñan, *Cautiverio feliz y razón individual de las guerras dilatadas del Reino de Chile.* (Santiago: Editorial Universitaria, 1973), 80–84.

53. Padden, "Cultural Adaptation and Militant Autonomy," 78.

54. Rosales, *Historia general*, 2:805.

55. Zavala Cepeda and Dillehay, "El 'Estado de Arauco,'" 439.

56. Dillehay, *Monuments, Empires and Resistance*, 123.

57. Dillehay, *Monuments, Empires and Resistance*, 93.

58. Dillehay, *Monuments, Empires and Resistance*, 16.

59. Dillehay, *Monuments, Empires and Resistance*, 137.

60. Barros Arana, *Historia general*, 2:58–59.

61. Barros Arana, *Historia general*, 2:102.

62. Barros Arana, *Historia general*, 2:259.

63. Mario Góngora, "Vagabundaje y sociedad fronteriza en Chile (siglos XVII a XIX)," *Cuadernos del Centro de Estudios Socioeconómicos* 2 (1966): 5.

64. Góngora, "Vagabundaje y sociedad fronteriza," 5.

65. Góngora, "Vagabundaje y sociedad fronteriza," 5.

66. Jane Landers, *Black Society in Spanish Florida.* (Urbana: University of Illinois Press, 1999), 164.

67. Góngora, "Vagabundaje y sociedad fronteriza," 6.

68. Góngora, "Vagabundaje y sociedad fronteriza," 6.
69. Barros Arana, *Historia general,* 2:337–38.
70. Rosales, *Historia general,* 2:221–22.
71. Rosales, *Historia general,* 2: 221–22.
72. Rosales, *Historia general,* 2:221–22.
73. Mapuches who did not attend these cahuínes in person but whose help was required in an attack would often be sent an arrow dipped in the sacrificed animal's blood. *Pasando la flecha* (passing the arrow) would initiate a gifting cycle where the recipient would be obligated to join an impending attack.
74. Rosales, *Historia general,* 2:221–25.
75. Rosales, *Historia general,* 2:228.
76. Rosales, *Historia general,* 2:247–48. Alonso de Ovalle, *Histórica Relación del Reino de Chile* (Santiago: Zig-Zag, 1961), 253–55.
77. Barros Arana, *Historia general,* 3:112–113.
78. Rosales, *Historia general,* 2: 260.
79. Rosales, *Historia general,* 2:261.
80. Pierina Pighi Bel, "El Matrimonio entre la "Última Gran Princesa Inca" y un Capitán Español que Selló la Conquista de Perú," BBC News Mundo, January 26, 2020.
81. Rosales, *Historia general,* 2:272–80.
82. Rosales, *Historia general,* 2:286.
83. Rosales, *Historia general,* 2:293.
84. Rosales, *Historia general,* 2:296.
85. Guevara, *Historia de la civilización de Araucanía,* 247.
86. Guevara, *Historia de la civilización de Araucanía.* Ovalle, *Histórica Relación del Reino de Chile.* González de Nájera, *Desengaño y reparo de la guerra.* These are just three of the many sources that discuss the assassination of the governor in detail.
87. Rosales, *Historia general,* 2:688.
88. Osvaldo Silva Galdames, *Atlas de historia de Chile* (Santiago: Editorial Universitaria, 1983), 48.
89. Diego de Ocaña, *Relación del viaje a Chile, año de 1600, contenida en la crónica intitulada "A través de la América del Sur"* (Santiago: Editorial Universitaria, 1995), 42. This six-thousand-soldier figure is Father Ocaña's own estimate, but, based on the observations of other chroniclers and on the destruction caused, we can state almost without a doubt that the invading army was composed of thousands of soldiers. Villarrica and Arauco were held during the initial assault but were abandoned a few years later. Villarrica would not be refounded until the nineteenth century.
90. This is of course how the Spanish described it, but more recently, historians have begun to drop "disaster" label or replace it with "victory" as this attack was manifestly a great success for the Mapuche.
91. González de Nájera, *Desengaño y reparo de la guerra,* in Marqués de Miraflores and D. Miguel Salva, eds. *Colección de documentos inéditos para la historia de España,* vol. 48 (Madrid: Imprenta de la Viuda de Calero, 1866), 124.

Chapter 2

1. Barros Arana, *Historia general,* 3:419–20.
2. Lewis Hanke, *The Imperial City of Potosí: An Unwritten Chapter in the History of Spanish America* (The Hague: Martinus Nijhoff, 1956), 29.

3. Reséndez, *Other Slavery*, 123–24.

4. Lyle N. McAlister, *Spain and Portugal in the New World* (Minneapolis: University of Minnesota Press, 1989), 52. Once it was rationalized, "just war" saw a rather seamless transition to the Americas largely because of its long tradition in Europe. There are several examples of how concepts, strategies, and traditions were transferred piecemeal from the Crusades to the Conquest. In an example relevant to our South American case, the Spanish referred to the Juríe Indians of Juyjuy as *alárabes* (or *A la Arabe*) believing that the members of this seminomadic Andean group resembled Arabs. Gonzalo Fernández de Oviedo y Valdés, *Historia general y Natural de las Indias, Biblioteca de Autores Españoles*, vol. 121 (Madrid: Ediciones Atlas, 1959), 133.

5. McAlister, *Spain and Portugal*, 155–56.

6. Bartolomé de las Casas, *An Account, Much Abbreviated, of the Destruction of the Indies*, trans. Stafford Poole, ed. Franklin W. Knight (Indianapolis: Hackett, 2003), xli.

7. McAlister defines *repartimiento* as an "allotment" of Indians. McAlister, *Spain and Portugal*, 81.

8. Pope Paul III, *Sublimis Deus*, June 1537, in Las Casas, *An Account*, xxvii–xxviii.

9. Reséndez, *Other Slavery*, 81.

10. J. H. Elliot, "Spanish Conquest and Settlement," 183.

11. Elliot, "Spanish Conquest and Settlement," 194.

12. Jara, *Guerra y sociedad*, 43–47.

13. Henry Stevens, ed. *The New Laws of the Indies* (London: Chiswick Press, 1893). Elliot, "Spanish Conquest," 194.

14. Indigenous slavery persisted even into the eighteenth century in a handful of regions, especially in frontier areas like the south of Chile, where enslaved Africans were hard to come by and where imperial authority was weak. One of the causes of the Acaxee rebellion of 1601 in Nueva Vizcaya was Acaxee frustration over Spanish raids to enslave. Susan M. Deeds, "Indigenous Rebellions on the Northern Mexican Mission Frontier: From First-Generation to Later Colonial Responses," in *Contested Ground: Comparative Frontiers on the Northern and Southern Edges of the Spanish Empire*, edited by Donna J. Guy and Thomas E. Sheridan (Tucson: University of Arizona Press, 1998), 36–37. In the early years of the eighteenth century, the Choctaws and Chicksaws sought an alliance with the French at Mobile, Alabama, to strengthen their defenses against British dealers in enslavement from Carolina and the new Spanish presence at Pensacola. Daniel Usner, *Indians, Settlers, and Slaves in a Frontier Exchange Economy: The Lower Mississippi Valley before 1783* (Chapel Hill: University of North Carolina Press, 1992), 17–19. While the French may have protected the Choctaw, they were soon involved in trade of the enslaved indigenous people, buying Apache women and children from the Pawnee. Brooks, *Captives and Cousins*, 61. Even as late as the 1780s, the Spanish sought to end their "just war" against the Apaches by shipping enslaved captives to Havana. Richard Slatta, "Spanish Colonial Military Strategy and Ideology," in Guy and Sheridan, *Contested Ground*, 90–91.

15. Reséndez, *Other Slavery*, 89–90.

16. Christine Hunefeldt, *A Brief History of Peru* (New York: Facts on File, 2004), 49.

17. Korth, *Spanish Policy*, 27.

18. Korth, *Spanish Policy*, 27.

19. Korth, *Spanish Policy*, 29.

20. Jara, *Guerra y sociedad*, 28–29.

21. Alvaro Jara, "Importación de trabajadores indígenas en el siglo XVII," *Revista Chilena de Historia y Geografía* 124 (1958): 179.

22. Miguel de Aguirre, *Población de Valdivia: Motivos y medios para aquella fundación* [. . .] , in *Colección de historiadores de Chile y documentos relativos a la historia nacional*, vol. 45: *Los Holandeses en Chile* , ed. Sociedad Chilena de Historia y Geografía (Santiago: Imprenta Universitaria, 1923), 75.

23. In 1528, the Ordinances of Toledo had banned the removal of Indians from their homes, with or without their consent, which was reinforced in 1541. Aguirre, *Población de Valdivia*, 23–31.

24. Historian Mario Góngora claims that this practice helped create a class of itinerant workers in Chile known as the *roto* or *huaso* that had a major presence in the republican period and that even exists in some form to this day. Góngora, "Vagabundaje y sociedad fronteriza," 5.

25. Real cédula comunicada al adelantado don Jerónimo Alderete, gobernador de Chile, sobre beneficiar las minas de aquella provincia, September 4, 1555, in J. T. Medina, ed., *Colección de documentos inéditos para la historia de Chile desde el viaje de Magallanes hasta la Batalla de Maipo: 1518–1818: Tomo XXVIII* (Santiago: Imprenta Elzeviriana, 1901), 24.

26. Medina, *Colección de documentos inéditos*, 33.

27. Arnoldo Pacheco Silva, "Una Economía de conquista: Concepción Siglo XVI," *Revista de Historia (Concepción)* Año 1, 1 (1991): 25.

28. Pacheco Silva, "Una Economía de conquista," 36.

29. Pacheco Silva, "Una Economía de conquista," 37.

30. Pacheco Silva, "Una Economía de conquista," 39.

31. Pacheco Silva, "Una Economía de conquista," 35.

32. Pacheco Silva, "Una Economía de conquista," 39–40.

33. Góngora, *Encomenderos y estancieros*, 3. Góngora, "Urban Social Stratification in Colonial Chile," *Hispanic American Historical Review* 55, no. 3 (1975): 421–48.

34. Flusche, *Two Families*, 112.

35. Vicuña Mackenna, *Los Lisperguer y la Quintrala*, 148–49.

36. Rolando Mellafe, *La Introducción de la esclavitud negra en Chile: Tráfico y rutas.* (Santiago: Universidad de Chile, 1959), 123.

37. AGI, Chile, 60, *Cartas y expedientes de los Obispos de Santiago y Concepción*, Obispo de Santiago de Chile a SM, May 16, 1626.

38. Feliú Cruz, *Las encomiendas*, 111–12.

39. Melchor Hernández de la Serna, Escribano Público, "Convenio entre Andres Enríquez y Lorenzo Núñez de Silva Sobre Cambio de un Indio de Encomienda por un Indio Esclavo Cogido en la Guerra. 11 de Septiembre de 1604," in Alvaro Jara and Sonia Pinto, eds., *Fuentes para la historia del trabajo en el Reino de Chile: Legislación, 1546–1810: II* (Santiago: Editorial Bello, 1983), 159–60.

40. Willam St. Clair, *The Door of No Return: The History of Cape Coast Castle and the Atlantic Slave Trade* (New York: BlueBridge, 2006), 133–35.

41. Feliú Cruz, *Las encomiendas*, 132.

42. Feliú Cruz, *Las encomiendas*, 155.

43. Feliú Cruz, *Las encomiendas*, 132–33.

44. Matthew Restall, "Black Conquistadors: Armed Africans in Early Spanish America," *Americas* 57, no. 2 (2000): 171–205.

45. Gregory E. O'Malley estimates that at least fifteen percent of enslaved Africans saw a second voyage after their transatlantic crossing. O'Malley, "Beyond the Middle Passage: Slave Migration from the Caribbean to North America, 1619–1807," *William and Mary Quarterly*, 3rd ser., 66, no. 1 (January 2009): 125–72.

46. Herbert S. Klein, *The Atlantic Slave Trade*, 2nd ed. (New York: Cambridge University Press, 2010), 25.

47. AGI, Lima 36, Cartas y expedientes de virreyes de Perú. 1611–1615, Marqués de Montesclaros, letter to S. M. Callao. April 17, 1613, foja 57.

48. BN, M. M. Pieza, 1981, Juan Fernández de Castillo. Instrucciones . . . de La Serena al muy Reverendo . . . , guardián de la casa y convento de San Francisco de la cuidad de Santiago, sobre las cosas que necesista el Reino de Chile, Abril 1, 1613, fojas 52v.–53v.

49. BN, M. M. Pieza, 1981, fojas 52v.–53v.

50. Mellafe, *Introducción de la esclavitud Negra*, 195.

51. Mellafe, *Introducción de la esclavitud Negra*, 226.

52. Guillermo Feliú Cruz, *La abolición de la esclavitúd en Chile: Estudio histórico y social*, 2nd. ed. (Santiago: Editorial Universitaria, 1973), 32–34.

53. Gustavo Valdes Bunster, *El poder económico de los Jesuitas en Chile, (1593–1767)* (Santiago: Imprenta Pucará, 1985), 70.

54. As of 1767, there were 120 enslaved individuals on the hacienda. An inventory of the hacienda also listed a number of clocks ready to be delivered to prominent buildings in the capital. Horacio Aránguiz Donoso, "Notas para el estudio de la hacienda de La Calera de Tango, 1685–1783," *Historia. Universidad Católica de Chile* 6 (1967), 229.

55. Benjamín Vicuña Mackenna, *Historia de Santiago*, vol. 2: *Obras completas de Vicuña Mackenna Volumen XI* (Santiago: Universidad de Chile, 1938), 391.

56. Feliú Cruz, *La Abolición de la esclavitud en Chile*, 32–34.

57. Vicuña Mackenna, *Historia de Santiago*, 2:390–91.

58. *Institución del Mayorazgo Aguirre*, October 12, 1744, in Domingo Amunátegui Solar, *Mayorazgos y títulos de Castilla: Tomo Segundo* (Santiago: Imprenta Barcelona, 1901), 61.

59. Vicuña Mackenna, *Historia de Santiago*, 2:430.

60. Ovalle, *Histórica relación del Reino de Chile*, 85–86.

61. Gonzalo Vial Correa, *El Africano en el Reino de Chile: Ensayo histórico—jurídico* (Santiago: Universidad Catolica de Chile, 1957), 52–56.

62. Mellafe, *La introducción de la esclavitud negra*, 166.

63. Vial Correa, *El Africano en el Reino de Chile*, 73.

64. Until 1791, an enslaved man seeking manumission had to pay his value, *alcabala*, the deed, and in some cases the man-hours lost with his own freedom. Vial Correa, *El Africano en el Reino de Chile*, 167.

65. Vial Correa, *El Africano en el Reino de Chile*, 156.

66. Della M. Flusche and Eugene H. Korth, *Forgotten Females: Women of African and Indian Descent in Colonial Chile, 1535–1800* (Detroit: Blaine Ethridge Books, 1983), 6.

67. Letter from Bishop Alday of March 7, 1757, to "M.I.S. Presidente de esta Real Audiencia, gobernador y capitán jeneral de este reino, . . ." in Vicuña Mackenna, *Historia de Valparaíso*, 2:427n.

68. Fernando Márquez de la Plata, "Documentos relativos a la introducción de esclavos negros en América," *Revista Chilena de Historia y Geografía* 61–63 (1928): 212–13.

69. Liliana Crespi, "Comercio negrero en el Río de la Plata durante el siglo XVII. Comerciantes y rutas de distribución hacia las provincias internas, Chile y Perú," paper

presented at Reunión: La ruta del esclavo en Hispanoamérica," San José, Costa Rica, February 24–26, 1999.

70. Elena F. S. de Studer, *La trata de negros en el Río de la Plata Durante el siglo XVIII* (Montevideo: Libros de Hispanoamérica, 1984), 331, appendix, "Buques negreros llegados al Río de la Plata desde 1742 hasta 1806." Despite losing ground in their rivalry with Buenos Aires, Lima was still receiving significant shipments of enslaved Africans. The Spanish ship *San Felipe* arrived in Montevideo in 1797 with 229 *cabezas* (heads) aboard, under the license granted to the conde de premio real in Lima. The ships destination was listed as Callao. In another case, 70 enslaved individuals from the English ship *Neptune,* which arrived in Montevideo in 1804, were sold and placed aboard the *Santa Eulalia,* also destined for Callao.

71. Due to fears of contraband, ships that anchored in Buenos Aires were not typically allowed to continue on to Valparaíso or Callao. In addition, a quick return to Europe with hides and or tallow was much more profitable than a trip through the Strait of Magellan, with a half-full hold of enslaved people, who could fall ill or go unsold on the Pacific side of the continent. Before traders in enslaved people even set out for the interior of the continent, they were faced with a fifty to sixty peso per head surcharge that applied to any enslaved individual who was to be sold *tierra adentro* (to the interior). This surcharge could be offset by the higher prices offered for enslaved people in the interior. Mendoza prices were usually fifty pesos above those in Buenos Aires, and Santiago one hundred above during the 1730s. Studer, *La trata de negros,* 225. This surcharge could not be recovered, however, if an enslaved individual fell ill in the harsh climate of the Andes.

72. Studer, *La trata de negros,* 258.

73. Greg Grandin, *The Empire of Necessity* (New York: Picador, 2014), 120–21.

74. Carta del cirujano Patricio Gedd, "a los directores," March 26, 1733, in Archivo General Nacional (hereafter AGN), *Asiento de los Ingleses, 1727,* legajo no. 2, quoted in Studer, *La trata de negros,* 223.

75. AGN, *Asiento de los Ingleses,* leg. no. 2.

76. Flusche and Korth, *Forgotten Females,* 6.

77. A list of prices in BN, Archivo de la Real Audiencia, vol. 1805, pieza 1, a, page 21, lists among others, "Una negra criolla, de 34 años, en 800 pesos, Un esclavo mulatto, de 16 años, en 650 pesos, Una zamba esclava, de 6 años, en 300 pesos." Quoted in Domingo Amunátegui Solar, "La trata de negros en Chile," *Revista Chilena de Historia y Geografía* 91, no. 46, (1922): 33.

78. Rolf Foerster, *Introducción a la religiosidad Mapuche* (Santiago: Editorial Universitaria, 1993), 17–20.

79. Francisco de Núñez de Pineda y Bascuñán, *Cautiverio feliz y razón individual de las guerras dilatadas del Reino de Chile* (Santiago: Editorial Universitaria, 1973), 19–21.

80. In Sociedad Chilena de Historia y Geografía and Academia Chilena de la Historia, eds., *Colección de historiadores de Chile y de Documentos Relativos a la historia Nacional,* vol. 20, *Actas del Cabildo de Santiago: Tomo V* (Santiago: Imprenta Elzeviriana, 1900), 212.

81. Jara, *Guerra y sociedad,* 154.

82. Letter of Cisneros to Philip II, December 17, 1590, cited in Korth, *Spanish Policy,* 75.

83. Bengoa, *Historia de los antiguos Mapuches,* 566.

84. Bengoa, *Historia de los antiguos Mapuches,* 566.

85. Korth, *Spanish Policy,* 75.

86. Rosales, *Historia general,* 2:282, 288.

87. Rosales, *Historia general*, 2:282.

88. David J. Weber, *Bárbaros: Spaniards and Their Savages in the Age of Enlightenment* (New Haven, CT: Yale University Press, 2005), 8.

89. Murdo J. MacLeod, "Spain and America: The Atlantic Trade 1492–1720," in *The Cambridge History of Latin America*, vol 1, ed. Leslie Bethell (Cambridge: Cambridge University Press, 1984), 368.

90. Jara, *Guerra y sociedad*, 181.

91. AGI, Chile, 60, Cartas y expedientes de los Obispos de Santiago y Concepción. 1564–1633, Bishop of Santiago, Francisco de Salcedo, letter to S. M. Santiago, January 20, 1630.

92. Foerster, *Jesuitas y Mapuches*, 178.

93. The Spanish soldier Diego Serrano and Pehuenche chief Juan Millanchingue had agreed to attack a rebel tribe together. When Millanchingue arrived with his people to carry out the attack, Serrano had all of them imprisoned. Villalobos, *Los Pehuenches en la Vida Fronteriza*, 30. The soldier-poet Diego Arias de Saavedra referred to the incident in his *Purén indómito*: "Llegado a él, a los demás vendieron como a esclavos herrados de Guinea, dándolos a quien más por ellos dieron, que creo que no habrá quién esto crea; cual ésta otra maldad gentes no vieron en todo cuanto el délfico rodea, ni codicia tan grande que hiciese que por esclavo el libre se vendiese." Arias de Saavedra, *Purén indomito* (Concepción, Chile: Universidad de Concepción, 1984), 527.

94. Jara, *Guerra y sociedad*, 162.

95. Feliú Cruz, *Las encomiendas*,122.

96. Feliú Cruz, *Las encomiendas*,131–32.

97. Jaime Valenzuela Márquez, "Esclavos Mapuches. Para una historia del secuestro y deportación de indígenas en la colonia," in *Historias de racismo y discriminación en Chile*, ed. Rafael Gaune, Martín Lara, and Margarita Alvarado (Santiago: Uqbar Editores, 2009), 251n.

98. Valenzuela Márquez, "Esclavos Mapuches," 243–44.

99. "Carta de Gregorio Sánchez al virrey don Francisco de Toledo refiriéndose a los indios desterrados a La Serena, cuya administración le encomendó Rodrigo de Quiroga" in José Toribio Medina, ed., *Colección de documentos inéditos para la historia de Chile: Segunda serie, t. II* (Santiago: Fondo Historico y Bibliográfico J. T. Medina, 1956), 371–72.

100. Korth, *Spanish Policy*, 75.

101. Juan Guillermo Muñoz Correa, "La esclavitud indígena, El caso de Colchagua," *Revista de Historia Social y de las Mentalidades* 2, no. 7 (2003): 116.

102. Bengoa, *Historia de los antiguos Mapuches*, 573.

103. Jara, *Guerra y sociedad*, 177.

104. BN, Manuscritos Medina, tomo 113, pieza 1946, letter from Alonso García Ramón, a S.M., August 9, 1608, Fort Levo, foja 257.

105. Santiago de Tesillo, *Guerra de Chile, Causas de su duración, medios para su fin exempilicado en el gobierno de Don Francisco Lasso de la Vega* (Madrid: Imprenta Real, 1647), 43.

106. González de Nájera says five hundred Spanish women were taken captive. *Desengaño y reparo*, 124, 128.

107. Miguel de Contreras and Noble David Cook, eds. *Padrón de indios de Lima en 1613* (Lima: Universidad Nacional Mayor de San Marcos, 1968).

108. Andrés Reséndez attributes this to both sexual exploitation and a preference for

skills that were traditionally taught to girls like "weaving, food gathering and child rearing." Reséndez, *Other Slavery*, 6.

109. Contreras and Cook, *Padrón de indios*, 138.

110. Contreras and Cook, *Padrón de indios*, 222.

111. Contreras and Cook, *Padrón de indios*, 197.

112. Contreras and Cook, *Padrón de indios*, 276.

113. Contreras and Cook, *Padrón de indios*, 279.

114. Contreras and Cook, *Padrón de indios*, 516.

115. Jimena Obregón Iturra, "'Indios en *collera*,' Deportaciones coloniales de trabajadores Huarpes y Aucaes razón de estado e intereses particulares. Chile, 1598–1658," *Revista Tiempo Historico* 9, no. 16 (Enero–Junio 2018): 28.

116. Reséndez, *Other Slavery*, 5.

117. AGI, Lima, 46, no. 7-A, Cartas y expedientes de virreyes de Perú. El Gobernador de Chile Don Francisco Lasso de la Vega contradice los inconvenientes que el fiscal alega para vender fuera de aquella provincia los indios cautivados en la guerra April 15, 1633. The recapture part of this story may be apocryphal as it fits the governor's narrative that prisoners would return to their homes and cause havoc a bit too conveniently. Unless the prisoners were *caciques principals*, it is unlikely also that they would be recognized as escaped fugitives.

118. Obregón Iturra, "'Indios en *collera*,'" 27.

119. Hernán Ramírez Necochea, *Antecedentes económicos de la independencia de Chile* (Santiago: Universidad de Chile, 1967), 65–67n.

120. Ovalle, *Histórica relación de Chile*, 19–21.

121. Barros Arana, *Historia general*, 4:198–99.

122. AGI, Chile, 56, 1671–87, Expediente de la actuación del Gobernador Don Juan Henríquez, Santiago, March 4, 1673.

123. Vicuña Mackenna, *Historia de Valparaíso*, 145.

124. Vicuña Mackenna, *Historia de Valparaíso*, 1:153.

125. Vicuña Mackenna, *Historia de Valparaíso*, vol. 1.

126. Rolando Mellafe, *Historia social de Chile y América: Sugerencias y aproximaciones* (Santiago: Editorial Universitaria, 1986), 86.

127. Pablo Lacoste, ed. *Sistema Pehuenche: Frontera, sociedad y caminos en los Andes centrales Argentinos Chilenos (1658–1997)* (Mendoza Argentina: Universidad Nacional de Cuyo, 1998), 46.

128. Archivo Nacional de Chile (AN), Escribanos de Santiago, vols. 20, 40, 48.

129. Vicuña Mackenna, *Historia de Valparaíso*, 1:388.

130. Góngora, "Urban Social Stratification," 430–31.

131. Mellafe, *Introducción de la esclavitud negra*, 133.

132. Mellafe, *Introducción de la esclavitud negra*, 160–62.

133. Núñez de Pineda, *Cautiverio felíz*.

134. Mark Meuwese, trans. *To the Shores of Chile: The Journal and History of the Brouwer Expedition to Valdivia in 1643* (University Park: Pennsylvania State University Press, 2019), 69.

Chapter 3

1. González de Nájera, *Desengaño y reparo*.

2. González de Nájera, *Desengaño y reparo*, 49.

3. Quoted in Jorge Pinto Rodríguez, *Misioneros en la Araucanía, 1600–1900* (Bogotá: Consejo Episcopal Latinoamericano, 1990), 103.

4. Pinto Rodríguez, *Misioneros en la Araucanía,* 103

5. Melchior Calderón, *Tratado de la importancia y utilidad que ay en dar por esclavos a los indios rebelados de Chile* (Madrid: 1607), Memoria Chilena.

6. AGI, Lima, 46, Cartas y expedientes de virreyes de Perú, no. 7, el V, a S.M., inconvenientes de que los indios que se cautivan en la guerra de Chile se saquen a vender fuera de aquella provincia, Lima, November 24, 1635.

7. AGI, Lima, 40, Real provisión del May 26, 1608, en que se dieron por esclavos los indios de Chile, fojas 218–19.

8. Jara, *Guerra y sociedad,* 183–84.

9. Archivo Nacional de Chile (AN), Morla Vicuña, vol. 50, pieza 26, Carta de Nicolás Blanco de Santillán a S. M., de 7 de mayo de 1633, sobre la marca que se le pone en el rostro a los indios esclavos, foja 206.

10. AGI, Lima, 44, Cartas y expedientes de virreyes de Perú, 1633, Luis Fernández de Cabrera, Viceroy of Peru, n. 4, lib. 4, letter to S.M, in n. 4, lib. 4 is V. to S. M. Duda sobre si se han de herrer en el rostro los indios que se cautiven en la guerra de Chile, Lima, 6 de Abril, 1633, foja 300v. The practice was banned except for enslaved individuals who were considered flight risks by the viceroy in 1635. Lima, 47, Cartas y expedientes de virreyes de Perú. 1635–36, n.1, lib III. Auto from Viceroy, Ciudad de los Reyes, October 16, 1635, foja 340v.

11. BN, Manuscritos Medina, tomo 133, pieza 2413, Junta de Guerra del Consejo de Indias, Sobre que los indios, varones o hembras, que se tomen prisioneros en las guerras de Chile se tengan por esclavos, Madrid, 24 Abril 1635, fojas 47–51.

12. Jara, *Guerra y sociedad,* 235.

13. Jara, *Guerra y sociedad,* 146.

14. Domingo de Eraso, Papel sobre la esclavitud de los indios de Chile. Del capitán, . . . , in Miraflores and Salva, *Colección de documentos inéditos,* 229–30.

15. Barros Arana, *Historia general: III,* 309.

16. Margarita Gascón, "Frontier Societies: A View from the Southern Frontier of the Indies. *International Seminar on the History of the Atlantic World, 1500–1800.* Harvard University, Working Paper No. 02-04, 11. (Used with permission of the author.)

17. AGI, Chile, 4, Consultas de la Junta de Guerra, 1602–1699, Madrid, September 20, 1633.

18. AGI, Chile, 55, Expediente de los excesos del Gobernador Francisco Meneses (1664–1668), testimony from Maestre de Campo General Geronimo de Molina Vasconcelos, Concepción, March 23, 1665, fojas 2v.-3.

19. AGI, Chile, 55, fojas 4–20.

20. Barros Arana, *Historia general,* vol. 4.

21. González de Nájera, *Desengaño y reparo,* 124, 150.

22. González de Nájera, *Desengaño y reparo,* 309.

23. Bernd Schröter, "La frontera en hispanoamérica colonial: Un estudio historiográfico comparativo," *Colonial Latin American Historical Review,* Summer 2001, 380.

24. Barros Arana, *Historia general,* 3:363.

25. Barros Arana, *Historia general,* 3:363.

26. Jara, *Guerra y sociedad,* 131.

27. González de Nájera, *Desengaño y reparo,* 1st ed. (1866), 451.

28. Zacarias Moutoukias, "Power, Corruption and Commerce: The Making of the Local Administrative Structure in Seventeenth-Century Buenos Aires," *Hispanic American Historical Review* 68, no. 4 (November 1988): 789.

29. Gascón, "Frontier Societies."

30. Góngora, "Vagabundaje y sociedad Fronteriza," 7.

31. AGI, Lima, 38, Cartas y expedientes de virreyes de Perú, 1618–19, (Francisco de Borja y Aragón, Principe de Esquilache), Virrey a S.M., Marzo, 27 1619, Lima, foja 456v.

32. AGI, Chile,129, Expediente relativo al Ejército de Chile y su situado, 1680–99, Memoria de los ynstrumentos que el lcdo D. Pablo Vazquez de Velasco Cavo del orden de Santiago y fiscal de la R. Audiencia de Chile remite a su Magd. en comprobazion de lo que en carta de 25 de Septte de 1690 escribe en orden a lo obrado en la distribuzion del situado del exercito de chile y de los fraudes y malas administraziones que reconosco y experimento en el dispendio del caudal de dicho situado y lo demas que en dha carta se contiene.

33. AGI, Chile, 35, Cartas y expedientes de personas seculares, 1632–60, Francisco de la Fuente Villalobos letter to V.M., 4 de Abril 1640, Concepción.

34. Reséndez, *Other Slavery*, 92.

35. Angel Esteban, Introduction to Catalina de Erauso, *Historia de la Monja Alférez, Catalina de Erauso, Escrita por ella misma* (Madrid: Ediciones Cátedra, 2002), 93n.

36. Esteban, in Erauso, *Historia*, 109.

37. Esteban, in Erauso, *Historia*, 111.

38. Erauso, *Historia*, 106.

39. Erauso, *Historia*, 107.

40. Two soldiers who served with her confirmed her wounding at Purén in sworn declarations. Both gave the declarations in Lima on her behalf after she had confessed that she was a woman and was facing punishment for the murders she had committed. Certificación de Don Francisco Pérez de Navarrete (1624), and Certificación de Don Juan Cortés de Monroy (1625), in Erauso, *Historia*.

41. Mellafe, *Introducción de la esclavitud negra*, 98.

42. Mario Góngora, *Encomenderos y estancianceros: Estudios acerca de la constitución social aristocrática de Chile después de la Conquista: 1580–1660* (Santiago: Universidad de Chile, 1970), 103.

43. Mellafe, *Introducción de la esclavitud negra*, 126.

44. Jaime Valenzuela Márquez, *Las liturgias del* poder: *Celebraciones públicas y estrategias persuasivas en Chile Colonial (1609–1709)* (Santiago: LOM Ediciones, 2001), 79.

45. Feliú Cruz, *Las encomiendas*, 191.

46. Muñoz Correa, "La esclavitud indígena."

47. See Gascón, "Frontier Socieities," 21. See also Socolow, "Spanish Captives in Indian Society," 73–99. Socolow's article is a fascinating study of captive taking on the other side of the Andes where Spanish women were kidnapped to bolster indigenous populations in the pampa well into the republican era.

48. Barros Arana, *Historia general*, 3:309.

49. Gascón, "Frontier Societies," 11.Barros Arana, *Historia general*, 3:323.

50. Bengoa, *Historia de los antiguos Mapuches*, 341.

51. Bengoa, *Historia de los antiguos Mapuches*, 341–42.

52. Leonardo León Solís, *Maloqueros y conchavadores en Araucanía y las Pampas, 1700–1800* (Temuco, Chile: Ediciones Universidad de la Frontera, 1990), 15. The Mapuche

language (*mapudungún*) term *maloca* was commonly used to describe a raid from either side well into the eighteenth century.

53. BN, Manuscritos Medina, tomo 129, pieza 2317, Carta del Licenciado don Alonso Pérez de a S. M. el Rey, fecha en Lima en 24 de Junio de 1628.

54. Jara, *Guerra y sociedad*, 149.

55. Reséndez, *Other Slavery*, 76.

56. Reséndez, *Other Slavery*, 99.

57. Mellafe, *Historia social*, 86–90.

58. Mellafe, *Historia social*, 90–92. For more on the consumption habits and daily life of the Army of Arauco, see Hugo Contreras Cruces, "Fortificaciones, logística, y vida de cuartel en el Real Ejército de Chile durante el siglo XVII," *Boletín Americanista* 2, no. 77 (2018): 203–23.

59. Moutoukias, "Power, Corruption and Commerce," 789.

60. Juan Eduardo Vargas Cariola, "Financiamiento del Ejército de Chile en el siglo XVII," *Historia* 19 (1984): 179–80.

61. Vargas Cariola, "Financiamiento del Ejército," 192–93.

62. Diego de Rosales, *Historia general del Reino de Chile, Flandes indiano*, vol. 1 (Santiago: Imprenta del Mercurio, 1877), 283.

63. Before sending the rescue fleet, the viceroy had ordered the governor of Chile to gather all his troops and march on Valdivia, driving the Dutch out to sea. This order merely revealed "the viceroy's imperfect knowledge of Chile's situation" and was impossible to carry out. Gathering the Army of Arauco together as one force would have meant abandoning Spanish forts and exposing the column to a series of ambushes as they marched the hundreds of kilometers to Valdivia where they would meet an unknown number of Dutch and Indian enemies. Barros Arana, *Historia general*, 4:289–90.

64. AGI, Lima 52, Cartas y Expedientes, fojas 185–186v.

65. Bengoa, *Historia de los antiguos Mapuches*, 382.

66. There were still occasional raids across the Bío-Bio in both directions during this period, but they cannot be referred to as "campaigns." Chillán, for example, a growing town near the Bío-Bío, was a target of Mapuche *malocas* in 1616 and 1623. Rosales, *Historia general*, 2:949–50.

67. Rosales, *Historia General*, 2:649–50.

68. Archivo Nacional de Chile, Fondo Morla Vicuña, Vol. 19 N. 34. Carta de D. Luis Fernandez de Córdova: Da noticia de los indios de la otra banda de la cordillera. 1629. Fojas 245–46.

69. Barros Arana, *Historia general*, 4:162.

70. Bengoa, *Historia de los antiguos Mapuches*, 443.

71. See Lisa Voigt, *Writing Captivity in the Early Modern Atlantic: Circulations of Knowledge and Authority in the Iberian and English Imperial Worlds* (Chapel Hill: University of North Carolina Press, 2009).

72. Núñez de Pineda, *Cautiverio feliz*, 27.

73. Ralph Bauer, "Imperial History, Captivity and Creole Identity in Francisco Núñez de Pineda y Bascuñán's *Cautiverio feliz*," *Colonial Latin American Review* 7, no. 1 (June 1998): 59–60.

74. José Anadón, "Estudio preliminar," in Núñez de Pineda, *Suma y epilogo de lo más esencial que contiene el libro intitulado: Cautiverio feliz y guerras dilatadas del Reino de Chile*, ed. Robert A. McNeil (Santiago: Ediciones Universidad Católica de Chile, 1984), 25.

75. Anadón, "Estudio preliminar," 26–27.

76. In *Cautiverio feliz,* Núñez de Pineda refers to Butapichón as Putapichun.

77. Núñez de Pineda, *Cautiverio feliz,* 38–39.

78. Francisco does not name the unfortunate victim, referring to him only as "mi compañero."

79. Núñez de Pineda, *Cautiverio feliz,* 41.

80. Núñez de Pineda, *Cautiverio feliz,* 131–32.

81. Núñez de Pineda, *Cautiverio feliz,* 132.

82. Boccara, "Etnogénesis Mapuche," 437.

83. Geertz, *Negara,* 103.

84. José Manuel Zavala Cepeda, ed. *Los parlamentos Hispano-Mapuches, 1593–1803: Textos fundamentales* (Temuco, Chile: Universidad Católica de Temuco, 2015), 18.

85. Zavala Cepeda, *Los parlamentos,* 41–44. Brett Rushforth writes of a similar development in early eighteenth-century New France. In 1711, the French invited the Fox indigenous people to live near Detroit, but the Fox were concerned that would leave them vulnerable to invasion from indigenous enemies like the Ottawa and Huron. Rushforth, *Bonds of Alliance,* 211.

86. Zavala Cepeda, *Los parlamentos,* 44.

87. Zapater, *La búsqueda de la paz,* 19–22.

88. Barros Arana, *Historia general,* 3:449.

89. Rosales, *Historia general,* 2:563.

90. Rosales, *Historia general,* 2:965.

91. Zapater, *La búsqueda de la paz,* 25.

92. Korth, *Spanish Policy,* 118–19.

93. Zapater, *La búsqueda de la paz,* 25.

94. Zapater, *La búsqueda de la paz,* 19–22.

95. Zavala Cepeda, *Los parlamentos,* 63–65.

96. Korth, *Spanish Policy,* 130–31.

97. "Real Cédula para los Caciques de la Araucanía, en favor del P. Luis de Valdivia," in Claudio Gay, ed. *Historia física y politica de Chile: Documentos,* vol. I(Paris: Imprenta de Maulde Y Renou, 1846), 261.

98. Luis de Valdivia, "Relación de lo que sucedió en la jornada que hizimos el Señor Presidente Alonso de Ribera, Governador deste Reyno, y yo, desde Arauco a Paicaví, a concluir las pazes de Elicura, última regua de Tucapel, y las de Purén, y la Imperial. Escrita por mi el Padre Luis de Valdivia, al Salir de Paicaví, de Vuelta a Levo," in *Americana Series; Photostat Reproductions by the Massachusetts Historical Society,* no. 223 [Lima?, 1613?].

99. Rosales, *Historia general,* 2:960.

100. I write "rarely" because Anganamón killed three Jesuits at Elicura in 1612. He explained that the killing was a response to the Jesuits holding several women from his levo against their will at Fort Paicaví. The Jesuits responded that the women had fled to be baptized and did not wish to return to Elicura. This episode is complicated by the fact that the only details available of the developments come from other Jesuits, who of course refer to the murdered priests as "martyrs." Foerster, *Jesuitas y Mapuches,* 140–41. Anganamón's ire may also have derived from a legitimate concern for Mapuche women alone in a Spanish fort as "Euro-American men indulged in sexual violence against captives with much greater frequency than Native men. . . . Rape had long been a prerogative of invading warriors." Snyder, *Slavery in Indian Country,* 90.

101. Solar Correa, *Semblanzas literarias de la colonia*, 162.
102. Bengoa, *Historia de los antiguos Mapuches*, 454.
103. Bengoa, *Historia de los antiguos Mapuches*, 465.
104. Bengoa, *Historia de los antiguos Mapuches*, 468–69.
105. Zavala Cepeda, *Los parlamentos*, 123–34.
106. Bengoa, *Historia de los antiguos Mapuches*, 470.
107. Ignacio Chuecas Saldías, "Esclavitud indígena y economías familiares en el Chile del siglo XVII," in Valenzuela Márquez, *América en diásporas*, 319–80.
108. Bengoa, *Historia de los antiguos Mapuches*, 476–77.
109. Bengoa, *Historia de los antiguos Mapuches*, 492.
110. Rosales, *Historia general del Reyno de Chile*, 162
111. Bengoa, *Historia de los antiguos Mapuches*, 496; Zavala Cepeda, *Los parlamentos*, 107–20.
112. Barros Arana, *Historia general*, 2:311.
113. Rosales, *Historia general*, 2:339.
114. Kris Lane, *Pillaging the Empire: Piracy in the Americas, 1500–1750* (Armonk, NY: M.E. Sharpe, 1998), 75.
115. Diego de Rosales, *Historia general del Reino de Chile, Flandes indiano*, vol. 2, 2nd ed. (Santiago: Editorial Andrés Bello, 1989), 721–73.
116. This Dutch threat from the south is quite ironic in that Magellan's motivation for finding the strait that bears his name was an alternate route to the East Indies. This Spanish sponsored expedition had only paved the way for a century of Dutch and English navigation of the route when Spanish attention shifted to American gold and silver. Captured or deserting Dutch sailors were interviewed ad nauseum about the plans for their voyage, which meant that officials in Chile and Peru were well aware of Dutch motives. W. S. Barclay, *The Land of Magellan* (New York: Brentano's Publishers, 1926), 39.
117. AGI, Patronato, 268, N.2, R.3, foja 1, Declaración que hizo Rodrigo Giraldo, capitán de filibote flamenco, que se rindió al capitán Jerónimo de Molina despues de haber entrado con otros dos buqes holandeses por el Estrecho de Magallanes en el Mar del Sur, Stog., Feb. 10, 1600. Ralph Lee Woodward, *Robinson Crusoe's Island: A History of the Juan Fernández Islands* (Chapel Hill: University of North Carolina Press, 1969), 18–21.
118. Lane, *Pillaging the Empire*, 74–75.
119. Lane, *Pillaging the Empire*, 79–80.
120. Rosales, *Historia general*, 2:612.
121. Rosales, *Historia general*, 2:945.
122. BN, Manuscritos Medina, Declaraciones que hacen diez piratas que quedan prisioneros en la plaza de la Concepción de sus carrerías en las costas de Chile, fechas en 5 de Diceimbre de 1630, Signed Geronimo de Quiroga, 37v, 38.
123. Benjamin Schmidt, *Innocence Abroad: The Dutch Imagination and the New World, 1570–1670* (Cambridge: Cambridge University Press, 2001), 192.
124. Schmidt, *Innocence Abroad*, 205–6.
125. Schmidt, *Innocence Abroad*, 198.
126. Peter T. Bradley, *The Lure of Peru: Maritime Intrusion into the South Sea, 1598–1701* (London: Palgrave Macmillian, 2014).
127. Lane, *Pillaging the Empire*, 87–88.
128. Schmidt, *Innocence Abroad*, 205–6.
129. Rosales, *Historia general*, 2:1163; Lane, *Pillaging the Empire*, 87–90.

130. Rosales, *Historia general,* 2:1164.

131. Schmidt, *Innocence Abroad,* 208–9.

132. AGI, Lima, 52, Cartas y expedientes de virreyes de Perú. Pedro de Toledo, Marqués de Mancera, 1644–45, no. 4-B, Copia de carta que el General Olandes Elas Harquemans escribió a Manqueante caçique de Mariquina en 14 de otubre de 1643.

133. Rosales, *Historia general,* 2:1168–69.

134. AGI, Lima 52, no. 4-D, Declaración de un prisionero holandés que hizo traer de Chiloé el Marqués de Vaides, Concepción, November 23, 1643, fojas 3–3v.

135. AGI, Lima, 52, Cartas y expedientes de virreyes de Perú. Pedro de Toledo, Marqués de Mancera. 1644–45, no. 43, lib. III, El V, a S.M., noticia de holandeses en Valdivia, Fortificación del puerto, May 24, 1645.

136. AGI, Lima, 52, no. 52, El V, a S.M, noticias de una armada que se prevenía en Holanda para Pernambuco y pasar al Mar del Sur, Propone medios para la defensa de las provincias del Puerú y Nueva España, November 25, 1645.

137. The governor went on to describe Chile as the "key" to Spain's retaining power in all of the Americas. From Valdivia, the Dutch could begin to take over Spanish trade in the Pacific. Valdivia's proximity to the Strait of Magellan would facilitate communication and cooperation with their forces in Brazil to cut off Spain's Atlantic trade as well. The marquis claimed that with this increasing Dutch control, no American silver would reach Spain. Also, Valdivia's distance from Spanish forces, its fertile soil, and cooperative local Indians made a permanent Dutch presence there seem all the more possible. The governor challenged those who "had tried to say that (the loss of Chile) would be of little import." If Chile were to fall, "(God forbid)," they would know the "true affliction" that would befall so many Spanish "provinces and kingdoms." AGI, Lima, 52, Cartas y expedientes de virreyes de Perú, Pedro de Toledo, Marqués de Mancera, 1644–45, no. 4-A, El Marqués de Vaides, gobernador de Chile, a V. sobre los navíos holandeses que habían llegado a Chiloé, Concepción, November 16, 1643, foja 3.

138. Barros Arana, *Historia general,* 4:290–91.

139. This message did have some truth to it, as the Dutch believed that gold in Valdivia would bring more settlers. AGI, Lima, 52, 4-D, Declaración de un prisionero . . . , Concepción, November 23, 1643, fojas 10–10v.

140. AGI, Lima, 52, 4-E, . . . sobre el enemigo holandes . . . , Concepción, December 3, 1643.

141. BN, Manuscritos Medina, tomo 138, pieza 2533, Copia de carta que el Marqués de Baides, gobernador de Chile, escribió al Marqués de Mansera, Virrey del Perú, fecha en la ciudad de Concepción en 4 de Marzo de 1645.

142. Barros Arana, *Historia general,* 4:297–98n.

143. Juan Luis Espejo, *La Provincia de Cuyo del Reino de Chile* (Santiago: Fondo Historico y Bibliografico José Toribio Medina, 1954), 177.

144. Rosales, *Historia general,* 2:1333.

Chapter 4

1. Sergio Villalobos, Tres siglos y medio de vida fronteriza (Santiago: Editorial Universidad Católica de Santiago, 1982), 43.

2. The term *indios amigos* is a bit misleading as, at least in the beginning, the aborigines did not help the Spanish out of "friendship." In the late sixteenth century, most indios amigos were in fact encomienda Indians aiding their encomendero in performing his

obligatory military service. By the seventeenth century, most indios amigos were no longer attached to encomiendas and had a good deal of autonomy as long as they lived near a Spanish settlement or with a Spanish *capitán de amigos* supervising them. Groups of indios amigos were scattered throughout Chile's central valley and the Araucanía, so mapping their settlements or counting them is more than difficult. However, we do know that the indios amigos serving as soldiers on the Spanish side in the War of Arauco far outnumbered troops of European extraction. Some chroniclers added that indios amigos were essential for their quantity and quality, as with their local knowledge and zeal in battle; one indio amigo soldier was worth a dozen of his Spanish allies. Andrea Ruíz-Esquide Figueroa, *Los indios amigos en la frontera Araucana* (Santiago: Editorial Universitaria, 1993), 23. Indios rebeldes and indios de paz had not been *reducidos* (conquered) by the Spanish, but as the name suggests, indios de paz had no quarrel with the Spanish and helped them occasionally.

3. For examples of these alliances in New Spain, see Laura E. Matthew and Michael R. Oudijk, eds. *Indian Conquistadors: Indigenous Allies in the Conquest of Mesoamerica* (Norman: University of Oklahoma Press, 2012).

4. Ruíz-Esquide, *Los indios amigos*, 22.

5. Jara, *Guerra y sociedad*, 155.

6. Ruíz-Esquide, *Los indios amigos*, 25.

7. Mario Góngora's list of major seventeenth-century encomenderos includes many who maintained business interests in both Santiago and La Araucanía. The family of Gaspar de Ahumada for example, had dozens of enslaved peoples and servants, properties in Choapa and Conchalí, and an important sausage and tallow business in Valdivia. Góngora, *Encomenderos y Estancieros*, 141–42.

8. Ruíz-Esquide, *Los indios amigos*.

9. Vargas Cariola, "Financiamiento del Ejército," 184–85.

10. Ruíz-Esquide, *Los indios amigos*, 26–27.

11. Ruiz-Esquide, *Los indios amigos*, 32.

12. Espejo, *La Provincia de Cuyo*, 57.

13. Ruíz-Esquiduide, *Los indios amigos*, 21–24.

14. Ruiz-Esquide, *Los indios amigos*, 22.

15. Mellafe, *Introducción de la esclavitud Negra*, 119.

16. These instructions involved some hyperbole in the sense that Remulta was being asked to spy on all aspects of this regua's activities. However, games, of course, can often be preparation for warfare, or organization of games can conceal the gathering of soldiers without raising suspicion.

17. Tesillo, *Guerra de Chile*, 18–19.

18. Tesillo, *Guerra de Chile*, 19.

19. Tesillo, *Guerra de Chile*, 38.

20. Archivo Nacional de Chile, Morla Vicuña, vol. 20, pieza 11a, fojas 91–101, Carta del virrey del Perú a S.M., de 28 de abril de 1675 (Posible colonización inglesa en el Estrecho; dilgencias relaizadas para saber efectivamente; medios que utilizará para desalojar a los ingleses), foja 93.

21. Archivo Nacional de Chile, Morla Vicuña, vol. 20, pieza 11a, fojas 91–101.

22. Ruíz-Esquide, *Los indios amigos*, 23.

23. Slatta, "Spanish Colonial Military Strategy and Ideology," 85.

24. AGI, Lima, 38, Cartas y expedientes de virreyes de Perú, 1618–1619 (Francisco de Borja y Aragón, Principe de Esquilache), Virrey a S.M., 27 Marzo 1619, foja 456v.

25. "No era el fuerte el que se disponía para abrigo de los amigos, sino los amigos los que se venían a vivir al abrigo del fuerte." Ruíz-Esquide, *Los indios amigos*, 66.

26. Barros Arana, *Historia general*, 4:268.

27. Chuecas Saldías, "Esclavitud indígena y economías familiares," 239.

28. Contreras and Cook, *Padrón de indios*, 288.

29. Christina Snyder observes a similar phenomenon among the Chicksaw in England's North American colonies. Snyder estimates that in the late seventeenth and early eighteenth centuries, the Chicksaw, "sometimes acting in concert with their allies, captured a minimum of 1,200 captives." Snyder, *Slavery in Indian Country*, 63.

30. Lacoste, *Sistema Pehuenche*, 47–48.

31. AGI, Chile, 4, Antonio de [Ubilla], Es de parecer que en atención a los méritos y servicios de Don Martín de las Cuebas Palan Cacique en el Reyno de Chile, 20 de [Setiembre] de 1696.

32. "Informe de la Real Audiencia sobre el estado de Chile (1639)," in Gay, *Historia física y politica*, 413.

33. BN, Manuscritos Medina, tomo 141, pieza 2636, Carta del Gobernador de Chile don Antonio de Acuña y Cabrera a S.M. el Rey, fecha en Santiago a 1º de Mayo de 1651.

34. BN, Manuscritos Medina, tomo 142, pieza 2654, Carta de la Real Audiencia de Chile a S.M. el Rey, fecha en Santiago a 22 de Mayo de 1651.

35. Feliú Cruz, *Las encomiendas*, 191.

36. AGI, Chile, 57, "Expediente de la libertad de los indios esclavos de guerra. 1674–1683," Fray Dionysio, Concepción, August 1659.

37. AGI, Lima, 55, Cartas . . . 1651, García Sarmiento de Sotomayor, "El V. a S.M., Defensa del Puerto de Buenos Aires," Lima, September 2, 1651.

38. Feliú Cruz, *Las encomiendas*, 191.

39. Barros Arana, *Historia general*, 4:338.

40. BN, Manuscritos Medina, tomo 138, pieza 2533, "Copia de Carta que el Marqués de Baides, Gobernador de Chile, Escribió al Marqués de Mansera, Virrey del Perú," Concepción, 4 de Marzo de 1645.

41. In his 1651 exit interview, the viceroy explained usanza to his successor. He added that he had only recently learned of it and that the Audiencia of Chile had already requested that it be banned. Relación de Estado en que deja el Gobierno de estos reinos el Conde de Salvateirra al Sr. Virrey Conde de Alba de Sesta, Los Reyes, March, 22, 1651. Angel Altolaguirre y Duvalle, ed., *Colección de las memorias o relaciones que escribieron los Virreyes del Perú: Tomo II* (Madrid: Imp. del Asilo de Huérfanos del S.C. de Jesús, 1921), 300.

42. BN, Manuscritos Medina, tomo 143, pieza 2705, Información sumaria que está mandada hacer sobre la pérdida y alzamiento general del Reino de Chile, en la causa que sigue el general Martín Ruíz de Gamboa al Gobernador de Chile, don Antonio de Acuña y Cabrera y al Maestre de Campo, don Juan Salazar y Solís Henríquez, tomada al testigo don Ignacio de Carrera, Sargento Mayor del Reino, en la ciudad de la Concepción en 27 de Junio de 1656, foja 242 v.

43. AGI, Chile, 57, Letter from Viceroy Conde de Alba. Lima, March 14, 1659. AGI, Escribanía, 932 A, Comisiones Audiencia de Chile. 1660–1685, pieza 1a, Comisión a Pedro de Azaña Solís y Palacio, oidor de la Audiencia de Chile, para proceder en la continuación de la causa que de oficio comenzó Martín de Mújica, Presidente de la Audiencia de Chile, contra Antonio Ramírez de Laguna, fiscal y protector general de indios, sobre el mal

uso de su oficio en tratos y contratos y los azotes que mandó ejectutar en Gonzalo de Aculco, cacique principal del pueblo de Aculco, Testimonio de la causa que segui sobre que los Indios de servidumbre no se vendesen en conformidad de la cedula de su Magd. Antonio Ramírez de Laguna, December 2, 1659, foja 359.

44. Gaspar Mayo, Santiago, February 6, 1652, in Jara and Pinto, *Fuentes para la historia del trabajo*, 169–70.

45. AGI, Escribanía, 932 B, pieza 19, Testimonio en Relación de la Culpa . . . , fojas 4v.–5. For a larger discussion of the process of usanza and the role of Governor Acuña y Cabrera in the practice of enslaving people, see Eugene Clark Berger, "War on Peru's Periphery: Frontier Identity and the Politics of Conflict in 17th Century Chile," PhD diss., Vanderbilt University, 2006.

46. AGI, Escribanía, 932 C, pieza 22, Testimony of Padre Diego de Rosales . . . given to General Martín Ruíz de Gamboa, July 3, 1656, Concepción, fojas 536–38.

47. AGI, Chile, 57, Expediente de la libertad de los indios esclavos de guerra. 1674–1683, Letter from Bishop of Concepción, Fray Dionysio, Concepción, August 1659.

48. AGI, Escribanía, 932 C, pieza 22, Testimony of Captain Juan de Salazar, fojas 611v.–12. With the sheer number of enslaved people and raids to enslave being discussed here, it would have been impossible for Rosales or any of the other Jesuits at Boroa to combat all the abuse being committed. Rosales worked to bring justice to the Puelches because he had worked closely with them for years. Other groups went without help, and as Alvaro Jara details, ecclesiastics played a role in Chile's indigenous slavery. Jara, *Guerra y sociedad,* ch. 9, "La justificación doctrinal de la esclavitud de los indios." This study, however, concerns the actions of Spanish soldiers who existed in far greater numbers and had far greater access to Indians than did missionaries in Chile's south.

49. Beyond strategic and economic motives for enslaving Indians, Margarita Gascón reminds us that prostitution often appears with standing armies. Gascón, "Frontier Societies," 21. With the numbers of young females enslaved in the War of Arauco, it is reasonable to assume that the Army of Arauco also engaged in it.

50. BN, Manuscritos Medina, tomo 143, pieza 2706, Información sumaria que está mandada haver sobre la pérdida y alzamiento general del Reino de Chile, en la causa que sigue el General Martín Ruíz de Gamboa al gobernador de Chile, don Antonio de Acuña y Cabrera y el Maestre de Campo don Juan de Salazar y Solís Henríquez, tomada al padre Diego de Rosales, Rector de la Compañía de Jesús, en la ciudad de la Concepción en 3 de Jul(?)io de 1656, fojas 283–283v.

51. AGI, Escribanía, 932 C, pieza 22, Testimony of Don Francisco de Pineda Bascuñán, Concepción, June 29, 1656, fojas 380–380v.

52. BN, Manuscritos Medina, tomo 143 pieza 2706, Información sumaria que está mandada haver sobre la pérdida y alzamiento general del Reino de Chile, en la causa que sigue el general Martín Ruíz de Gamboa al gobernador de Chile, don Antonio de Acuña y Cabrera y el Maestre de Campo don Juan de Salazar y Solís Henríquez, tomada al padre Diego de Rosales, Rector de la Compañía de Jesús, en la ciudad de la Concepción en 3 de Jul(?)io de 1656, fojas 293v.–94.

53. BN, Ms., vol. 142, "Instrucción del Fiscal del Consejo de Indias a Juan Salazar y Solís, 22 de enero de 1654. Cited in Ruíz-Esquide, *Los Indios Amigos*, 35.

54. AGI, Escribanía, 932 C, pieza 22, Martín Ruíz de Gamboa, Querellas against Antonio de Acuña y Cabrera and Juan de Salazar, Concepción, June 26, 1656, foja 138v.

55. AGI, Escribanía, 932 B, pieza 19, Testimonio en relación de la culpa . . . , fojas 4v.–5.

56. AGI, Escribanía, 932 C, pieza 22. Testimony of Don Francisco de Pineda Bascuñán, Concepción, June 29, 1656, foja 384v.

57. BN, Manuscritos Medina, tomo 143, pieza 2706, Información sumaria que está mandada haver sobre la pérdida y alzamiento general del Reino de Chile, en la causa que sigue el genreal Martín Ruíz de Gamboa al gobernador de Chile, don Antonio de Acuña y Cabrera y el Maestre de Campo don Juan de Salazar y Solís Henríquez, tomada al padre Diego de Rosales, Rector de la Compañía de Jesús, en la ciudad de la Concepción en 3 de Jun(l?)io de 1656, fojas 281–82.

58. Rosales, *Historia general,* 2:1295.

59. AGI, Escribanía, 932 C, pieza 22, Martín Ruíz de Gamboa, Querellas against Antonio de Acuña y Cabrera and Juan de Salazar, Concepción, June 26, 1656, foja 138v.

60. María Ximena Urbina Carrasco, *La frontera de arriba en Chile colonial: Interacción hispano-indígena en el territorio entre Valdivia y Chiloé e imaginario de sus bordes geográficos, 1600–1800* (Valparaíso, Chile: Ediciones Universitarias de Valparaíso, 2009), 103.

61. AGI, Escribanía, 932 C, pieza 22, Testimony of Don Francisco de Pineda Bascuñán, Concepción, June 29, 1656, fojas 385–87.

62. "Que busquen al enemigo en los llanos de Osorno Cunco el alto a donde quiera que estuvieren de suerte que aunque se halla retirado a los más escondido de los bosques le ha de buscar y pelear con el hasta rendirle y por donde quiera que pasase le han de talar sus mieses quemar sus ranchos y coger todo el Ganado que pudiere destruyendo todo lo que toparen de suerte que sientan el castigo en todo lo que tuvieren no se han de retirar hasta que el dicho Maestre de campo lo hordene y el Yndio que fuere preso de diez años arriva se á de pasar a cuchillo sin que en esto se haga otra cosa y loas mujeres y niños de menor hedad se traygan presos á esclavitud perpetua." Alamiro de Ávila Martel, ed., "Instrucciones para la Guerra de Arauco dadas por Acuña y Cabrera para las compañas de 1654 y 1655," *Revista Chilena de Historia del Derecho: Número 2,* 1961, 74.

63. AGI, Escribanía, 932B, pieza 8a, Querella del fiscal de Lima, Don Bernardo de Yturricarra, (1655?), foja 28. Salazar denied that there were any children swimming in the river. Pieza 8, Testimony of Juan de Salazar, Ciudad de Los Reyes, November 20, 1655, foja 124v.

64. AGI, Escribanía, 932 B, pieza 19, Testimonio en Relación de la Culpa que resulta contra el Maese de Campo General Don Juan de Salazar, en razón del Alçamiento general que subçedio en el Reyno de Chile a los 14 de febrero de 1655, Reyes, August 14, 1656, foja 3v.

65. AGI, Escribanía, 932 B, pieza 8. . Querella del fiscal de Lima, (October 1655), fojas 27–27v. Urbina Carrasco, *La frontera de arriba,* 103.

66. AGI, Escribanía, 932 B, pieza 19, Testimonio en Relación de la Culpa . . . , foja 3v.

67. AGI, Escribanía, 932 B, foja 3.

68. AGI, Escribanía, 932 B, foja 27v.

69. AGI, Escribanía, 932 B, pieza 8, testimony of Juan de Salazar, Ciudad de Los Reyes, November 20, 1655, fojas 132v—136v.

70. AGI, Chile, 53, "Interrogatorio para examinar los testigos que supieren y tubieren visto de lo sucedido en la xornada y castigo a los enemigos deesta vanda del rio bueno para que al tenor de las preguntas digeronn los testigos en la información mandada hacer son las siguientes," Juan de Salazar y Solís Enríquez, Mariquina Fort, January 22, 1654.

71. AGI, Escribanía, 932 B, pieza 8, Testimony of Juan de Salazar, Ciudad de Los Reyes, November 20, 1655, foja 124v.

72. AGI, Chile, 5, "Interrogatorio para examinar los testigos que supieren. . . ."

73. See Urbina Carrasco, *La frontera de arriba.*

74. BN, Manuscritos Medina, tomo 142, pieza 2665, Instrucciones que el Fiscal del Real Consejo de las Indias da a don Juan de Salazar y Solís, en fecha 22 de Enero de 1654, fojas 89v–91v.

75. Dillehay, *Monuments, Empires and Resistance*, 37.

76. Espejo, *La Provincia de Cuyo*, 196. AGI, Escribanía, 932 B, pieza 9, Protesta en nombre de Juan de Salazar por Antonio Pérez de Villaroel (Lima, 1656), foja 28v.

77. AGI, Escribanía, 932 C, pieza 22, Martín Ruíz de Gamboa, Querellas against Antonio de Acuña y Cabrera and Juan de Salazar, Concepción, June 26, 1656, foja 155. José, who was killed in the aftermath of the 1655 uprising, was also named in documents as "Joseph."

78. AGI, Escribanía, 932 B, pieza 8, Testimony of Juana de Sotomayor, Ciudad de los Reyes, November 18, 1655, foja 81v.

79. AGI, Escribanía, 932 B, pieza 19, Testimonio en Relación de la Culpa . . . , fojas 5v.–6.

80. AGI, Chile, 53, Expediente de la destitución del Gobernador de Chile, Letter from El Provincial de la Compañía de Jesus, Vicente Modele(?), Santiago, June 13, 16[55].

81. BN, Manuscritos Medina, tomo 143, pieza 2705, Información sumaria que está mandada hacer sobre la pérdida y alzamiento general del Reino de Chile, en la causa que sigue el general Martín Ruíz de Gamboa al Gobernador de Chile, don Antonio de Acuña y Cabrera y al Maestre de Campo, don Juan Salazar y Solís Henríquez, tomada al testigo don Ignacio de Carrera, Sargento Mayor del Reino, en la ciudad de la Concepción en 27 de Junio de 1656, foja 251v. AGI, Escribanía, 932 C, pieza 22, Martín Ruíz de Gamboa, Querellas en contra de Antonio de Acuña y Cabrera and Juan de Salazar, Concepción, June 26, 1656, fojas 156–156v. There are a number of striking similarities to the 1655 uprising in the 1680 Pueblo Revolt or "Great Southwest Rebellion" in New Mexico. Principal among them was the role of excessive indigenous slave taking by the Spanish. A Pueblo army emissary asked for the head of Maese de Campo Francisco Javier as their "first demand" in seeking a possible end to the violence. Like Acuña and the Salazars, Francisco Javier had guaranteed "safe conduct" to a group of Plains Apaches but proceeded to disarm and distribute "them among his friends as captives, retaining some to sell south in Parral." Brooks, *Captives and Cousins*, 52.

82. AGI, Chile, 53, Expediente de la destitución del Gobernador de Chile, Confesión del Capitan Jerónimo de Molina Basconcelos, Concepción, March 17, 1654, foja 38v. AGI, Escribanía, 932 B, pieza 9, Dated Ciudad de los Reyes, April 10, 1656, Letter (series of protests) "en nombre de" Juan de Salazar by Antonio Perez de Villaroel (Reyes, April 10, 1656, foja 28. AGI, Escribanía, 932 C, pieza 22, Testimony of Don Francisco de Pineda Bascuñán, Concepción, June 29, 1656, fojas 372–73.

83. Barros Arana, *Historia general*, 4:358.

84. Some said that as many as 5,400 horses were killed. AGI, Escribanía, 932 B, pieza 19, Testimonio en Relación de la Culpa . . . , fojas 3v–5v.

85. BN, Manuscritos Medina, tomo 143, pieza 2694, Informe del Consejo de Indias, fechado en Madrid en 30 de Octubre de 1556 [*sic*] a S.M, foja 45.

86. AGI, Escribanía, 932 C, pieza 22, Testimony of Captain Juan de Salazar (not to be confused with the aforementioned maestre de campo of the same name), July 6, 1656, Concepción, foja 610.

87. No charges were brought against José, as he had been killed in the 1655 rebellion.
88. Barros Arana, *Historia general*, 4:368.
89. BN, Los terremotos en Chile (1570–2010), Memoria Chilena.
90. Barros Arana, *Historia general*, 5:16–18.
91. AGI, Chile, 126, Captain Pedro de Anpuero, Santiago, April 27, 1664.
92. Zavala Cepeda, *Los parlamentos*, 139.
93. AGI, Chile, 126, Captain Pedro de Anpuero, Santiago, April 27, 1664.

Chapter 5

1. AGI, Lima, 58, Cartas y expedientes de virreyes de Perú, "Embiando testimonio de lo que ha empecado a obrar Don Alvaro de Ibarra en las caussas del Gobernador de Chile, Don Antonio de Acuña y Cabrera, y repressentando lo que se ha ofrecido en algunas reslutas dellas tocantes al dcho Governador y Don Juan de Salacar, y la fuga que este hico de la Carcel," Conde de Alba, 20 Agosto 1656.
2. Reséndez, *Other Slavery*, 96.
3. Reséndez, *Other Slavery*, 98.
4. Reséndez, *Other Slavery*, 99.
5. AGI, Chile, 53, Testimony of Francisco de Ovalle. Valparaíso, November 9, 1657.
6. AGI, Escribanía, 932 A, Verdict of the Audiencia de Chile, Santiago, June 26, 1660, fojas 578–80.
7. Julio Retamal Ávila, "El concepto del honor en Chile colonial," in *Estudios Coloniales* II, ed. Julio Retamal (Santiago: Editorial Biblioteca Americana, 2002), 43.
8. Archivo Histórico Nacional, "Pruebas para la concesión del Título de Caballero de la Orden de Calatrava de Juan de Salazar y Solís Enríquez," fojas 7r–12v.
9. Slatta, "Spanish Colonial Military Strategy and Ideology," 83.
10. AGI, Escribanía, 932 C, pieza 22, Martín Ruíz de Gamboa. Querellas against Antonio de Acuña y Cabrera and Juan de Salazar, Concepción, June 26, 1656, foja 140; AGI, Escribanía, 932 C, pieza 22, Testimony of Don Francisco de Pineda Bascuñán, Concepción, June 29, 1656, foja 375. Another witness heard Acuña say he wished to force the Indians to rebel in order to justify a counterattack and to "quemarlos a todos." (burn them all). AGI, Escribanía, 932 C, pieza 22, Sargento Mayor Ignacio de Carrera, Información sumaria . . . , Concepción, June 27, 1656, foja 306.
11. AGI, Escribanía, 932 C, pieza 22, Sargento Mayor Ignacio de Carrera, Información sumaria . . . , Concepción, June 27, 1656, fojas 306–6v.
12. AGI, Escribanía, 932 C, pieza 22, Testimony of Don Francisco de Pineda Bascuñán, Concepción, June 29, 1656, fojas 385–87.
13. AGI, Chile, 53, Expediente de la destitución del Gobernador de Chile, Letter from El Provincial de la Compañía de Jesus, Vicente Modele(?), Santiago, June 13, 16[55].
14. AGI, Chile, 57, Real Cédula of April 9, 1662.
15. AGI, Chile, 57, Real Cédula of April 9, 1662.
16. AGI, Chile, 57, Letter from Conde de Santisteban Diego de Benavides a S.M., Lima, November 20, 1662.
17. Feliú Cruz, *Las encomiendas*, 210.
18. Korth, *Spanish Policy*, 190.
19. Barros Arana, *Historia general*, 5:10–11.
20. Barros Arana, *Historia general*, 5:16–17.
21. AGI, Chile, 22, Cartas de Gobernadores, November 2, 1663, Buenos Aires.

22. It appears that Maleo was at least as corrupt as Meneses proved to be. There were at least three judgments against Maleo in the 1660s, one involving the smuggling of non-Spaniards into the Spanish Americas. AGI, Contratación, 5781, no. 202, October 10, 1661.

23. AGI, Chile, 22, Cartas de Gobernadores, November 2, 1663, Buenos Aires, fojas 14r–v.

24. AGI, Chile, 22, November 2, 1663, foja 16r.

25. AGI, Chile, 22, November 2, 1663, fojas 18v–19r.

26. AGI, Chile, 22, November 2, 1663, foja 17v.

27. AGI, Chile, 22, November 2, 1663, foja 26v.

28. AGI, Chile, 22, November 2, 1663, fojas 23v–25v.

29. AGI, Chile, 22, November 2, 1663, fojas 22r–v.

30. Barros Arana, *Historia general,* 5:59.

31. AGI, Chile, 55, Expediente de los excesos del Gobernador Francisco Meneses (1664–1668), Letter from Audiencia de Chile, Santiago, August 9, 1665, fojas 10–11.

32. Barros Arana, *Historia general,* 5:32.

33. AGI, Chile, 126, Pedro de Anpuero, Escribano Público, Santiago, April 27, 1664.

34. AGI, Chile, 55A, Carta de Audiencia, August 9, 1665.

35. AGI, Chile, 55A, Francisco de Meneses and others, Concepción, April 8, 1665.

36. AGI, Chile, 55, Letter to V.M. from Audiencia de Chile, Santiago, February 10, 1666, fojas 2v–3.

37. AGI, Chile, 55A, Juan de la Peña Salazar, et. al. Santiago, February 10, 1666, "Buelbe la Rl Audiencia de Santiago de Chile a dar quenta a VM del miserable estado en que tiene a todo el Reno el Govnernador Don Francisco Meneses," *Expediente de los excesos del Gobernador Francisco Meneses (1664–1668).*

38. AGI, Chile, 55A, Santiago, August 9, 1665, Carta de Audiencia.

39. AGI, Chile,126, Expediente de la actuación del Gobernador de Chile, 1663–65, Fr. D(iego?), Obispo de Santiago de Chile, Letter to S.M., Santiago, August 9, 1664.

40. AGI, Chile, 55A, Santiago, December 20, 1665, Carta de Audiencia.

41. AGI, Chile, 55A, Santiago, December 20, 1665, Carta de Audiencia. Barros Arana, *Historia general,* 5:56–58.

42. AGI, Chile, 55A, Expediente de los excesos del Gobernador Francisco Meneses, (1664–68) (Contenido: Expediente relativo a los excesos cometidos por el Gobernador y Capitán de Chile, Don, . . . durante su mandato. . . . Letter from Audiencia leveling their accusations against him, August 9, 1665.

43. Barros Arana, *Historia general,* 5:69–70.

44. Kris Lane writes that "Clerque" may have been his last name or his occupation (clerk). Lane, *Pillaging the Empire,* 132–33. AGI, Lima, 73, Copy of testimony dated March 12, 1671, in Balparaiso from Dn. Carlos Enríquez Clerque, foja 6.

45. AGI, Lima, 73, Declaration of Don Juan Fortiscue, dated Valdivia, March 14, 1671.

46. AGI, Lima, 73, Declaration of Don Carlos Enríquez, Reyes, April 28, 1671, fojas 47–49.

47. AGI, Chile, 57, Expediente de la libertad de los indios esclavos de guerra, 1674–83, Letter from Jesuit Rosales that he titled, "Memoria de los caciques de paz, que degollo el Capan Pedro de Ripete y de las piezas de paz, que cautivo en esta campeada del año de 1672 . . . ," July 25, 1672.

48. AGI, Chile, 85, Cartas y expedientes de los Virreyes de Lima (sobre asuntos de Chile), Letter from Virrey Conde de la Monclova, Lima, July 15, 1696.

49. Valenzuela, *Las liturgias del poder*, 56.

50. Góngora, *Encomenderos y estanciancieros*, 16–17.

51. Góngora, *Encomenderos y estanciancieros*, 17–18.

52. Not all members of the Audiencia had a conflict with Meneses. While royal regulations prohibited judges from receiving gifts or having property or business, Chile was a small colony with an even smaller aristocracy, and judges could not help but have a close relationship with governors, landowners, and army officers. There were no such prohibitions on members of the town council, however. In fact, typically, prominent landowners were elected to the cabildo. Barros Arana, *Historia general*, 4:175.

53. Valenzuela, *Las liturgias del poder*, 85.

54. AGI, Chile, 55A, Expediente de los excesos del Gobernador Francisco Meneses (1664–68), Expediente relativo a los excesos cometidos por el Gobernador y Capitán de Chile, Don . . . , durante su mandato, Letter from Audiencia (leveling their accusations against him), August 9, 1665, fojas 3, 7v.

55. AGI, Chile, 56, 1671–87, Expediente de la actuación del Gobernador Don Juan Henríquez, Lima, October 27, 1672, Capitán Pedro de la Barreda Zevallos, dueño y maestre del navío nombrado *San Joseph*.

56. Barros Arana, *Historia general*, 4:130–31.

57. AGI, Chile, 56, 1671–87, Expediente de la actuación del Gobernador Don Juan Henríquez, April 12, 1672, and June 20, 1672, Fray Dionisio.

58. AGI, Chile, 56, April 30, 1672, Juan Henríquez.

59. AGI, Chile, 56, Lima, December 4, 1671, Sargento Gno [Geronimo, Genaro] Ruvio.

60. AGI, Chile, 56, October 25, 1672, "Don Feliz de Bustamante Zeballos vecino rregor del cabildo de la cuidad de la Concepción y residente en esta cuidad."

61. AGI, Chile, 56, November 9, 1671, Capn Don Cristobal de Gaona.

62. AGI, Chile, 56, November 9, 1671, Diego Revollo de Alvelda [Aluelda] abogado de la Real Audiencia de Chile.

63. AGI, Chile, 56, October 25, 1672, "Don Feliz de Bustamante Zeballos."

64. AGI, Chile, 56, "Don Feliz de Bustamante Zeballos."

65. AGI, Chile, 56, November 9, 1671, Cappn Don Cristobal de Gaona.

66. AGI, Chile, 56, 1671–87, Expediente de la actuación del Gobernador Don Juan Henríquez, October 25, 1672, "Don Feliz de Bustamante Zeballos."

67. Valenzuela, *Las liturgias del poder*, 51–52.

68. AGI, Chile, 56, November 9, 1671, Diego Revollo de Alvelda [Aluelda].

69. AGI, Chile, 55A, Expediente de los excesos del Gobernador Francisco Meneses, December 4, 1671, Sargento Gno [Geronimo, Genaro] Ruvio.

70. AGI, Chile, 55A, November 9, 1671, Diego Revollo de Alvelda [Aluelda].

71. Larry H. Spruill, "Slave Patrols, 'Packs of Negro Dogs' and Policing Black Communities," *Phylon* 53, no. 1 (2016): 42–66.

72. Jaime Valenzuela Márquez, "Indias esclavas ante la real Audiencia de Chile (1650–1680): Los caminos del amparo judicial para mujeres capturadas en la Guerra de Arauco," in Valenzuela Márquez, *América en Diásporas*, 319–80.

73. In 1631, the Santiago cabildo prohibited non-Europeans in Santiago from using imported clothing. In 1675, the same local authorities specifically limited the use of long hair and capes to Spaniards. Valenzuela, *Las liturgias del poder*, 51–52.

74. Mellafe, *Historia social*, 91–92.

75. One of the accusers was Maestre de Campo Domingo Sánchez Chaparo. AGI, Escribanía, 932 A, Response to charges against him, Antonio Ramírez de Laguna [Santiago, 1659], fojas 324v.–325.

76. AGI, Escribanía, 932 A, Verdict of the Audiencia de Chile, Santiago, June 26, 1660, fojas 578–80.

77. AGI, Chile, 57, Letter from Conde de Santisteban Diego de Benavides a S.M., Lima, November 20, 1662

78. AGI, Chile, 57, Expediente de la libertad de los indios esclavos de guerra, 1674–83, Letter from Rosales, "Memoria de los caciques de paz, que degolló el Capan Pedro de Ripete del año de 1672 . . . ," July 25, 1672.

79. AGI, Chile, 57, Diego de Rosales, S.J., Memoria de los Caciques e indios, que vinieron a dar la paz . . . al Capn Bartholome de Villagrán en esta campeada de 1672 . . . [1672].

80. Feliú Cruz, *Las encomiendas*, 211

81. AGI, Chile, 57, Consejo de Indias, November 6, 1674, Madrid.

82. For more on the campaign to end indigenous slavery after the 1655 uprising, see Andrés Reséndez, "An Early Abolitionist Crusade" *Ethnohistory* 64, no. 1 (2017).

83. AGI, Chile, 57, Letter from S.M. to Audiencia de Chile, Madrid, April 2, 1676.

84. AGI, Chile, 57, Letter from S.M., Madrid, July 15, 1676. Uzanza was an agreement between a colonist and an Indian where the latter would "rent" the labor of a neighbor or family member to the colonist for a period of time. Often, however, the "agreement" involved the colonist kidnapping the Indian or the colonists keeping the "rented" laborer indefinitely. In some cases, the uzanza laborer was even enslaved and sold out of Chile.

85. Feliú Cruz, *Las Encomiendas*, 215–16.

86. Manuel de Odriozola, ed., *Terremotos: Colección de las relaciones de los más notables que ha sufrido esta capital* (Lima: Tipografía de Aurelia Alfaro, 1863), x.

87. Juan de Barrencechea, *Reloj Astronómico de Temblores de la Tierra*, in Odriozola, *Terremotos*, 27.

88. Peter F. Klarén, *Peru: Society and Nationhood in the Andes* (New York: Oxford University Press, 2000), 81.

89. Most historians agree that *ustilago segetum* (black powder) fungus caused this blight, although it is unclear whether the fungus was caused by the earthquake or whether its appearance was a terrible coincidence. At the time, of course, all manner of explanations were offered including the argument that the earthquake released nitrates and sulfates in the soil and the belief that this was a punishment from God. Barros Arana, *Historia general*, 5:220n.

90. Barros Arana, *Historia general*, 5:219n.

Conclusion

1. Collier and Sater, *A History of Chile*, 9.

2. In Chile in 1700, an *arroba* (about 11 kilograms) of wheat was five times more valuable than a head of cattle. Barros Arana, *Historia general*, 5:218–20.

3. Foerster, *Jesuitas y Mapuches*, 140.

4. Barros Arana, *Historia general*, 5:194.

5. Barros Arana, *Historia general*, 5:194.

6. The authoritative work on eighteenth-century parleys is León Solís, *Maloqueros y conchavadores*.

7. Kristine Jones points out that much of this raiding simply moved to the more volatile

Argentine pampa. She adds that this raiding economy persisted into the nineteenth century and had an important role in the formation of the "modern nation states" of Chile and Argentina. Kristine Jones, "La Cautiva: An Argentine Solution to Labor Shortage in the Pampas," in *Brazil and Río de la Plata: Challenge and Response*, ed. Luis Felipe Clay Mendez and Lawrence W. Bates (Charleston: Eastern Illinois University, 1983), 91–94. Just war doctrines provided a number of exceptions to the ban in New Mexico as well. Padre Juan Amondo Niel claimed in 1694 that "Carlos II himself condoned the use of royal funds to ransom Pawnee and Jumano boys and girls held captive by Navajo raiders," who were often destined for beheading if not purchased. Brooks, *Captives and Cousins*, 123.

8. AGI, Chile, 85, Cartas y expedientes de los Virreyes de Lima (sobre asuntos de Chile), Letter from Virrey Conde de la Monclova, Lima, July 15, 1696.

9. AGI, Chile,129, Expediente relativo al Ejército de Chile y su situado, 1680–99, no. 12 in Memoria de los ynstrumentos que el lcdo D. Pablo Vazquez de Velasco Cavo del orden de Santio y fiscal de la R. Auda de Chile remite a su Magd. en comprobazion de lo que en carta de 25 de Septte de 1690 escribe en orden a lo obrado en la distibuzion del situado del exto de chile y de los fraudes y malas administraziones que reconosco y experimento en el dispendio del caudal de dho situado y lo dmas que en dha carta se contiene, Maestre de Campo Geronimo de Quiroga, Letter to Licenciado Don Pablo Vazquez de Velasco . . . Fiscal de la Real Audiencia . . . de Chile, Concepción, February 28, 1690.

10. AGI, Chile, 28, Pedro Correal and other members of the cabildo de Mendoza, Mendoza, November 4, 1692.

11. Cristián Gazmuri, "Rasgos de nuestra mentalidad: Perspectiva pretérita. Nuestra historia y geografía," *El Mercurio*, September 15, 2002.

12. Ward, "A Colonial Woman in a Republican's Chilean History," 85.

13. Collier and Sater, *History of Chile*, 46.

14. Collier and Sater, *History of Chile*, 53.

15. Zavala Cepeda, *Los parlamentos*, 169, 215.

Bibliography

Archival Sources

Chile

Archivo General Nacional (AGN)
Biblioteca Nacional (BN)

Spain

Archivo General de Indias (AGI), Seville
Archivo Histórico Nacional, Madrid

Published Works

Adams, Jerome R. *Notable Latin American Women: Twenty-Nine Leaders, Rebels, Poets, Battlers and Spies, 1500–1900.* Jefferson, NC: McFarland, 1995.

Aguirre, Miguel de. *Población de Valdivia: Motivos y medios para aquella fundación* [. . .]. In *Colección de historiadores de Chile y documentos relativos a la historia nacional*, vol. 45: *Los Holandeses en Chile*, ed. Sociedad Chilena de Historia y Geografía. Santiago: Imprenta Universitaria, 1923.

Aldunate del Solar, Carlos. *Cultura Mapuche*. Santiago: Editorial Gabriela Mistral, 1978.

———. *Mapuche, Seeds of the Chilean Soul: An Exhibit at the Port of History Museum at Penn's Landing, Philadelphia, Pennsylvania, March 27–June 30, 1992.* Translated by Richard C. Baker and Peter W. Kendall. Santiago: Museo Chileno de Arte Precolombiano, 1992.

Altoagurrie y Duvalle, Angel, ed. *Colección de las memorias o relaciones que escribieron los Virreyes del Perú: Tomo II.* Madrid: Imp. del Asilo de Huérfanos del S.C. de Jesús, 1921.

Álvarez, Gregorio. *Neuquén, su historia, su geografía, su toponimia.* Neuqén, Argentina: Universidad de Neuquén, 1972.

Amunátegui Solar, Domingo. "La trata de negros en Chile." *Revista Chilena de Historia y Geografía* 91, no. 46 (1922): 25–41.

———. *Mayorazgos y títulos de Castilla: Tomo Segundo.* Santiago: Imprenta Barcelona, 1901.

Aránguiz Donoso, Horacio. "Notas para el estudio de la hacienda de La Calera de Tango, 1685–1783." *Historia. Universidad Católica de Chile* 6 (1967): 221–62.

Arias de Saavedra, Diego. *Purén Indómito.* Concepción, Chile: Universidad de Concepción, 1984.

Armond, Louis de. "Frontier Warfare in Colonial Chile." In *Where Cultures Meet. Frontiers in Latin American History*. 2nd ed., edited by David J. Weber and Jane M. Rausch. 115–22. Wilmington, DE: Jaguar Books, 1994.

Ávila Martel, Alamiro de, ed. "Instrucciones para la Guerra de Arauco dadas por Acuña y Cabrera para las compañas de 1654 y 1655." *Revista Chilena de Historia del Derecho, Número 2*, 1961, 68–79.

Barclay, W. S.. *The Land of Magellan*. New York: Brentano's Publishers, 1926.

Barrencechea, Juan de. "Reloj astronómico de temblores de la Tierra." In Odriozola, *Terremotos*, 5–6 and [i]–xxiii.

Barros Arana, Diego. *Historia general de Chile*. Vols. 1–5. 2nd. ed. Santiago: Editorial Universitaria, 1999.

———. "La Monja Alférez-Algunas observaciones críticas sobre su historia-Noticias desconocidas acerca de su muerte." *Revista de Santiago* 1 (1872): 225–34.

Bauer, Ralph. "Imperial History, Captivity and Creole Identity in Francisco Núñez de Pineda y Bascuñán's *Cautiverio feliz*." *Colonial Latin American Review* 7, no. 1 (June 1998): 59–83.

Beltrán y Rózpide, Ricardo, ed. *Colección de las memorias o relaciones que escribieron los Virreyes del Perú acerca del estado en que dejaban las cosas generales del reino*. Vol. 1. Madrid: Imp. Del Asilo de Huérfanos del S.C. de Jesús, 1921.

Bengoa, José. *Historia de los antiguos Mapuches del sur*. Santiago: Catalonia, 2003.

———. *Historia del pueblo Mapuche*. Santiago: Ediciones Sur, 1985.

Berger, Eugene Clark. "Permanent War on Peru's Periphery: Frontier Identity and the Politics of Conflict in 17th Century Chile." PhD diss., Vanderbilt University, 2006.

Berlin, Ira. *Many Thousands Gone: The First Two Centuries of Slavery in North America*. Cambridge, MA: Harvard University Press, 1998.

Boccara, Guillaume. "Etnogénesis Mapuche: Resistencia y restructuración entre los indígenas del centro-sur de Chile (Siglos XVI-XVIII)." *Hispanic American Historical Review* 79, no. 3 (August 1999): 425–61.

Bolton, Herbert. "Defensive Spanish Expansion and the Significance of the Borderlands: An Address Delivered at the Boulder Conference on the History of the Trans-Mississippi West." June 1929. Reprinted from the Proceedings.

———. *The Spanish Borderlands: A Chronicle of Old Florida and the Southwest*. Whitefish, MT: Kessinger Publishing, 1921.

Bradley, Peter T. *The Lure of Peru: Maritime Intrusion into the South Sea, 1598–1701*. London: Palgrave Macmillan, 2014.

Brioso Santos, Héctor. *América en la prosa literaria Española de los siglos XVI y XVII*. Huelva, Spain: Diputación Provincial de Huelva, 1998.

Brooks, James F. *Captives and Cousins: Slavery, Kinship and Community in the Southwest Borderlands*. Chapel Hill: University of North Carolina Press, 2002.

Calderón, Melchior. *Tratado de la importancia y utilidad que ay en dar por esclavos a los indios rebelados de Chile*. Madrid, 1607.

Campos Harriet, Fernando. "La destitución del Gobernador Acuña y Cabrera en 1655." *Boletín de la Academía Chilena de Historia* 56, no. 100 (1989): 121–35.

Canals Frau, Salvador. *Las poblaciones indígenas de la Argentina: Su origen—su pasado—su presente*. Buenos Aires: Editorial Sudamericana, 1953.

Carvallo Goyeneche, Vicente. *Descripción-histórico-jeográfica del reino de Chile*. In *Colección de historiadores de Chile y documentos relativos a la historia nacional*. Vol. 8.

Santiago: Imprenta del Ferrocarril, 1875. Disponible en Memoria Chilena, Biblioteca Nacional de Chile.

Chuecas Saldías, Ignacio. "Esclavitud indígena y economías familiares en el Chile del siglo XVII." In Valenzuela Márquez, *América en diásporas*, 197–250.

Collier, Simon. *Ideas and Politics of Chilean Independence: 1808–1833*. Cambridge: Cambridge University Press, 1967.

Collier, Simon, and William F. Sater. *A History of Chile, 1808–1994*. Cambridge: Cambridge University Press, 1996.

Contreras, Miguel de, and Noble David Cook, eds. *Padrón de indios de Lima en 1613*. Lima: Universidad Nacional Mayor de San Marcos, 1968.

Contreras Cruces, Hugo. "Fortificaciones, logística, y vida de cuartel en el Real Ejército de Chile durante el siglo XVII." *Boletín Americanista* 2, no. 77 (2018): 203–23.

Corporación Latinobarómetro. "Latinobarómetro libro de códigos: 2017." *Latinobarómetro: Opinión pública latinoamericana*. Chile_v20181701.

Crespi, Liliana. "Comercio negrero en el Río de la Plata durante el siglo XVII. Comerciantes y rutas de distribución hacia las provincias internas, Chile y Perú." Paper presented at Reunión: La ruta del esclavo en hispanoamérica, San José, Costa Rica, February 24–26, 1999.

Cruz, Nicolás de la. "Diario de viaje de Talca a Cádiz, 1783." Edited by Rafael A. Soto. Santiago: Imprenta Universitaria, 1942.

Deeds, Susan M. "Indigenous Rebellions on the Northern Mexican Mission Frontier: From First-Generation to Later Colonial Responses." In *Contested Ground: Comparative Frontiers on the Northern and Southern Edges of the Spanish Empire*, edited by Donna J. Guy and Thomas E. Sheridan, 32–51. Tucson: University of Arizona Press, 1998.

Deverell, William. *Whitewashed Adobe: The Rise of Los Angeles and the Remaking of Its Mexican Past*. Berkeley: University of California Press, 2005.

Dillehay, Tom D., ed. *Late Prehispanic and Hispanic Ceramics in the Purén, Lumaco, and Liucura Valleys, La Araucanía, Chile*. Nashville: Vanderbilt University Publications in Anthropology, 2010.

———. *Monuments, Empires and Resistance*. Cambridge: Cambridge University Press, 2012.

———. "Reflections on Araucanian/Mapuche Resilience, Independence, and Ethnomorphosis in Colonial (and Present-Day) Chile." *Chungara, Revista de Antropología Chilena* 48, no. 4 (2016): 691–702.

Dillehay, Tom D., and Carlos Aldunate del Solar. *Araucanía: Presente y Pasado*. Santiago: Editorial Andrés Bello, 1990.

Douglass, Frederick. "The Constitution of the United States: Is It Pro-Slavery or Anti-Slavery?" March 26, 1860. Teaching American History.

Elliot, J. H. *Imperial Spain: 1469–1716*. London: Penguin, 1963.

———. "The Spanish Conquest and Settlement of America." In *The Cambridge History of Latin America*, vol 1, edited by Leslie Bethell, 149–206. Cambridge: Cambridge University Press, 1984.

Eltis, David. *The Rise of African Slavery in the Americas*. Cambridge: Cambridge University Press, 2000.

Ercilla, Alonso de. *The Araucaniad: A Version in English Poetry of Alonso de Ercilla Zúñiga's La Araucanca*. Translated by Charles M. Lancaster and Paul T. Manchester. Nashville, Vanderbilt University Press, 2013.

———. *La Araucana*. Santiago: Editorial Andrés Bello, 1983.

Espejo, Juan Luis. *La Provincia de Cuyo del Reino de Chile*. Santiago: Fondo Histórico y Bibliográfico José Toribio Medina, 1954.

Erauso, Catalina de. *Historia de la Monja Alférez, Catalina de Erauso, Escrita por ella misma*. Edited by Angel Esteban. Madrid: Ediciones Cátedra, 2002.

Feliú Cruz, Guillermo. *La Abolición de la esclavitúd en Chile: Estudio histórico y social*. 2nd ed. Santiago: Editorial Universitaria, 1973.

———. *Las encomiendas según tasas y ordenanzas*. Buenos Aires: Talleres Jacobo Peuser, 1941.

Fernández de Oviedo y Valdés, Gonzalo. *Historia general y natural de las Indias, biblioteca de autores Españoles*. Vol. 121. Madrid: Ediciones Atlas, 1959.

Flusche, Della M. *Two Families in Colonial Chile*. Lewiston, NY: Edwin Mellen Press, 1989.

Flusche, Della M., and Eugene H. Korth. *Forgotten Females: Women of African and Indian Descent in Colonial Chile, 1535–1800*. Detroit: Blaine Ethridge Books, 1983.

Foerster, Rolf G. *Introducción a la religiosidad Mapuche*. Santiago: Editorial Universitaria, 1993.

———. *Jesuitas y Mapuches, 1593–1767*. Santiago: Editorial Universitaria, S.A., 1996.

Furlong, Guillermo. *Nicolás Mascardi, S.J. y su Carta-Relación. (1670)*. Buenos Aires: Ediciones Theoria, 1963.

Gallay, Alan. *The Formation of a Planter Elite: Jonathan Bryan and the Southern Colonial Frontier*. Athens: University of Georgia Press, 2007.

———. *The Indian Slave Trade: The Rise of the English Empire in the American South, 1670–1717*. New Haven, CT: Yale University Press, 2002.

———. "Jonathan Bryan's Plantation Empire: Land, Politics, and the Formation of a Ruling Class in Colonial Georgia." *William and Mary Quarterly* 3rd ser., 45, no. 2 (April 1988): 253–79.

Ganson, Barbara. *The Guaraní under Spanish Rule in the Río de la Plata*. Stanford, CA: Stanford University Press, 2003.

Garcilaso de la Vega, Inca. *Historia general del Peru: Segunda Parte de los Comentarios Reales*. Vol. 1. Lima: Editorial Universo S.A., 1970.

———. *Los Comentarios Reales de los Inkas*. Vol. 2. Lima: Imprenta y Librería Sanmarti y Ca., 1918.

Gascón, Margarita. "Comerciantes y redes mercantiles del siglo XVII en la frontera sur del Virreinato del Perú." *Anuario de Estudios Americanos* 57, no. 2 (July/December 2000): 413–48.

———. "Frontier Societies: A View from the Southern Frontier of the Indies." *International Seminar on the History of the Atlantic World, 1500–1800*. Harvard University, Working Paper No. 02–04.

———. "La frontera sur del Virreinato del Perú en el siglo XVII. Recursos, catastrophes y estrategias imperiales." Paper presented at the Encuentro de historiadoes Argentinos y Peruanos, Lima, September 2004.

Gay, Claudio, ed. *Historia fisica y politica de Chile: Documentos. Tomo primero*. Paris: Imprenta de Maulde Y Renou, 1846.

———, ed. *Historia fisica y politica de Chile: Documentos sobre la historia, la estadistica y la geografía*. Vol. 2. Santiago: Museo de Historia Natural, 1852.

Gazmuri, Cristián. "Rasgos de nuestra mentalidad: Perspectiva pretérita. Nuestra historia y geografía." *El Mercurio*, September 15, 2002.

Geertz, Clifford. *Negara: The Theatre and State in Nineteenth Century Bali*. Princeton, NJ: Princeton University Press, 1980.

Glave, Luis Miguel. *De rosa y espinas: Economía, sociedad y mentalidades, siglo XVII*. Lima: IEP, 1998.

Góngora, Mario. *Encomenderos y Estancianceros: Estudios acerca de la constitución social aristocrática de Chile después de la Conquista: 1580–1660*. Santiago: Universidad de Chile, 1970.

———. *Orígen de los inquilinos de Chile central*. Santiago: Instituto de Capacitación e Investigación en Reforma Agraria, 1974.

———. "Urban Social Stratification in Colonial Chile." *Hispanic American Historical Review* 55, no. 3 (1975): 421–48.

———. "Vagabundaje y sociedad fronteriza en Chile (Siglos XVII a XIX)." *Cuadernos del Centro de Estudios Socioeconómicos* 2 (1966): 1–41.

Góngora Marmolejo, Alonso de. *Historia de Chile desde su descubrimiento hasta el año de 1575*. In *Colección de historiadores de chile y documentos relativos a la historia nacional*. Vol. 2. Santiago: Imprenta del Ferrocarril, 1862. Disponible en Memoria Chilena, Biblioteca Nacional de Chile.

González de Gispert, Jaime. "'Aquí no hay negros': Cómo se borró de la historia de Argentina y Chile el aporte de los esclavos y los afrodescendientes." BBC News Mundo, June 11, 2019.

González de Nájera, Alonso. *Desengaño y reparo de la guerra del Reino de Chile*. Santiago: Editorial Universitaria, 1970.

———. *Desengaño y reparo de la guerra del Reino de Chile*. Santiago: Imprenta Ercilla, 1889.

González Vargas, Carlos, and Hugo Rosati Aguerre. "Métodos y formas de resistencia indígena en la crónica de Gerónimo de Bibar." *Diálogo Andino* 38 (2011): 45–73.

Grandin, Greg. *The Empire of Necessity*. New York: Picador, 2014.

Guevara, Ernesto "Che." *The Motorcycle Diaries: Notes on a Latin American Journey*. Translated and edited by Alexandra Keeble. New York: Ocean Press, 2003.

Guevara, Tomás. *Historia de la civilización de Araucanía*. Vol. 1: *Antropolojía Araucana*. Santiago: Imprenta Cervantes, 1898.

Hale Shields, Robert. *The Legend of the Caesars and the Patagonaian Expedition of Gerónimo Luis de Cabrera, 1620–1621*. Unpublished PhD diss., University of California, Berkeley, [1940?].

Hanke, Lewis. *The Imperial City of Potosí: An Unwritten Chapter in the History of Spanish America*. The Hague: Martinus Nijhoff, 1956.

———. "An Unpublished Document on the Junta de Hacienda de Indias." *Revista de Indias* 20 (1960): 134–141.

Hunefeldt, Christine. *A Brief History of Peru*. New York: Facts on File, 2004.

Invernizzi Santa Cruz, Lucía. "'Los trabajos de la guerra' y 'Los trabajos del hambre': Dos ejes del discurso narrativo de la cnquista de Chile (Valdivia, Vivar, Góngora Marmolejo)." *Revista Chilena de Literatura* 36 (1990): 7–15.

Jara, Alvaro. *Fuentes para la historia del trabajo en el Reino de Chile* Vol. 3: *Alquileres y ventas de indios, 1599–1620*. Santiago: Editorial Universidad Católica, 1958.

———. *Guerra y sociedad en Chile y otros temas*. 3rd ed. Santiago: Editorial Universitaria, 1984.

———. "Importación de trabajadores indígenas en el siglo XVII." *Revista Chilena de Historia y Geografía* 124 (1958): 177–212.

Jara, Alvaro, and Sonia Pinto. *Fuentes para la historia del trabajo en el Reino de Chile: Legislación, 1546–1810: II*. Santiago: Editorial Bello, 1983.

Jones, Kristine L. "La Cautiva: An Argentine Solution to Labor Shortage in the Pampas." In *Brazil and Río de la Plata: Challenge and Response*, edited by Luis Felipe Clay Mendez and Lawrence W. Bates, 91–94. Charleston: Eastern Illinois University, 1983.

———. "Warfare, Reorganization, and Readaptation at the Margins of Spanish Rule: The Southern Margin (1573–1882)." In *The Cambridge History of the Native Peoples of the Americas*. Vol 3: *South America, Part II*, edited by Frank Salomon and Stuart B. Schwartz, 138–87. Cambridge: Cambridge University Press, 2008.

Klarén, Peter F. *Peru: Society and Nationhood in the Andes*. New York: Oxford University Press, 2000.

Klein, Herbert S. *The Atlantic Slave Trade*. 2nd ed. New York: Cambridge University Press, 2010.

Korth, Eugene. *Spanish Policy in Colonial Chile: The Search for Social Justice, 1535–1700*. Stanford, CA: Stanford University Press, 1968.

Lacoste, Pablo, ed. *Sistema Pehuenche: Frontera, sociedad y caminos en los Andes centrales Argentinos Chilenos (1658–1997)*. Mendoza, Argentina: Universidad Nacional de Cuyo, 1998.

Landers, Jane. *Black Society Spanish Florida*. Urbana: University of Illinois Press, 1999.

Lane, Kris. *Pillaging the Empire: Piracy in the Americas, 1500–1750*. Armonk, NY: M. E. Sharpe, 1998.

Langfur, Hal. "Moved by Terror: Frontier Violence as Cultural Exchange in Late-Colonial Brazil." *Ethnohistory* 52, no. 2 (Spring 2005): 255–89.

Las Casas, Bartolomé de. *An Account, Much Abbreviated, of the Destruction of the Indies*. Translated by Stafford Poole. Edited by Franklin W. Knight. Indianapolis: Hackett, 2003.

León Echaiz, René. *El Toqui Lautaro*. Santiago: Talleres de Ricardo Neupert, 1971.

León Solís, Leonardo. "Expansión Inca y resistencia indígena en Chile, 1470–1536." *Chungara: Revista de Antropología Chilena* 10 (1983): 95–115.

———. *Maloqueros y conchavadores en Araucanía y las Pampas, 1700–1800*. Temuco, Chile: Ediciones Universidad de la Frontera, 1990.

Lewis, Stephen E. "Myth and the History of Chile's Araucanians." *Radical History Review* 58 (Winter 1994): 113–141.

MacLeod, Murdo J. "Spain and America: The Atlantic Trade 1492–1720." In *The Cambridge History of Latin America*, vol. 1, edited by Leslie Bethell, 341–88. Cambridge: Cambridge University Press, 1984.

Marimán, Pablo, Sergio Caniuqueo, José Millalén, Rodrigo Levil. *¡ . . . Escucha Winka . . . !: Cuatro ensayos de historia nacional Mapuche y un epílogo sobre el futuro*. Santiago: LOM Ediciones, 2017.

Mariño de Lobera, Pedro. *Crónica del Reino de* Chile. Santiago: Editorial Universitaria, 1970.

Márquez de la Plata, Fernando. "Documentos relativos a la introduccíon de esclavos negros en América" *Revista Chilena de Historia y Geografía* 61–63 (1928): 226–49.

Matthew, Laura E., and Michael R. Oudijk, eds. *Indian Conquistadors: Indigenous Allies in the Conquest of Mesoamerica*. Norman: University of Oklahoma Press, 2012.

McAlister, Lyle N. *Spain and Portugal in the New World*. Minneapolis: University of Minnesota Press, 1989.

Medina, José Toribio, ed. *Colección de documentos inéditos para la historia de Chile: Desde el viaje de Magallanes hasta la Batalla de Maipo: 1518–1818*. Santiago: Imprenta y Encuardernación Barcelona, 1895.

———, ed. *Colección de documentos inéditos para la historia de Chile: Segunda Serie*. Vol. 2. Santiago: Fondo Historico y Bibliográfico J. T. Medina, 1956.

Mellafe, Rolando. *Historia social de Chile y América: Sugerencias y aproximaciones*. Santiago: Editorial Universitaria, 1986.

———. *La introducción de la esclavitud negra en Chile: Tráfico y rutas*. Santiago: Universidad de Chile, 1959.

Meuwese, Mark, trans. *To the Shores of Chile: The Journal and History of the Brouwer Expedition to Valdivia in 1643*. University Park: Pennsylvania State University Press, 2019.

Miraflores, Marqués de, and D. Miguel Salva, eds. *Colección de documentos inéditos para la historia de España*. Vol. 48. Madrid: Imprenta de la Viuda de Calero, 1866.

Molina, Giovanni Ignazio. *The Geographical, Natural and Civil History of Chili*. Vol. 2. Middletown, CT: I. Riley, 1808.

Molina, Raul. *Territorio y comunidades Pehuenches del Alto Bío-Bío*. Santiago: Corporación Nacional de Desarrollo Indígena, 1996.

Monardes, Dr. Nicoloso de. *Dos libros, El uno que trata de todas las cosas que traen de nuestras Indias Occidentales, que sirven al use de la medicina, y el otro quetTrata de la piedra bezaar, y de la yerba escuaerconera. Compuestos por el doctór . . . Medico de Sevilla*. Seville: Hernando Díaz, 1569.

Monteiro, John M. *Blacks of the Land: Indian Slavery, Settler Society, and the Portuguese Colonial Enterprise in South America*. Translated and edited by James Woodard and Barbara Weinstein. Cambridge: Cambridge University Press, 2018.

Moore, Jerry D. *A Prehistory of South America: Ancient Cultural Diversity on the Least Known Continent*. Boulder: University Press of Colorado, 2014.

Morales, Raul. *La Monja Alférez: Crónica de una vida que tuvo perfil de romance*. Santiago: Excelsior, 1938.

Moreno, Pedro, ed. *La Monja Alférez Doña Catalina de Erauso: Dos manuscritos autobiográficos inéditos de su autobiografía conservados en el archivo de la Santa Iglesia Catedral de Sevilla*. Seville: Ediciones del Cabildo Metropolitano de la Catedral de Sevilla, 1995.

Morgan, Edmund S. *American Slavery, American Freedom: The Ordeal of Colonial Virginia*. New York: Norton, 1975.

Moutoukias, Zacarias. "Power, Corruption, and Commerce: The Making of the Local Administrative Structure in Seventeenth-Century Buenos Aires." *Hispanic American Historical Review* 68, no. 4 (November 1988): 771–801.

Mulcahy, Matthew. *Hubs of Empire: The Southeastern Lowcountry and British Caribbean*. Baltimore: Johns Hopkins University Press, 2014.

Muñoz Correa, Juan Guillermo. "La esclavitud indígena, El caso de Colchagua." *Revista de Historia Social y de las Mentalidades* 2, no. 7 (2003): 113–47.

Núñez de Pineda y Bascuñán, Francisco. *Cautiverio feliz y razón individual de las guerras dilatadas del Reino de Chile*. Santiago: Editorial Universitaria, 1973.

———. *Suma y epilogo de lo mas esencial que contiene el libro intitulado: Cautivero feliz, y guerras dilatiadas del Reino de Chile*. Edited by Robert A. McNeil. Santiago: Ediciones Universidad Católica de Chile, 1984.

Obregón Iturra, Jimena. "'Indios en *collera*,' Deportaciones coloniales de trabajadores Huarpes y Aucaes razón de estado e intereses particulares. Chile, 1598–1658." *Revista Tiempo Historico* 9, no. 16 (Enero–Junio 2018): 15–38.

Ocaña, Diego de. *Relación del viaje a Chile, año de 1600, contenida en la crónica intitulada "A través de la América del Sur."* Santiago: Editorial Universitaria, 1995.

Odriozola, Manuel de, ed., *Terremotos: Colección de las relaciones de los más notables que ha sufrido esta capital.* Lima: Tipografía de Aurelia Alfaro, 1863.

O'Malley, Gregory E. "Beyond the Middle Passage: Slave Migration from the Caribbean to North America, 1619–1807." *William and Mary Quarterly*, 3rd ser., 66, no. 1 (January 2009): 125–72.

Operé, Fernando. *Indian Captivity in Spanish America: Frontier Narratives.* Translated by Gustavo Pellón. Charlottesville: University of Virginia Press, 2008.

Ovalle, Alonso de. *Histórica relación del Reino de Chile.* Santiago: Zig-Zag, 1961.

Pacheco Silva. "Una economía de conquista: Concepción Siglo XVI." *Revista de Historia (Concepción)* Año 1, 1 (1991): 25–44.

Padden, Robert Charles. "Cultural Adaptation and Militant Autonomy among the Mapuches of Chile." In *The Indian in Latin American History: Resistance, Resilience and Acculturation*, edited by John E. Kicza, 71–92. Wilmington, DE: Scholarly Resources, 1993.

Payás Puigarnau, Gertrudis. "¿Qué hacen las mujeres Mapuches y Españolas en los parlamentos Hispano-Mapuches." In *Mujeres: Olvidos y memorias en los márgenes: Chile y América, siglos XVII-XXI*, edited by Yéssica González Gómez, 153–68. Temuco, Chile: Ediciones Universidad de la Frontera, 2020.

Paul III. *Sublimis Deus.* June 1537. In Las Casas, *Account*, xxvii–xxviii.

Pérez-Mallaína, Pablo E. "La fabricación de un mito: El terremoto de 1687 y la ruina de los cultivos de trigo en el Perú." *Anuario de Estudios Americanos* 57, no. 1 (2000): 69–88.

Pighi Bel, Pierina. "El matrimonio entre la "Última Gran Princesa Inca" y un Capitán Español que selló la conquista de Perú." BBC News Mundo, January 26, 2020.

Pinto Rodríguez, Jorge. *Misioneros en la Araucanía, 1600–1900.* Vol. 1. Bogotá: Consejo Episcopal Latinoamericano, 1990.

———. "Producción e intercambio en un espacio fronterizo. Araucanía y Pampas en el siglo XVIII." In *Mercados indígenas en México, Chile y Argentina*, edited by Jorge Silva Riquer and Antonio Escovar Ohmstede, 148–76. Mexico City: Desarrollo Gráfico Editorial, 2000.

Pocock, H. R. S. *The Conquest of Chile.* New York: Stein and Day, 1967.

Powell, Philip Wayne. *Mexico's Miguel Caldera: The Taming of America's First Frontier, 1548–1597.* Tucson: University of Arizona Press, 1977.

Ramírez Necochea, Hernán. *Antecedentes económicos de la independencia de Chile.* Santiago: Universidad de Chile, 1967.

Ramos, Demetrio. *Trigo chileno, navieros del Callao y hacendados limeños entre la crisis agrícola del siglo XVII y la comercial de la primera mitad del XVIII.* Madrid: Instituto "Gonzalo Fernández de Oviedo," 1967.

Reséndez, Andrés. *The Other Slavery: The Uncovered Story of Indian Enslavement in America.* Boston: Mariner Books, Houghton Mifflin, 2016.

Restall, Matthew. "Black Conquistadors: Armed Africans in Early Spanish America." *Americas* 57, no. 2 (2000): 171–205.

Retamal Ávila, Julio. "El concepto del honor en Chile colonial." In *Estudios Coloniales*, vol. 2, edited by Julio Retamal, 41–56. Santiago: Editorial Biblioteca Americana, 2002.

Retamal Favereu, Julio. *Familias fundadoras de Chile—1540–1600: Colonos en la frontera.* Santiago: Zig-Zag, 1992.

Rivera, Mario A. "Prehistory of the Southern Cone." In *The Cambridge History of the Native Peoples of the Americas.* Vol 3: *South America, Part I*, edited by Frank Salomon and Stuart B. Schwartz, 734–68. Cambridge: Cambridge University Press, 2008.

Rock, David. *Argentina 1516–1987.* Berkeley: University of California Press, 1987.

Rodríguez Fernández, Mariano. "Estudio Preliminar." In *Purén indómito*, edited by Diego Arias de Saavedra, 99–102. Concepción: Universidad de Concepción, 1984.

Rosales, Diego de. *Historia general del Reino de Chile, Flandes indiano.* Vol. 1. 2nd ed. Santiago: Editorial Andrés Bello, 1989.

———. *Historia general del Reyno de Chile: Flandes indiano.* Vol. 3. Valparaíso, Chile: Imprenta del Mercurio, 1878.

Ruíz-Esquide Figueroa, Andrea. *Los Indios Amigos en la frontera Araucana.* Santiago: Editorial Universitaria, 1993.

Rushforth, Brett. *Bonds of Alliance: Indigenous and Atlantic Slaveries in New France.* Chapel Hill: University of North Carolina Press, 2014.

Sánchez Pérez, Macarena. "De cautivos a esclavos: Algunos problemas metodológicos para el estudio de los indios cautivos en la Guerra de Arauco." In Valenzuela Márquez, ed., *América en diásporas*, 133–60.

Schmidt, Benjamin. *Innocence Abroad: The Dutch Imagination and the New World, 1570–1670.* Cambridge: Cambridge University Press, 2001.

Schröter, Bernd. "La frontera en Hispanoamérica colonial: Un estudio historiográfico comparativo." *Colonial Latin American Historical Review*, Summer 2001, 351–85.

Silva Galdames, Osvaldo. *Atlas de Historia de Chile.* Santiago: Editorial Universitaria, 1983.

———. "¿Detuvo la Batalla del Maule la expansión Inca hacía el sur de Chile?" *Cuadernos de Historia* 3 (Julio 1983): 7–25.

———. "Guerra y trueque como factores de cambio en la estructura social." In *Economía y comercio en América Hispana*, edited by Guillermo Bravo Acevedo, 83–95. Santiago: Departamento de Ciencias Histórica, Facultad de Filosofía y Humanidades, Universidad de Chile, 1990.

Silva Galdames, Osvaldo, and José Luis Schroeder Gutiérrez. *Historia de Chile ilustrada.* Santiago: La Tercera, 1998.

Slatta, Richard. "Spanish Colonial Military Strategy and Ideology." In *Contested Ground: Comparative Frontiers on the Northern and Southern Edges of the Spanish Empire*, edited by Donna J. Guy and Thomas E. Sheridan, 83–96. Tucson: University of Arizona Press, 1998.

Snyder, Christina. *Slavery in Indian Country: The Changing Face of Captivity in Early America.* Cambridge, MA: Harvard University Press, 2012.

Sociedad Chilena de Historia y Geografía and Academia Chilena de la Historia, eds. *Colección de historiadores de Chile y de documentos relativos a la historia nacional.* Vol. 20, *Actas del Cabildo de Santiago.* Vol. 5. Santiago: Imprenta Elzeviriana, 1900.

———. *Colección de historiadores de Chile y de documentos relativos a la historia nacional.* Vol. 45, *Los Holandeses en Chile.* Santiago: Imprenta Universitaria, 1923.

Socolow, Susan Migden. "Spanish Captives in Indian Societies: Cultural Contact along the Argentine Frontier, 1600–1835." *Hispanic American Historical Review* 72, no. 1 (February 1992): 73–99.

Solar Correa, Eduardo. *Semblanzas literarias de la colonia*. Santiago: Editorial Difusión Chilena S.A., 1945.

Spruill, Larry H. "Slave Patrols, 'Packs of Negro Dogs' and Policing Black Communities." *Phylon* 53, no. 1 (2016): 42–66

St. Clair, William. *The Door of No Return: The History of Cape Coast Castle and the Atlantic Slave Trade*. New York: BlueBridge, 2006.

Stevens, Henry, ed. *The New Laws of the Indies*. London: Chiswick Press, 1893.

Studer, Elena F. S. de. *La trata de negros en el Río de la Plata Durante el siglo XVIII*. Montevideo: Libros de Hispanoamérica, 1984.

Tapson, Alfred J. "Indian Warfare on the Pampa during the Colonial Period." *Hispanic American Historical Review* 42, no. 1 (February 1962): 1–28.

Te Paske, John. "The Costs of Empire Spending Patterns and Priorities in Colonial Peru, 1581–1820." *Colonial Latin American Historical Review* 2 (Winter 1993): 1–34.

Tesillo, Santiago de. *Guerra de Chile, causas de su duración, medios para su fin exempilicado en el gobierno de Don Francisco Lasso de la Vega*. Madrid: Imprenta Real, 1647.

Thayer Ojeda, Tomás, and Carlos Larraín de Castro. *Valdivia y sus compañeros*. Santiago: Academia Chilena de la Historia, 1950.

Urbina Carrasco, María Ximena. *La frontera de arriba en Chile colonial: Interacción Hispano-indígena en el territorio entre Valdivia y Chiloé e imaginario de sus bordes geográficos, 1600–1800*. Valparaíso, Chile: Ediciones Universitarias de Valparaíso, 2009.

Usner, Daniel. *Indians, Settlers, and Slaves in a Frontier Exchange Economy: The Lower Mississippi Valley before 1783*. Chapel Hill: University of North Carolina Press, 1992.

———. "Rescuing Early America from Nationalist Narratives: An Intra-Imperial Approach to Colonial Canada and Louisiana." *Historical Reflections/Réflexions Histoirques* 40, no. 3 (Winter 2014): 1–19.

Utley, Robert M. *The Last Sovereigns: Sitting Bull and the Resistance of the Free Lakotas*. Lincoln, NE: Bison Books, 2020.

Valdes Bunster, Gustavo. *El poder económico de los Jesuitas en Chile (1593–1767)*. Santiago: Imprenta Pucará, 1985.

Valdivia, Luis de. "Relación de lo que sucedió en la jornada que hizimos el Señor Presidente Alonso de Ribera, Governador deste reyno, y yo, desde Arauco a Paicaví, a concluir las Pazes de Elicura, última regua de Tucapl, y las de Purén, y la Imperial. Escrita por mi el Padre Luis de Valdivia, al salir de Paicaví, de vuelta a Levo." In *Americana Series; Photostat Reproductions by the Massachusetts Historical Society*, no. 223. [Lima?, 1613?]

Valdivia, Pedro de. "Cartas de Pedro de Valdivia que tratan del descubrimiento y conquista del Reino de Chile." *Crónicas del Reino de Chile*. Madrid: Atlas, 1960.

Valenzuela Márquez, Jaime, ed. *América en diásporas: Esclavitudes y migraciones forzadas en Chile y otras regiones Americanas (Siglos XVI-XIX)*. Santiago: RIL Editores, 2017.

———. "Esclavos Mapuches. Para una historia del secuestro y deportación de indígenas en la colonia." In *Historias de racismo y discriminación en Chile*, edited by Rafael Gaune, Martín Lara, and Margarita Alvarado, 225–62. Santiago: Uqbar Editores, 2009.

———. "Indias esclavas ante la Real Audiencia de Chile (1650–1680): Los caminos del

amparo judicial para mujeres capturadas en la Guerra de Arauco." In Valenzuela Márquez, *América en diásporas*, 319–80.
———. *Las liturgias del poder: Celebraciones públicas y estrategias persuasivas en Chile colonial (1609–1709)*. Santiago: LOM Ediciones, 2001.
Vallbona, Rima R. "Realidad histórica y ficción en *Vida y sucesos de la Monja Alférez*." PhD. diss., Middlebury College, 1981.
Vargas Cariola, Juan Eduardo. "Financiamiento del Ejército de Chile en el Siglo XVII." *Historia* 19 (1984): 159–202.
Vega, Garcilaso de la. *Los comentarios reales de los Incas*. Vol. 2. Lima: Imprenta y Librería Sanmarti y Ca., 1918.
Vial Correa, Gonzalo. *El Africano en el Reino de Chile: Ensayo histórico—jurídico*. Santiago: Universidad Catolica de Chile, 1957.
Vicuña Mackenna, Benjamín. *Historia de Santiago*. Vol. 2. *Obras completas de Vicuña Mackenna Volumen XI*. Santiago: Universidad de Chile, 1938.
———. *Historia de Valparaíso*. Vol. 1. Santiago: Universidad de Chile, 1936.
———. *Los Lisperguer y la Quintrala: (Doña Catalina de los Ríos): Episodio histórico-social con numerosos documentos inéditos*. Valparaíso: Imprenta del Mercurio, 1877.
Villalobos, Sergio. *Los Pehuenches en la vida fronteriza*. Santiago: Ediciones Universidad Católica de Chile, 1989.
———. *Tres siglos y medio de vida fronteriza*. Santiago: Editorial Universidad Católica de Santiago, 1982.
Villanueva Soberal, Alonso. "Planta de la nueva población de Angol." In *Atlas cartográfico del Reino de Chile*, edited by Pablo Gran López. CD. Santiago: Instituto Geográfico Militar, 2002.
Vivar, Jerómino de. *Crónica de los Reinos de Chile*. Madrid: Dastin, 2001.
Voigt, Lisa. *Writing Captivity in the Early Modern Atlantic: Circulations of Knowledge and Authority in the Iberian and English Imperial Worlds*. Chapel Hill: University of North Carolina Press, 2009.
Wachtel, Nathan. *The Vision of the Vanquished, The Spanish Conquest of Peru through Indian Eyes*. Translated by Ben Reynolds and Siân Reynolds. Hassocks, Sussex: Harvester Press, 1977.
Walker, Charles F. *Shaky Colonialism: The 1746 Earthquake-Tsunami in Lima, Peru, and Its Long Aftermath*. Durham, NC: Duke University Press, 2008.
Ward, Ronda. "A Colonial Woman in a Republican's Chilean History: Benjamín Vicuña Mackenna and La Quintrala." *Journal of Women's History* 13, no. 1 (2001): 83–107.
Weber, David J. *Bárbaros: Spaniards and Their Savages in the Age of Enlightenment*. New Haven, CT: Yale University Press, 2005.
———. *The Spanish Frontier in North America*. New Haven, CT: Yale University Press, 1992.
White, Richard. *The Middle Ground: Indians, Empires and Republics in the Great Lakes Region, 1650–1815*. Cambridge: Cambridge University Press, 1991.
Woodward, Ralph Lee. *Robinson Crusoe's Island: A History of the Juan Fernández Islands*. Chapel Hill: University of North Carolina Press, 1969.
Zapater, Horacio. *La búsqueda de la paz en la Guerra de Arauco: Padre Luis de Valdivia*. Santiago: Editorial Andrés Bello, 1992.
Zavala Cepeda, José Manuel, ed. *Los parlamentos Hispano-Mapuches, 1593–1803: Textos fundamentales*. Temuco, Chile: Universidad Católica de Temuco, 2015.

Zavala Cepeda, José Manuel, and Tom Dillehay. "El 'Estado de Arauco' frente a la conquista Española: Estructuración sociopolítica y ritual de los Araucano-Mapuches en los valles nahuelbutanos durante los siglos XVI y XVII." *Chungara, Revista de Antropología Chilena* 42, no. 2 (2010): 433–50.

Index

Page numbers in italics refer to figures.